BEHAVIOURAL SCIENCES
FOR MANAGERS

KU-797-713

To: Judy, Inger and Celia

BEHAVIOURAL SCIENCES FOR MANAGERS

R. L. Boot, A. G. Cowling
and M. J. K. Stanworth

Edward Arnold

© R. L. Boot, A. G. Cowling and
M. J. K. Stanworth 1977

First published 1977 by
Edward Arnold (Publishers) Ltd.
25 Hill Street, London W1X 8LL

British Library Cataloguing in Publication Data
Boot, R. L.
  Behavioural sciences for managers.
  1. Management   2. Social sciences
  I. Title   II. Cowling, A. G.   III. Stanworth, Michael Jon Kenneth
  658.4   HD 38
  ISBN 0–7131–3382–1
         0–7131–3383–X Pbk

All Rights Reserved. No part of this
publication may be reproduced, stored in
a retrieval system, or transmitted in any
form or by any means, electronic, mechanical,
photocopying, recording or otherwise, without
the prior permission of Edward Arnold (Publishers) Ltd.

Set in 11 on 12 pt Photon Times and printed by
The Camelot Press Ltd, Southampton

PREFACE

This book has been written for students of management and practising managers interested in the application of the behavioural sciences to the field of work. The expansion of management education in recent years has led to a demand for publications which present practical guides for management based on an analysis of both empirical and theoretical considerations.

Accordingly, *Behavioural Sciences for Managers* has been written with a variety of audiences in mind. It should prove particularly useful to students taking Part I of the Diploma in Management Studies Course and the Applied Behavioural Science Course in Part II of the Institute of Personnel Management Membership examinations. It should also interest students taking an industrial or commercial course, with a behavioural science content, leading to a degree or professional qualification. We have also considered practising managers who find themselves unable to vacate their positions in industry for long enough to undertake a formal course of study but who are concerned with decision-making and who pursue an interest in the management literature. Amongst others, we have tried to keep the small firm owner-manager and his management team in mind.

The value of the behavioural sciences to the manager lies in the fact that their subject matter is concerned with one of the most important, if not the most important, aspect of his work—human resources. The practising manager may feel that there is more to be learned about the tasks of management by actually pursuing them than by reading about them. He is sometimes prompted to make this claim by a feeling that the theoreticians he criticizes are intent on obscuring their ideas within fortresses of jargon.

In this book, we do not attempt to belie the importance of practical experience but hope to complement it. It has been written for managers and students of management who probably have no intention of becoming specialists in the behavioural sciences but who wish to become familiar with them. In addition to examining the practical implications of the behavioural sciences at work, we introduce readers to many of the concepts and terms used in behavioural science literature so that they may be understood when they are encountered again either in the work situation or in other published materials.

It is doubtful whether any single book can cope with so wide a range of topics in sufficient detail to satisfy fully the interests of a broad and diversified readership. The interested reader will, however, be able to extend his appreciation of topics of particular interest through the references given at the end of each chapter.

The authors would like to acknowledge the contribution to this book by James Curran, Senior Lecturer, School of Sociology, Kingston Polytechnic, for his co-authorship of Chapter X and his assistance in the preparation of Chapters II and VI.

CONTENTS

I

INTRODUCTION

This is a book about the behavioural sciences and their application to work and work organizations. But what are the behavioural sciences? That would seem to be a simple question but it is one to which, unfortunately, there is no straightforward answer. In this introduction we shall attempt to clarify what we mean by the term and also to highlight some of the problems inherent in the field of study.

Problems of definition

Many of the problems of definition stem from the fact that 'the behavioural sciences' or 'behavioural science' are terms used to refer to a collection of basic academic disciplines which, although all concerned one way or another with the study of man, each have their differing perspectives, theories and methods. There are other such collective terms, for example 'the social sciences' or 'social science'. Indeed, quite frequently these terms are regarded as interchangeable and are used to include such subjects as psychology, social-psychology, sociology, anthropology, politics and economics. In such cases, which term is used seems simply to be a question of preference or perhaps fashion. Also quite frequently, however, the terms are used to refer to slightly different areas of study. So, for example, social science will sometimes be defined to exclude psychology, that subject being regarded as concerned solely with the individual. Behavioural science, on the other hand, will often exclude politics and economics, and is sometimes assumed to imply a more applied or even consultancy perspective. It is certainly true the term seems to be more fashionable when applied to the study of organizations than when applied to other social phenomena where its synonym still seems to hold greater currency. In this book we are primarily interested in the contributions to our understanding of work and work organizations made by psychologists, social-psychologists, sociologists and management theorists. This interdisciplinary approach has its advantages—reality, after all, is not conveniently segmented to suit the lines of demarcation that academics have drawn between their areas of study. It does, however, also have disadvantages which we shall look at later.

The term behavioural science(s), although convenient, does have some major semantic problems in that both *behavioural* and *science* create difficulties and are potential sources of misunderstanding. Let us look at the first of these. It is true that in this book we are concerned with people's behaviour at work. But that is not our sole interest. Some behavioural scientists in their quest for objectivity maintain that the only legitimate subject matter for 'scientific' study is the observable behaviour or overt acts of individuals. That is not a position taken in this book. In other words we are also concerned with how the individual experiences his world of work, the way he perceives his physical and social environment and the meanings he attributes to them. Thus, following Porter *et al.*[1] we believe:

> The fact that a goal of science in this area is to be as objective as possible should not, however, mislead us into ignoring or downgrading the very real importance of subjective phenomena.

It will be seen, for example, that such subjective phenomena play an important part in motivation (Chapter III) in interaction with other people (Chapter IV) and in the taking of work roles (Chapter VI).

Our field of study also extends beyond observable elements of behaviour in another direction. We are also concerned with stable patterns of relationships within organizations. That is, we are interested in social structures as well as social actions. So we shall be examining the structure of groups (Chapter V) and the structure of organizations (Chapter VII). An understanding of organizational behaviour, then, involves more than the study of behaviour in organizations.

Let us now turn to that other troublesome term—*science*. To what extent can our field of study be regarded as scientific. Certainly if we regard a science as being a body of general laws governing a particular aspect of nature then behavioural 'science' is a misnomer. There is little or nothing to approximate to the general laws of the physical sciences. Even if we do not demand the status of 'law' for our body of knowledge but will settle for verifiability, the behavioural scientist still encounters problems. For information to be verified it must be gained in a form and under conditions which are replicable; that is, other people should be able to reproduce the same situation in which the original observations were made, make similar observations and come up with the same results. Such is the variability of human nature that genuine replicability is never really attainable. This means that even if a researcher is able to control every aspect of a situation (itself extremely difficult) perfect matching of human subjects is, as yet, not possible. Different people will perceive and react to the same situation differently. This problem cannot be overcome simply by placing the same person in the same situation on different occasions because, as Smith[2] points out:

> people remember some of what happens to them, thereby making each separate experience distinctive.

This last discussion leads us to an alternative view of science; that is, seeing it not so much as a collection of 'facts' but rather as what scientists do. It may be identified by the methods of enquiry adopted. According to Sills[3] such enquiry takes the form of 'systematic exploration, description and explanation'. The aims of such enquiry, Allport[4] maintains, are 'understanding, prediction and control above the levels achieved by unaided commonsense'. In the natural sciences the dominant method for meeting these aims is the experiment. In its basic form the experiment involves the investigator manipulating one aspect of the environment (the independent variable) and observing and measuring its effect on another (the dependent variable) while holding all other variables constant. We have already seen the problems associated with attempting to hold all things constant in the behavioural sciences. There is, however, an additional problem, and that is with measurement. Many of the important variables to be studied do not lend themselves to absolute or even direct measurement. The impact of this difficulty has, to some extent, been diminished by refinements in statistical analysis. Unfortunately, in some cases statistical sophistication seems to have become an end in itself. Thus Bass and Barrett[5] are drawn to say:

> we seem to place more emphasis on statistical correctness than on the practical significance of results. We escape through 'a flight into statistics' to avoid difficulties involved in working on the real problems. Often we invent problems to fit existing research methods rather than *vice versa*.

The representation of data in quantitative form undoubtedly makes it easier to manipulate but it does not make it any more objective or exact. This fact seems too often to have been overlooked. Nevertheless, the quest for scientific credibility has led many behavioural scientists into the attempt to imitate the assumed exactitude of the methods of the natural sciences. In recent years such approaches have come under increasing attack from within the ranks of behavioural scientists 'in that they prescribe methods which reduce the true complexity of experience by imitating the physical and the natural sciences'.[6] What is required then, is a greater emphasis on developing and refining methods which have their origin in our field of study and perhaps less emphasis on adapting the methods of the other sciences.

The methods of the behavioural sciences

At this stage it will be useful to elaborate a little on some of the methods that are used. A distinction can be made between research design and techniques for data collection. Any given research project may of course use more than one basic design and more than one data collection technique, but for our purposes we shall look at them separately. Each research design has its own advantages and disadvantages. The problem seems to be one of compromise between degree of control and degree of artificiality.

Laboratory experiments attempt to reproduce the controlled conditions of the natural sciences. Such conditions allow the researcher to manipulate one variable at a time and so more easily establish a causal relationship between variables, i.e. say that a change in A causes a change in B. In other words, it makes it easier to explain the phenomena being studied. Unfortunately such settings are rather artificial and therefore it is not possible to be certain of the applicability of the findings outside the laboratory. Some of the studies to be mentioned in Chapters IV and V are of this nature.

Attempts to overcome some of this artificiality have employed the *experimental field study* which is carried out in a real organizational setting. Here some variables are manipulated while holding others constant but since the experimenter is operating in a natural environment the chances are greater of uncontrolled variables influencing the results. The study carried out by Coch and French, which will be discussed in Chapter IX, is an example of such a design.

Both these approaches are however limited in the extent to which the findings can be generalized to other situations. The *survey method* makes it possible to include a much wider range of situations in the study. It means however that the researcher cannot manipulate variables and study the effect on other variables. It is possible for him, by statistical analysis, to establish that certain variables he is studying are correlated or in some way associated with each other, but he cannot be certain that one causes another. Many of the studies referred to in this book are of this type and the problems of establishing causality are discussed in Chapter V in connection with leadership effectiveness.

The final design which has been used fairly widely in the study of organizational behaviour is the *case study*. Here the researcher makes no attempt to manipulate variables but makes a study in depth, over a period of time, of a particular organizational setting. He then attempts to organize what he has observed into some meaningful generalizations. Obviously, in this situation, the researcher has virtually no control and the value of his study depends heavily on his skill in interpretation and freedom from bias. Potentially, however, such studies can be a rich source of understanding of a real situation and can be particularly useful for generating hypotheses that can subsequently be 'tested' in a more controlled manner.

With each of these designs a number of data collection techniques may be used. These vary in the extent that the researcher is personally involved in the actual situation being studied. The more involved the researcher, the less extensive can be his field of study; but probably it will be more intensive, i.e. he will be more capable of recording complexity in the data. The technique entailing most involvement is usually referred to as *participant observation*, in which the researcher actually becomes a part of the social situation which he is studying. The study on small groups carried out by Roy, which will be discussed more fully in Chapter V, used this approach. At the opposite extreme some studies employ secondary analysis of existing documentary information, such as company records and reports or government statistics. Ranged between these two extremes are unstructured interviews, structured interviews, non-participant observation, psychological tests and self-completion questionnaires.

None of the research designs or techniques mentioned are necessarily better or worse than any of the others. In fact they are probably best regarded as complementary to each other, the disadvantages of any one approach being reduced when used in combination with another. There is still however, plenty of room for improvement in the methodology of the behavioural sciences before they can attain the degree of objectivity and certainty claimed by some (but not all) for the methods of the natural sciences. On the other hand, referring back to Allport's statement quoted earlier, the systematic methods of enquiry developed by behavioural scientists do enable a level of understanding of social phenomena 'above the levels achieved by unaided commonsense'. The value, then, of the behavioural sciences to the manager do not rest on whether or not the label 'science' is justified, but rather on the fact that they do represent a genuine alternative to what Gellerman[7] refers to as 'the accumulated folklore, mythology and superstition that too often passes for traditional managerial wisdom'.

Problems of perspective

However, the fact that we are not dealing with a 'hard' science does create some difficulties which the reader should bear in mind. As indicated earlier, some of these difficulties stem from the multi-disciplinary nature of the subject. Behavioural scientists do not represent a unified body of specialists in total agreement about the nature of organizational reality. Far from it. They can bring to the same setting a range of different perspectives, seeking explanations for the same phenomena in quite different levels of analysis. One may emphasize the relationship of the individual to his job, another the flow of communication in the organization, and still another the distribution of power in society as a whole. Many behavioural scientists have their own particular 'hobby-horse' which they insist on riding, whatever the situation. This problem seems particularly prevalent with regard to the theoretical viewpoint from which to study organizations. As will become clear throughout this book the field is still full of controversy. So, for example, Chapters II and VII will discuss the debate between the 'systems' and 'action' approaches. The problem of 'universalism' versus a 'particularist' or 'contingency' approach will recur throughout. And the implications of adopting a 'unitary' or 'pluralist' frame of reference will be discussed in Chapter VIII.

Such diversity of and controversy between perspectives can be off-putting to the newcomer to the field, but there are major advantages. It is through controversy and debate that the behavioural sciences are likely to progress from their existing stage of development to a fuller understanding of work and work organizations. In addition, the more aware the manager is of the controversy and complexity in the field, the less likely he will be to demand oversimplified solutions to his problems and, perhaps more importantly, the more he will be protected from those who attempt to sell him ready made answers and instant solutions to human problems at work.

This book, then, does not attempt to provide definitive answers to organizational problems. Rather, it attempts to show how the application of the behavioural sciences can give greater insight into the nature of those problems. It aims to improve the quality and appropriateness of the questions the manager might ask in order to arrive at better solutions of his own.

Plan of the book

The book is structured to look at work and work organizations from a number of focus points. Chapter II explores the meanings that work has in our society and the implications of various orientations to it. Chapter III examines a number of different approaches to explaining the motivation of the individual at work and looks at their implications for financial rewards and job design. In Chapter IV the focus is moved away from the individual on to the interaction between individuals at work, particularly managers and subordinates. This is expanded further in Chapter V which looks at the dynamic processes of working in groups and at the manager's role as leader. The concept of work roles, regarded by many as the link between the study of individuals and study of whole organizations, is explored in Chapter VI and in particular it looks at the impact of role conflict and ambiguity. In Chapter VII the focus is expanded once more to look at organizations as a whole, examining different approaches to the structuring of work relationships. Chapter VIII explores more fully the nature of management and how it is affected by the distribution of power and the nature of conflict within organizations. Changes in the distribution of power, along with other environmental pressures for change, are examined in Chapter IX as are behavioural science based approaches for coping with, planning for and introducing change. Much of the literature on organizations has aimed at the large organization. Chapter X is intended to redress the balance somewhat by concentrating particularly on the small firm. The final chapter points to a few problems influencing the effectiveness of the behavioural scientist in organizational settings.

REFERENCES

1 PORTER, L. W., LAWLER, E. E., and HACKMAN, J. R., *Behaviour in Organizations*, McGraw-Hill, 1975.
2 SMITH, P. B., *Groups within Organizations*, Harper & Row, 1973.
3 SILLS, P., 'The behavioural sciences: their potential and limitations', *Personnel Review*, **4**, pp. 5–12, 1975.
4 ALLPORT, G. W., *The Use of Personal Documents in Psychological Science*, Social Science Research Council, 1947.
5 BASS, B. M., and BARRETT, G. V., *Man, Work and Organizations*, Allyn & Bacon, 1972.
6 GROSS, G., 'Unnatural selection', in ARMISTEAD, N. (Ed.), *Reconstructing Social Psychology*, Penguin, 1974.
7 GELLERMAN, S. W., *Behavioural Science in Management*, Penguin, 1974.

II

THE MEANING OF WORK

It cannot be exceptional in a full working life—whether as a manual or professional worker—to expend around 100,000 hours of physical and mental effort. The fact that this effort is concentrated into a period in the human life cycle when the individual is most physically and mentally able gives this figure even greater significance. Further, though the length of the standard working week has tended to decrease over time, the length of the average working week, including overtime, has declined relatively little since the 1930's.[1] So the clear strategic importance of work in the lives of most individuals in our society is apparent and, in this chapter, we shall examine the meaning that work has in the minds and lives of those people.

Occupational choice

We live in a complex industrial society with an ideology of free occupational choice. Education is now regarded as being open to all, and is widely seen as a medium for the identification of talent and ability, and subsequent occupational placement. This situation, it is argued, stands in marked contrast to that existing in developing societies where occupational positions held in adult life are often highly dependent on the individual's position at birth. Along with the process of industrialization, it is claimed, we have seen *achievement* replace *ascription* as a basis for occupational placement. However, this is in reality rather an oversimplification and an exaggeration for family influences still continue to play an important part in both the kind of education a person receives and the occupational roles held in adult life.[2] This is especially true for the higher roles in society. It is more accurate to say, therefore, that over the last century or so there has been a shift in emphasis *towards* achievement in occupational placement and away from ascription.

The ideal of free occupational choice does not always translate into reality. Certain positions in our society, e.g. those of Monarch and of Hereditary Peer, are still totally dependent on ascription rather than achievement as a basis of selection. In the field of industry, the owner-manager of the small firm is likely to look more favourably on the claims of his own sons to succeed him than those of perhaps more talented managers already working for the firm or, alternatively, available from the outside labour market. Even many medium-size and large firms remain firmly in the control of their founders or the latters' descendants, as an examination of the recent histories of companies such as the Ford Motor Company, Thompson Newspapers, Guinness, Pilkington Glass and Marks and Spencer demonstrates.

Further, few people who invest in private education would deny that they expect this investment to improve the life-chances of their children. Finally, even within the state system of education, many studies have shown the importance of the home, parental support and encouragement, and systems of selection, e.g. the 11-plus examination and its replacements, as factors influencing the issue of 'who ends up where' in our society.[3]

The remarks above on the limitations of free occupational choice are not intended so much as a social comment, but more as a reminder that the issue of occupational placement and occupational choice is much more complex than it would be if the super-efficient meritocracy underlying the ideology of free occupational choice had become a reality. Indeed, it is fair to say that reminders of this state of affairs lie all about us. To illustrate this point, we need look no further than the failure of the 11-plus system of selection to accurately identify our major intelligence resources, and the current political concern that the cream of our potential engineering talent is being diverted to occupational positions outside the field of engineering. The degree of polemic and the competing remedies surrounding these two issues alone are a reminder of their complexity and of our incomplete knowledge.

Nevertheless, the preceding comments do not mean that little or no attention has been devoted to the question of occupational choice and occupational selection. A great deal of work has been done though most of the theories and hypotheses resulting from it do not stand up very well to testing in practice. Lancashire[4] has conveniently grouped attempts at explaining processes of occupational placement into two basic schools of thought: the *differentialist* and the *developmentalists*.

The *differentialists* tend to assume that an individual's abilities, interests, and dispositions develop at a relatively early age and thereafter undergo little change. The requirements of various occupations are seen as being identifiable in terms of the demands made upon potential occupants, and it is assumed that congruence is achieved thereafter as a result of individuals gravitating towards the type of work best suited to them.[5]

However, such an approach poses certain problems. For instance, social forces in society often result in an individual's talents not being fully developed or, alternatively, being developed in different directions to those which the theories in question would indicate. So a person with the potential to become a brilliant engineer may, in reality, end up as an accountant, a dropout, or even a long-distance lorry driver, depending upon the play of social forces in his environment. Further, even if his or her strongest talents are properly identified and reinforced at school, forces in the labour market and/or inefficiencies in the selection and promotion procedures of employing organizations may lead to this talent being overlooked or misplaced.[6]

The strong influence of psychologists on the *differentialist* school of thought has led to a neglect of the importance of social and economic factors without which an understanding of occupational placement cannot hope to proceed very far. This has been corrected to some extent by the *developmentalists* who stress that, by the time that social class, sex, race, area of residence and nationality have been taken into account, expectations of work and subsequent occupational choice become much restricted.[7] However, within the limits of these constraints, models of occupational choice and adaptation to work are developed. These models typically involve several succeeding stages: the initial development of attitudes towards work by individuals whilst still at school, followed by entry into work, movement between jobs as a test of fit and suitability and, finally, adoption of a chosen job as the main life-time work role.[8]

Blau *et al.*[9] have drawn a clear distinction between *occupational choice* (those elements over which the individual has actual or potential control) and *occupational selection* (those elements over which the individual has no control since they are the province of employing organizations). They postulate that the individual develops a hierarchy of job preferences and an estimate of the likely probabilities of entry into the jobs concerned. Occupational choice then is the outcome of these two sets of considerations.

Theories of occupational and job selection amongst manual workers have been confronted with problems of explaining empirical data tending to show that the process of occupational placement is often haphazard and based upon a highly imperfect knowledge, on the part of the worker, of the labour market and of the employment opportunities available.[10]

A further problem here is that the notion of a career,[11] implicit in many theories of occupational choice, is not relevant to many workers. The term 'career' tends to imply the notion of a prolonged commitment to one particular form of work and, in addition, upward movement between the various levels in a pre-defined career hierarchy. However, in considering manual workers, the majority do not even serve an apprenticeship and so are unlikely to be afforded opportunities for advancement comparable with those of a career. Even skilled workers who serve apprenticeships cannot realistically aspire to vertical career progression higher than first-line supervisor, and statistically may not even reach this far.

For managerial and specialist 'white-collar' positions, however, the notion of career does have more relevance; patterns of career development are nevertheless likely to vary from occupation to occupation. Progress in a career in line management may well be possible within the context of a single organization whereas, in more specialized areas, e.g. finance or personnel management, considerable movement between organizations may be necessary (see the discussion on Locals and Cosmopolitans in Chapter VI).

It is perhaps fitting that we should conclude discussion of the issue of occupational choice with summaries from two writers on how well the various theories of occupational choice have met the demands made of them in predicting and explaining the practical realities of occupational placement. Lancashire, has written:

> Although various of the theories and hypotheses have not stood up particularly well to testing, nevertheless they have helped to change the climate of thinking which has affected both research programmes and practical occupational guidance.[12]

More recently, Dunkerley has written, perhaps over-optimistically:

> While it could be argued that there are deficiencies in most of the explanations, taken together a reasonably comprehensive picture does emerge. Furthermore, it is a refreshing sign that considerable empirical research has been and is currently being undertaken in this area.[13]

It can be said that there is no single theory of occupational choice but rather several partial theories; the usefulness of each particular approach varies with the situation and occupational grouping in question.

Orientations to work

Politicians and journalists frequently cite superficial and anecdotal evidence to support claims that 'people no longer want to work'. Whilst the people making such claims often have dubious credentials for speaking on such matters with authority, the fact that they do so underlines the importance of the relationship between the worker and his work.

Morse and Weiss,[14] in a classic study carried out in the United States on samples of both manual and white-collar workers concluded that, for most men, work is more than merely a means of providing an income:

... for most men, having a job serves other functions than the one of earning a living. In fact, even if they had enough money to support themselves, they would still want to work. Working gives them a feeling of being untied into the larger society, of having something to do, of having a purpose in life.[15]

They saw this conclusion as being consistent with the feelings of isolation and dislocation frequently experienced by the unemployed, and also the retired, even when the latter have an adequate income. Recent studies of unemployment in Britain[16] have reinforced the claim that those unable to work can experience severe psychological deprivations with detrimental effects for their personal relationships both within and outside the family.

Part of Morse and Weiss's research focused on the question, 'If by some chance you inherited enough money to live comfortably without working, do you think you would work anyway or not'? Eighty per cent of respondents claimed that they would continue working and two-thirds of those gave positive reasons for their decision, e.g. job interest, job satisfaction, maintaining self-respect, etc. The remaining one-third gave negative reasons, e.g. would otherwise feel bored and isolated; would feel lost; would not know what to do with their time. Morse and Weiss claim that one reason why such people may want to continue working is that, although they may not find their work intrinsically rewarding, they have few alternative ideas for making use of their energy.

The percentage of respondents who said they would opt to give up work increased quite markedly with age; perhaps this is not surprising given that older workers may already have begun to adjust to the idea of a life outside the work place. The kind of job held by respondents did not generally influence attitudes on wanting to continue working. The only exception to this was amongst unskilled workers; only about 50 per cent said they would continue working.

When asking how satisfied they were with their current job, 80 per cent claimed to be either 'satisfied' or 'very satisfied'.[17] However, this should not be taken as an indication that their jobs were intrinsically interesting and stimulating. Morse and Weiss in fact say:

> This finding suggests that most individuals accommodate themselves to their chances and possibliities in life and in general do not maintain, as conscious aspirations, chances and opportunities not within their scope to realise.[18]

Another, but not unrelated, suggestion as to why workers occupying relatively unrewarding jobs tend to claim fairly high levels of job satisfaction has been commented upon by Goldthorpe and Lockwood, *et al.*[19] They point out that numerous studies have revealed that workers, when asked how they like their jobs, tend to report favourably even in cases where they obviously experience quite severe deprivations in performing their jobs. However, they argue, it is difficult for a worker to admit that he dislikes his job without 'thereby threatening his self-respect'. An individual's work tends to have an important influence on his image of himself, and to say that he finds his job unacceptable can be tantamount to saying he finds himself unacceptable.

Morse and Weiss found that many respondents who claimed fairly high levels of satisfaction said that, if they inherited enough money to live comfortably without working, they would continue working but change jobs. Hence it appeared that commitment to their current jobs was weaker than their commitment to work in general. This was particularly true for manual-worker respondents, only 34 per cent of whom said they would continue in their current line of work (this compares with a figure of 61 per cent for white-collar respondents). Many of those in manual occupations expressed an interest in self-employment though they were often unsure as to what sort of business this would be. The appeal of self-employment appeared to lie in the prestige and autonomy to be gained without the necessity for additional formal education and training.

In a final summary of the meaning of work for the people they studied, Morse and Weiss said:

> To the typical man in a middle-class occupation, working means having a purpose, gaining a sense of accomplishment, expressing himself. He feels that not working would leave him aimless and without opportunities to create. To the typical man in a working-class occupation working means having something to do. He feels that not working would leave him no adequate outlet for physical activity; he would just be sitting or lying around.[20]

Work as a 'Central Life Interest'

Dubin, in another well known American study, points out that in the Western world work has long been considered a Central Life Interest for adults. Indeed, Weber has claimed that the capitalist system itself rests on the moral and religious justification that the Reformation gave to work. However, Dubin's own research[21] indicates that the kind of commitment to work required to make it a Central Life Interest is often absent amongst industrial workers and that it is the family and non-work life which are most frequently areas of Central Life Interest.

Dubin found amongst the workers he studied that only 24 per cent identified work as their main area of life interest. The remainder tended to see other areas of life interest—outside the workplace—as being more important for them. Further, only 9 per cent claimed the workplace as their most meaningful source of informal human associations. The rest attached more meaning and importance to the family and other non-work contacts as sources of preferred informal social relationships.

The majority of the workers studied regarded work as mandatory and some form of social interaction within the workplace as preferred. However, for the most part, these social contacts were not highly valued, and did not result in primary social relationships. Participation in the workplace was seen as being economically necessary but not important as a source of meaningful social experience. Nevertheless, in 63 per cent of cases, work was identified by respondents as their main focus of attachment in their organizational and technical environment.

Dubin also makes the interesting suggestion on the overall significance of work that:

> The characteristics of industrial work that are alleged to be disturbing to the individual (monotony, repetitiveness, mechanistic nature, and over-specialization) are the very features that make obvious to its participants the nature of symbiotic or technological interdependence. In short, industrial work may be functional for the society because it sharply etches for the individual some awareness of the division of labour and its resultant interdependence.[22]

The ideas examined so far—those put forward by Morse and Weiss on the one hand and Dubin on the other—indicate that the relationship between the individual and his work is often of a rather complex nature. Whilst degree of *attachment* to work may be high in the sense that worklife is regarded as both necessary and important, *commitment* to work is often of a lower order when work fails to measure up to the emotional significance of other areas of life.

Levels of satisfaction in work

Blauner,[23] in a wide ranging survey on work orientations and satis-factions, has shown that levels of job satisfaction are closely related to position in the industrial hierarchy. The most satisfied are professionals and senior managers and the least satisfied are manual workers, especially those employed in mass production.[24]

We may assume that job satisfaction is positively correlated with the degree to which the individual makes work a Central Life Interest. Blauner makes the point that the most senior occupational roles in industry confer on the individual high personal status. In such roles the individual has considerable autonomy and control over others, both of which make a considerable contribution to his self-esteem. It should therefore not be surprising that such roles, the content of which makes a positive contribution to the individual's self-identity, are also clearly linked with the individual's Central Life Interest. Confirmation of this point is provided by Parker who reports that individuals in senior occupational roles rarely make a sharp distinction between work and leisure (see section on Work and Leisure later in this chapter).

The car assembly worker   The car assembly-line has long been seen as representing the 'classic symbol of the subjection of man to the machine'.[25] The work typically involves a minute sub-division of tasks, mechanically controlled workpace, pre-determination of assembly tools and methods of assembly, repetition, low levels of skill, and only surface mental attention. In a study of car assembly workers reported in the 1950's, Walker and Guest[26] recorded low levels of intrinsic job satisfaction amongst their sample. Further, the majority of the workers studied expressed a desire to move off the assembly-line on to alternative jobs, e.g. maintenance, inspection and clerical jobs, in order to escape the pacing, repetition, and physical fatigue associated with assembly-line work.

Over 90 per cent of those concerned had previously worked in jobs where the workpace had not been machine controlled; 15 per cent had previously held white-collar jobs, and a further 26 per cent had held skilled manual jobs. Eighty per cent claimed economic factors as their main source of attachment to their assembly jobs. It is not unreasonable to suggest that there was an element of self-selection operating here, given that many of the workers could presumably have found more interesting work, although at a lower rate of pay.

A now famous study of workers in Britain strongly favours the notion that such workers are self-selecting. This study, by Goldthorpe and Lockwood *et al*,[27] indicates that workers with an *instrumental* orientation towards work[28] are likely to make a positive decision to maximize their earnings at the expense of intrinsic satisfactions. Thus, if the individual worker's goals and expectations centre around the extrinsic rewards associated with his job, i.e. money and security, this allows him a degree of satisfaction with his job despite the dissatisfying nature of the work itself.

Goldthorpe and Lockwood's research was carried out in Luton in the 1960's and involved manual workers from three firms: Vauxhall Motors, Laporte Chemicals and the Skefko Ball-Bearing Company. All the workers studied were male, married and living with their wives, mostly on private housing developments, and between the ages of 21 and 46. Their position in the life-cycle, plus the fact that they were married and usually buying their homes, meant that their need for income was as high as it was ever likely to be. All of the respondents were earning what were considered high wages for the period in question.

Though the research studied men working in different technologies involving various levels of skills, it is probably fair to say that the part of their findings dealing with assembly workers has provoked most interest.[29] Their results were, in many ways, not very surprising, and it is the interpretation that the researchers put on their results which has been responsible for their considerable impact.

The assembly-line workers studied found little to interest them in their jobs and their levels of intrinsic job satisfaction were low. Complaints involving monotony and physical fatigue were commonplace; the majority said they would have preferred alternative jobs off the 'track' which they saw as involving greater skill, variety and autonomy. The majority of the workers gave reasons for staying in their jobs which were consistent with the goal of long-term income maximization (i.e. income plus job security).[30]

This *instrumental orientation* towards work, by workers taking intrinsically unsatisfying jobs in order to maximize their income, would be seen by Marx, Dubin, Blauner, Chinoy,[31] and others as a classic symptom of the alienation of the worker from his work. Goldthorpe and Lockwood do not dispute this and their departure from previous thinking stems from their seeing the instrumental orientation of the workers concerned as something other than a *direct consequence* of an inherently alienating technology. They claim rather that, in a time of full employment and with a knowledge of the intrinsic deprivations associated with assembly-line work, their workers had deliberately chosen this kind of work in order to satisfy external needs. So, it was argued, it was the workers' instrumental orientation towards work which had led them to *seek* this kind of employment.

Goldthorpe and Lockwood stress that technology and the objective features of the workplace, do not operate as the *only* source of influence and meanings which the worker has towards his work. Attitudes and meanings which the worker brings into the workplace with him are likely to mediate between the objective features of technology and the workers' experience of his situation.

The formation of social groups amongst the assembly workers in the workplace was inhibited by their dispersal along the 'track', their relative physical immobility, the mechanical pacing of the work and, in addition, high noise levels. Because of these limits on social group formation,

Walker and Guest had earlier stressed the need for foremen to play a socially expressive role in an attempt to mitigate the anonymity and impersonality which workers otherwise experienced. However, the Luton researchers found that, whilst over 90 per cent of their respondents claimed to get on 'very well' or at least 'pretty well' with their foreman, a majority gave *infrequency of contact* as their reason. This the researchers interpreted as a reflection of the workers' prior instrumental orientation to work which resulted in their not expecting, or indeed looking for, satisfaction of social needs at work.

Finally, the researchers claimed that the importance which workers attached to income maximization, coupled with the employer's ability to furnish satisfaction of this goal, led to relatively favourable attitudes towards the employer. Levels of instrumental attachment to the organization were claimed to be high even if levels of commitment to the work itself were low.[32]

Whilst this study has provided a new and interesting view of the meaning of work for those studied, caution should be adopted in its interpretation. Sometimes teachers of management, and possibly sociology too, leave students with the impression that Goldthorpe and Lockwood were claiming that a prior instrumental orientation towards work shields or anaesthetizes workers against feelings of deprivation associated with intrinsic aspects of their jobs. Indeed Daniel,[33] in a comment upon the Luton studies, has claimed some 'grotesque caricatures' and interpretations of the researchers' findings by practising managers and businessmen leading to the view: 'We've always said that all the worker is interested in is money'. In fact, Daniel feels that Goldthorpe and Lockwood's original interpretation of their results did imply that instrumentality performs the role of an anaesthetic in the light of intrinsic deprivations in the job. However, such a view cannot be upheld on the basis of their published material.

Daniel claims that whilst pay, security and working conditions may attract people *to* a job and explain their attachment to it, it is the opportunity to use mental ability and experiences in problem resolution and learning that are the main sources of satisfaction *in* a job. Thus, we could say that the Luton workers experienced satisfaction *with* their jobs but dissatisfaction *in* their jobs. After all, Goldthorpe and Lockwood did find that a majority of their respondents would have welcomed a more interesting job off the 'track', though at no reduction in pay, and this hardly indicates that the desire for more challenging work (which most respondents had experienced in previous employment) was dead.

This being so, we should look for alternative interpretations of the main reason given by workers for getting on well with their foremen, i.e., infrequency of contact. After all, the span of control of the foreman in assembly-line work is typically very wide, and contacts between foremen and workers under these conditions are often confined to dealing with immediate problems. In these conditions, the worker is likely to feel vulnerable and this could explain, in part at least, why infrequency of contact with foremen was welcomed. For many of the workers who said that they got on well with their foreman because he 'left them alone' or 'didn't bother them',[34] this last vestige of autonomy could have been valued as a positive virtue rather than reflecting a desire to avoid social involvement. However, despite criticisms, the Luton study remains a classic of its kind.

The small firm worker   Like Goldthorpe and Lockwood, Ingham[35] has also taken up the idea of self-selection but with respect to employment in organizations of differing size. He has argued that small firms tend to offer lower levels of economic rewards than their larger counterparts but offer higher levels of non-economic rewards. This he sees as a basis for self-selection of individuals into organizations offering rewards congruent with their personal goals. Workers seeking high levels of intrinsic job satisfaction, who are willing to forgo the opportunity to maximize earnings, are likely to actively seek employment in small firms. In contrast workers deliberately seeking high levels of economic rewards and whose concern with intrinsic job satisfactions is of a lower order, are likely to seek work in large firms.

For such self-selection to operate, obviously the worker must be faced with a variety of employment possibilities. In situations of full employment, it is argued he is able to select a job congruent with his own goals. However, in situations of high unemployment, he may have little or no flexibility and may be obliged to take any job offered him.

In common with Goldthorpe, Ingham sees the individual's orientation towards work as influencing relationships in the workplace. For instance, he has reported research data indicating that worker-foreman relationships are more commonly perceived as being good (by workers) in the small firm than in the large firm. His control sample of large firm workers often gave 'infrequency of contact' as a reason for claiming to get on well with their foremen, but respondents in his small firm worker sample were much more likely to welcome contact with their foreman. In short, relationships in the small firm were seen as being generally more expressive.

The two studies referred to above, those of Goldthorpe and Lockwood and Ingham respectively, are based on a Social Action approach to organizational analysis (see Chapter VII). This approach contrasts radically with other approaches which tend to see society as external to the actor and which adopt a 'puppet on a string' approach to man's behaviour. The latter view sees man as being highly conditioned by forces external to him which govern his attitudes, aspirations, values and beliefs. The Social Action approach, on the other hand, does not accept this rather pessimistic view and instead sees society as a reflection of the views, interests and goals of individuals, with society shaped by them.

In the context of the workplace, Social Action theorists do not accept that all men in the same work situation will interpret their situation identically. Rather, they see individuals as interpreting their situation in the light of the satisfactions they seek at work and the meaning that work has for them. So that whilst certain kinds of work may prove unacceptable to some workers, they may prove acceptable to others with different goals. The same can be said of management policies. Whilst well-meaning 'human relations' policies on the part of management may appeal to certain groups of workers, they may engender feelings of unwelcome paternalism and claustrophobia in others.

This approach is not as radical as it may appear. If we adopt the standpoint that action derives from individual will and individual goals, these can in turn be traced back to the actor's historical experiences. These experiences may reveal him as more acted upon and influenced than independently acting and influencing. Further, the work of Goldthorpe and Lockwood and of Ingham could be regarded in anything but a radical light; they could be said to be justifying the *status quo* in situations where dissatisfaction might be expected, for example, in routine assembly-line work in the motor industry, and in low-paid work in small firms. However, writers who have used the Social Action perspective, do predict dissatisfaction for workers unable to find employment situations congruent with their own personal work goals. An interesting example of this is shown in the work of Cotgrove and Box (see Chapter VI) on role strain amongst scientists. In this example, levels of satisfaction in fairly high status professional positions are shown to vary quite considerably, depending on the values and orientations which the scientist takes into the workplace with him.[36]

Orientations and the context of work   Daniel and McIntosh, in more recent studies[37] have distinguished between two different contexts in which the worker may find himself, and in which he may have different sets of interests. One of the studies involved petro-chemical workers and the other nylon spinners. In each instance, fairly far-reaching changes in work procedures were made following productivity agreements.

In the case of the petro-chemical firm, management-worker

relationships prior to the change were said to be very good, and most of the workers concerned claimed to find their jobs interesting. Despite this, the productivity agreement was initially resisted because of fears of redundancy. However, after the deal had been in operation for several months, the workers reported favourably on their feelings about the change. For the majority, the main reason for their now favourable attitude was that a higher level of intrinsic satisfaction had resulted from the deal.

The second group studied were ICI nylon spinners and, before the change in the work scheme, 80 per cent claimed their jobs were monotonous. This time the productivity exercise was *consciously* designed to bring about an element of job enrichment but, whilst the workers accepted the new work scheme, they did so overwhelmingly on account of the economic benefits derived as distinct from the promise of an increase in job satisfaction. However, when interviewed again several months later, the workers expressed high levels of satisfaction with the new work scheme, largely because of the greater intrinsic job interest.[38]

For both the petro-chemical workers and the nylon spinners, attitudes towards productivity agreements changed *after* the bargaining phase was completed. It is in the light of these observations that Daniel and McIntosh draw a sharp distinction between the *negotiating* or contractual aspect of employment and the *work* aspect itself. In the former, the authors claim, the worker is essentially *extrinsically* orientated and pre-occupied with a concern for pay and security. In the latter, he is *intrinsically* orientated and concerned with issues of job content and working relations. This approach varies from that of Goldthorpe and Lockwood in that the latter tend to assume a consistent orientation to work as a whole. However, it could perhaps be argued that, if workers had greater trust, understanding, and experience of productivity agreements and schemes for job enrichment, then the *work* aspect might merge much more into the *negotiating* context of employment, both aspects becoming the concern of the negotiators.

Finally, Wedderburn,[39] in a study of workers in the north east, has concluded that for most manual workers the most dominant experience of work is the sense of being subjected to work discipline, to authority relationships and generally to a situation in which there is little autonomy. It is within this context, she claims, that workers respond to the technological constraints of their jobs, and to the strategies adopted by management in particular market situations.[40]

The complexity of orientations to work   Other studies of fishermen[41] and miners[42] show how complex the orientations of manual workers may be through their links with life in the wider society. The meaning of work, in other words, should not be thought of simply at the psychological level, it is in large part socially generated and socially sustained through the individual's socialization experiences in and out of work. For example, it is only possible to understand the meaning of work for the coal miner if we understand the way in which his definitions of work depend on the wider social environment of the mining community.

One other distortion which arises from the essentially static study of orientations to work among manual workers is the implicit assumption that they do not vary greatly throughout the individual's life. There is a good deal of evidence to suggest that orientations to work are closely linked to the life-cycle. Thus initial entry into work has been seen to be associated with orientations to work which strongly emphasise the intrinsic aspects.[43] This is not surprising given that the two main reference groups influencing the initial socialization of work orientations—parents and teachers—are likely to emphasize a preference for jobs 'with a future', or jobs which will give the individual a high level of intrinsic satisfaction.

However, when workers get married and especially when a family is started, they are often constrained to adopt a more material attitude towards work. Whatever their intrinsic wants, the acceptance of family and home as a Central Life Interest suggests that work will be increasingly seen as a material means to achieve a particular life style.[44] Most manual workers have reached an earnings plateau by the time they reach their mid-twenties and the possibility of occupational achievement which produces both high earnings and high intrinsic rewards are limited. This is especially true in Britain, where high earnings for manual workers are often linked to jobs such as car manufacture with its low intrinsic rewards.

Older workers may also be expected to have orientations reflecting their position in the life-cycle. By the time they reach their mid-forties their children may be grown up and much of the material needs of the individual's chosen life style will have been achieved. In addition, many manual occupations—particularly those associated with high earnings—are physically very demanding. These factors may therefore combine to induce older workers to re-define work in less material terms. Often such a re-definition is forced on the worker when he finds he can no longer cope with the demands of a stressful, physically demanding job and where he encounters age discrimination in seeking an alternative job.[45]

The meaning of work may also change because of changes in an occupation's social correlates. An example of this is provided by Lockwood in his well known study of the clerk;[46] this suggests that a decline in the market and status situations of the lower level white-collar worker may lead to a change in the meaning of such work for those involved. Subsequent research[47] has confirmed this change and it has been cited to partly explain the increase in unionization among this group of workers.

A similar change in orientation may be occurring among managers. As Bendix[48] has shown, this role has emerged comparatively recently in industrial society, and the great expansion in the number of managerial roles has probably occurred only since 1950. Discussions of managerial ideologies and the meaning of work for the manager implicitly assume that most managers have a similar view of their role but, as Fletcher has suggested,[49] internal stratification may be occurring among various levels of managers with each stratum having a distinct orientation to work. New graduates entering management have an orientation to work distinct from older, middle-level managers who have settled in a particular firm. The middle-level manager who recognizes that he is unlikely ever to achieve the most senior posts in the firm may develop a different orientation to work to both the younger ambitious new entrant into management and to those who constitute the senior strata of management.

In this section, we have explored the meaning of work using a number of dimensions and have shown that it is highly variable between different groups within the labour force; it may also change over time. We have also seen how such orientations are affected by changes in the social and economic structure of society. Clearly, the meaning of work for the individual is a complex subject and discussion on this topic is often either superficial or based upon unwarranted assumptions.

Alienation

The concept of alienation, as used in the study of work, has its main origins in the Marxian critique of private ownership and division of labour in capitalist society.[50] Marx saw private ownership of the means of production, and the division of labour in pursuance of profit, as a denial of the workers' needs for self-expression and self-fulfilment in work. Frustration of the 'instinct of workmanship'[51] and the relegation of labour to the status of a commodity have, it is claimed, resulted in work becoming an alienating experience. Here, work no longer represents the satisfaction of a need in itself (self-fulfillment) but merely a *means* to the *end* of satisfying other external needs.

Blauner[52] has attempted to operationalize the concept of alienation for research purposes by defining it on four dimensions:

Powerlessness: stemming from a lack of control over immediate work processes.

Meaninglessness: stemming from standardization and division of labour, removing opportunities for identification with the final product and for understanding the organization overall.

Isolation: stemming from the workers' inability to belong to a socially integrated work organization or social grouping in the wider society.

Self-estrangement: stemming from workers seeing work as a means to an end rather than an end in itself.

This conceptualization represents a departure from that of Marx who stressed much more the powerlessness of the worker on the issue of organizational control in the wider sense. However, in adopting the above dimensions of alienation, Blauner considered the alienating tendencies of four different technologies—craft technology, machine minding, assembly-line, and process technologies. He argued that, whilst there are alienating tendencies inherent in all modern bureaucratic organizations, the degree of alienation is likely to vary with the mode of technology adopted. Of the four technologies considered, he found craft technology (his example being printing) least alienating and assembly-line technology most alienating, with the other two technologies occupying intermediate positions.

So that, in all four cases, whilst workers were divorced from ownership of the means of production, differences in degrees of alienation occurred. This indicates that, even if alienation is an inevitable consequence of the capitalist ownership of industry, flexibility does exist in the form of the production process adopted to influence the degree of alienation.[53]. Further, Weber[54] has linked alienating tendencies with bureaucratization generally, which he sees as a characteristic of *any* industrialized society, regardless of forms of ownership. Further, there is no reason why feelings of alienation should necessarily be thought of as being the exclusive prerogative of *manual* workers.[55]

Work and leisure relationships

The gradual reduction in the length of the standard working week has led many people to talk of the coming 'crisis of leisure'. However, perhaps such concern is premature. Parker, a leading figure in the study of leisure in this country, has written:

> Faced with the choice of more leisure time or more income, a good many British workers still choose more income from over-time, a second job, or do-it-yourself activities which are hardly leisure.[56]

In a similar vein, Sillitoe, has written:

> The striking point . . . is how little the actual working week has shortened since the 1930's. What has happened is that although the 'basic' or negotiated working week has come down considerably, people have preferred to work as long as before but at overtime rates.[57]

Further, we cannot assume that all time spent outside of the place of employment is leisure time. Simple physiological functions such as eating and sleeping make obvious incursions into non-work time and activities associated with what DeGrazia[58] calls 'work-related time' make further incursions. Obvious examples here are travelling, personal grooming, and husbands doing a share of the housework.

It is not the intention in this concluding section to examine in detail the ways in which individuals spend their leisure time but, rather, to briefly examine the influence which the kind of work that people undertake has upon their attitudes towards leisure. There are two basic approaches frequently adopted in attempts at understanding work-leisure relationships.

First, the *segmentalists* approach, which tends to see the various areas of activity in peoples lives as being relatively independent of each other. Adopting this view leads us to think of work and leisure as being only weakly related, if at all, so that if we wished to answer questions on why people spend their leisure time as they do, we would have to look for other influences outside the workplace. The second basic approach, that of the *holists*, assumes that attitudes and behaviour in one sphere of activity are likely to spill over into other spheres.

Parker suggests that these two approaches towards an understanding of work-leisure relationships operate at too general a level, and that we should look more closely at occupational sub-cultures and work milieux. In doing so, he has suggested three basically different types of work-leisure relationship—the *extension*, *neutrality* and the *opposition* patterns.[59]

The *extension* pattern tends to occur amongst occupational groups where work is seen as a Central Life Interest, and involvement[60] in the job is high. Typical examples are successful businessmen, the self-employed, social workers, teachers and lecturers, and some skilled manual workers. The occupations concerned generally possess a high degree of autonomy, the use of a wide range of personal abilities, high levels of intrinsic work satisfaction, and high levels of ego involvement. Work and leisure tend not to be sharply demarcated. Leisure activities tend to display similarities with work activities and function to develop the individual's personality in particular ways.

The *neutrality* pattern tends to occur amongst occupational groups where family or leisure are seen as central life interests and involvement in the job is of a calculative nature. Typical examples are clerical workers, semi-skilled manual workers, and minor professionals. The occupations concerned generally have medium to low degrees of autonomy, limited opportunities to use personal abilities, stress on extrinsic job satisfactions (e.g. pay and working conditions) and limited ego involvement. Leisure activities differ from work activities and function essentially as a form of relaxation.

The *opposition* pattern tends to occur amongst occupational groups whose Central Life Interest is decidedly in the non-work field, and whose involvement in the job is of a low order, often alienative or hostile. Typical examples are unskilled manual workers and those in occupations such as mining and distant water fishing. The occupations concerned generally possess low degrees of autonomy, use of only a narrow range of personal abilities, work satisfaction (if any) based on extrinsic rewards, and little or no ego involvement. Work and leisure are sharply demarcated and the function of leisure is recuperation from work.[61] However, it will be remembered that people in similar or identical occupations may have different orientations towards work (see Cotgrove and Box's work on scientific identities—Chapter VI) and this may, in itself, lead to different work-leisure relationships.

It is obviously worthwhile, in any attempt to understand the importance and the meaning that work has for those concerned,[62] to devote at least some attention to the question of leisure. If future research reinforces the above picture of marked relationships between work and leisure, then the meaning of work itself will take on an even greater importance in the lives of those involved than is often realized.

REFERENCES

1 *see* BOSTON, R., 'What leisure?', *New Society*, Dec. 26th 1968 and SILLITOE, A. F. *Britain in Figures*, p. 106, Penguin, 1971. For more recent data, see the *Department of Employment Gazette* which regularly publishes statistics for hours worked in a wide variety of different occupations.

2 *see*, for example, HARRIS, C. C., *The Family: An Introduction*, Ch. 4, Allen & Unwin, 1967.

3 *see* WILLIAMS, W.M. (Ed.), *Occupational Choice: A Selection of Papers from the Sociological Review*, Allen & Unwin, 1974; CARTER, M., *Into Work*, Penguin Books, 1966; DOUGLAS, J. W. B., *The Home and the School*, MacGibbon & Kee, 1964 (and Panther Books, 1967); HALSEY, A. H., FLOUD, J. and ARNOLD ANDERSON, C. (Eds.), *Education, Economy and Society, A Reader in the Sociology of Education*, Collier-Macmillan, 1961; KEIL, E. T., RIDDELL, D. S. and GREEN, B. S. R., 'Entry Into the Occupational System', in BUTTERWORTH, E. B. and WEIR, D. (Eds.), *The Sociology of Modern Britain*, pp. 160–3, Fontana, 1970.

4 LANCASHIRE, R., 'Occupational choice theory and occupational guidance practice', in WARR, P. B. (Ed.), *Psychology at Work*, pp. 194–207, Penguin Books, 1971.

5 *see* LANCASHIRE, R. *op. cit.*, pp. 196–200.

6 *see* SILVERMAN, D. and JONES, J. 'Getting in: the managed accomplishment of

"correct" outcomes', in CHILD, J. (Ed.), *Man and Organization*, pp. 63–106, Allen & Unwin, 1973.

7 *see* MILLER, D. C. and FORM, W. H., *Industrial Sociology: an introduction to the sociology of work relations*, Harper and Row, 1964.

8 *see* LANCASHIRE, R., *op. cit.*, pp. 200–4, and MILLER, D. C. and FORM, W. H., *op. cit.*, Ch. XIII and XIV.

9 BLAU, P. M., GUSTAD, J. W., JESSOR, R., PARNES, H. S. and WILCOCK, R. C., 'Occupational choice: a conceptual framework', in ZYTOWSKI, D. G. (Ed.), *Vocational Behaviour*, pp. 358–70, Holt, Rinehart & Winston, 1968.

10 WILLIAMS, W. M. (Ed.)., *op. cit.*, and RIDDELL, D. S. and GREEN, B. S. R., *op. cit.*

11 *see* MANSFIELD, R., 'Career and individual strategies', in CHILD, J. (Ed.), *op. cit.*, pp. 107–32.

12 LANCASHIRE, R., *op. cit.*, p. 207.

13 DUNKERLEY, D., *Occupations and Society*, p. 21, Routledge & Kegan Paul, 1975.

14 MORSE, N. C., and WEISS, R. S., 'The function and meaning of work and the job', *American Sociological Review*, **20**, 1955. Also reprinted in VROOM, V. H. and DECI, E. L., *Management and Motivation* pp. 42–57, Penguin, 1970.

15 *ibid.*, p. 42.

16 *see*, e.g., HILL, M. J., *et al.*, *Men Out of Work: A Study of Unemployment in Three English Towns*, Cambridge University Press, 1973; WEDDERBURN, D., *Redundancy and the Railwaymen*, Cambridge University Press, 1965, and WEDDERBURN, D., 'Unemployment in the seventies', in BUTTERWORTH, E. and WEIR, D. (Eds.), *Social Problems of Modern Britain*, pp. 361–8, Fontana, 1972.

17 More recent studies in Britain have replicated this finding. For example, a large scale government sponsored survey in 1971 reported that among male workers 87% were either 'very satisfied' or 'fairly satisfied' with their jobs; among women the proportion was 91·8%. *see*: *The General Household Survey Introductory Report*, HMSO, 1973, Table 6·7, p. 192. Of course, the meaning of 'satisfaction' will vary from individual to individual and will depend a great deal on peoples' expectations in relation to work.

18 MORSE, N. C. and WEISS, R. S., *op. cit.*, p. 47.

19 GOLDTHORPE, J. H., LOCKWOOD, D., BECHHOFER, F. and PLATT, J., *The Affluent Worker: Industrial Attitudes and Behaviour*, Cambridge University Press, 1968, p. 11, and BLAUNER, R., 'Work satisfaction and industrial trends in industrial society', in BENDIX, R. and LIPSET, S. M. (Eds.), *Class, Status, and Power*, pp. 473–87, Routledge & Kegan Paul, 1967.

20 MORSE AND WEISS, *op. cit.*, p. 56.

21 DUBIN, R., 'Industrial workers' worlds: a study of the "Central Life Interests" of industrial workers', in ROSE, A. M. *Human Behaviour and Social Processes—An Interactionist Approach*, pp. 247–66, Routledge and Kegan Paul, 1962.

22 *ibid.*, p. 262.

23 BLAUNER, R., *op. cit.*

24 *see*, for parallel findings for Britain, *The General Household Survey Introductory Report*, *op. cit.*, Table 6.8, p. 193. For a more general survey of job satisfaction in Britain see, WEIR, M. (Ed.), *Job Satisfaction, Challenge and Response in Modern Britain*, Fontana, 1976.

25 WALKER, C. J. and GUEST, R. H., *The Man on the Assembly Line*, p. 9, Harvard, 1952.

26 *ibid.*

27 GOLDTHORPE, J. H. and LOCKWOOD, D., *et al., op. cit.*

28 *see* BROWN, R., 'Sources of objectives in work and employment', in CHILD, J. (Ed.), *op. cit.*, pp. 17–38.

29 GOLDTHORPE, J. H., 'Attitudes and behaviour of car assembly workers: a deviant case and a theoretical critique, *British Journal of Sociology*, pp. 227–44, Sept. 1966.

30 The deprivations of car assembly workers are further described in Beynon's recent study of Ford's Halewood plant in Liverpool, BEYNON, H., *Working for Ford*, Allen Lane, Penguin, 1973, especially Chs. 5 and 6. There is reason to believe that, due to a variety of factors, worker-management relations at Halewood are less harmonious than those at the Vauxhall factory studied by GOLDTHORPE, *et al.*, so the negative experiences of workers at Ford were further accentuated. Beynon also implicitly shows that the 'trade off' of material rewards as compensation for dislike of the job, widely reported as a major finding of the Goldthorpe study, may only operate under favourable circumstances. If this is the case, then the findings on the Luton assembly workers may understate the extent to the psychological costs of subjecting workers to mass production technology.

31 MARX, K. 'The notion of alienation', pp. 505–10 and SEEMAN, M., 'On the meaning of alienation', pp. 510–23, in COSER, L. A. and ROSENBURG, B., *Sociological Theory: A Book of Readings*, Collier-Macmillan, 1969. Also, MARX, K., 'Alienated labour', in FINIFTER, A. W. (Ed.), *Alienation and the Social System*, pp. 12–18, Wiley, 1972, and BANKS, J. A., *Marxist Sociology in Action*, Faber & Faber, 1970; DUBIN, R., *op. cit.*; BLAUNER, R., *Alienation and Freedom: The Factory Worker and His Industry*, University of Chicago Press, 1964; and CHINOY, E., *Automobile Workers and the American Dream*, Doubleday, 1955.

32 However, as noted above, Beynon's study of Ford's Liverpool factory showed that this relationship may not always occur.

33 DANIEL, W. W., 'Industrial behaviour and orientation to work', *Journal of Management Studies*, pp. 366–75, Oct. 1969. *see*, also in this journal: GOLDTHORPE, J. H., 'The social action approach to industrial sociology', pp. 199–208, May 1970; DANIEL, W. W., 'Productivity bargaining and orientation to work—A rejoinder to Goldthorpe', pp. 329–35, 1971; and GOLDTHORPE, J. H., 'Daniel on orientations to work—a final comment', pp. 266–73, Oct. 1972.

34 GOLDTHORPE, J. H., and LOCKWOOD, D., *et al., op. cit.*, pp. 64–8.

35 INGHAM, G. K., *Size of Industrial Organization and Worker Behaviour*, Cambridge University Press, 1970, and 'Organizational size, orientation to work and industrial behaviour', *Sociology*, pp. 239–58, Sept. 1967.

36 COTGROVE, S. and BOX, S., *Science, Industry and Society*, Allen & Unwin, 1970.

37 DANIEL, W. W. and McINTOSH, N., *The right to Manage?* MacDonald & Jane's, 1972, pp. 29–52 and DANIEL, W. W., 'What interests a worker?' *New Society*, pp. 583–6, March 23rd 1972.

38 However, not all of Daniel's fellow researchers in the project felt that the

change in levels of satisfaction was very marked. They argued that there was a
' . . . reduction in boredom rather than any major increase in intrinsic interest
in the job . . . basically the job remained unchanged'. Thus, while 62%
reported more interest, for many this appeared to mean merely less boredom.
Most of the respondents had never had a job with much intrinsic satisfaction
so even a slight improvement was recognized. *see* COTGROVE, S., *et al.*, *The
Nylon Spinners*, pp. 134–5, Allen & Unwin, 1971.

39 WEDDERBURN, D., 'What determines shopfloor behaviour?', *New Society*, pp.
    128–30, July 20th 1972; and WEDDERBURN, D. and CROMPTON, R., *Workers
    Attitudes and Technology*, Cambridge University Press, 1972.
40 This point is also a major theme in Nichols and Armstrong's recent study of
    workers in another chemical factory. *see* NICHOLS, T. and ARMSTRONG, P.,
    Workers Divided, Fontana, 1976.
41 TUNSTALL, J., *The Fisherman—The Sociology of an Extreme Occupation*,
    MacGibbon & Kee, 1962.
42 DENNIS, N., HENRIQUES, F. and SLAUGHTER, C., *Coal is Our Life*, Eyre &
    Spottiswode, 1957.
43 CARTER, M. P., *Into Work*, Ch. 2, Penguin, 1966.
44 HOLLOWELL, P. G., *The Lorry Driver*, Routledge & Kegan Paul, 1968 and
    GOLDTHORPE, *et al.*, *op. cit.*
45 DAVIS, D. R. and SHACKLETON, V. J., *Psychology at Work*, Ch. 7, Methuen, 1975.
46 LOCKWOOD, D., *The Blackcoated Worker*, Unwin University Books, 1958.
47 WEIR, D., 'Satisfactions in white collar work', in BUTTERWORTH, E. and WEIR, D.
    (Eds.), *Social Problems of Modern Britain*, pp. 374–83, Fontana, 1972.
48 BENDIX, R., *Work and Authority in Industry*, Wiley, 1956.
49 FLETCHER, C., 'The end of management', in CHILD, J. (Ed.), *op. cit*, pp. 135–57.
50 MARX, K., *op. cit.*
51 VEBLEN, T., *The Instinct of Workmanship*, Macmillan, 1914.
52 BLAUNER, R., *op. cit.*
53 Blauner offered an optimistic view in that he found process technology less
    alienating than assembly-line technology and since progress technology as one
    form of automation is likely to increasingly replace assembly-line technology
    in the future, there is also likely to be an overall reduction in levels of
    alienation. This view may, however, be unduly optimistic. After all,
    Goldthorpe *et al.* reported the self-selection of workers into mass production
    technology. In other words, if workers are alienated we perhaps ought to seek
    the source of such alienation outside the workplace. Whether Blauner's
    optimism on the likelihood of process technology being associated with
    generally lower levels of alienation is sound may also be questioned. Some
    studies of workers in this kind of technology, such as those of Cotgrove *et al.*
    and Nichols and Armstrong discussed above, lead to doubts on this issue.
54 *see* 'Marx and Weber', in GERTH, H. H. and MILLS, C. WRIGHT, *From Max Weber
    Essays in Sociology*, pp. 46–50, Routledge & Kegan Paul, 1970.
55 Studies carried out both in America and Britain suggest that white collar
    workers, often at the highest level, experience quite severe alienation under
    certain conditions. *see* MILLER, G., 'Professionals in bureaucracy: alienation

amongst industrial scientists and engineers', in GRUSKY, O. and MILLER, G. (Eds.), *The Sociology of Organizations*, pp. 503–15, Collier-Macmillan, 1970; PAHL, J. M. and PAHL, R. E., *Managers and Their Wives*, Penguin, 1971, and COTGROVE and BOX, *op. cit.* This observation is, of course, quite in line with Marx's original thinking on the nature of alienation since he stressed that the social organization of production in capitalist society led to alienation for all those involved regardless of their position in the organization.

56 PARKER, S., *The Future of Work and Leisure*, p. 11, Paladin, 1971.

57 SILLITOE, A. F., *op. cit.*, pp. 106–7.

58 DEGRAZIA, S., *Of Time, Work and Leisure*, Twentieth Century Fund, 1962.

59 PARKER, S., *op. cit. see also*: PARKER, S. R., 'Work and leisure', in PARKER, S. R. BROWN, R. K., CHILD, J. and SMITH, M. A. (Eds.), *The Sociology of Industry*, pp. 173–81, 1972.

60 The forms of worker involvement associated with the *extension, neutrality,* and *opposition* work-leisure relationships are, respectively, those which Etzioni termed *moral, calculative,* and *alienative*. See: ETZIONI, A., *A Comparative Analysis of Complex Organizations*, Free Press, 1961.

61 In the case of distant-water fishermen, Tunstall has described the function of leisure as 'explosive compensation' for the dangerous and physically damaging aspects of their work. *see* TUNSTALL, J., *op. cit.*, p. 137.

62 Many of the studies previously discussed in this chapter also discuss leisure patterns, e.g. GOLDTHORPE *et al.*, espec. Vol. III; HOLLOWELL, *op. cit.*, CHINOY, *op. cit.* and DENNIS, *et al.*, *op. cit.*

III

MOTIVATION AT WORK

In the preceding chapter we looked at the meaning of work and employment, their role in our society and differing orientations towards them. In this chapter we shall be examining more closely the work of behavioural scientists who have attempted to increase our understanding of the individual's motivation at work. Vroom has described motivation as:

> The process governing choices made by persons or lower organisms among alternative forms of voluntary activity.[1]

The manager's interest in the subject is likely to be more specifically in those factors influencing activities or behaviours that make a contribution to organizational effectiveness. Katz[2] has suggested that there are three basic types of behaviour which are essential for an organization to function effectively:

1. *People must be induced to enter and remain within the system.*

   Labour turnover and absenteeism can be costly and disfunctional if allowed to get out of control. But physical attendance alone is not sufficient.

2. *They must carry out their role assignments in a dependable fashion.*

   For organizations to function they rely to greater or less extent on a fairly stable pattern of interrelated activities. These activities must be carried out to some minimal level of quantity and quality of performance. But a fixed pattern of role prescriptions cannot cater for unforeseen environmental changes or operational contingencies.

3. *There must be innovative and spontaneous activity* in achieving organizational objectives which go beyond the role specifications.

   What then are the factors likely to influence an individual's decision to devote or not to devote his time and energy to any or all of these types of behaviour? Before attempting to suggest any specific answers to this question it will be useful to look at the basic components of the motivational process.

A basic model of motivation

Underlying many approaches to the study of motivation is some concept of equilibrium. Although our main concern is with complex work-related activities, the significance of the concept is most easily demonstrated by reference to physiological approaches to the subject.

In 1932 Cannon[3] coined the word *homeostasis* to refer to the physiological mechanisms set into action to restore the internal state of an organism (e.g. blood sugar level, body temperature, etc.) to its normal and optimal condition of functioning whenever such a condition has been disturbed. A simple example of this process would be the automatic response of perspiration when the human body temperature moves above its equilibrium state of 98·4°F. Extended to behavioural responses to internal disequilibrium the idea of homeostasis leads us to what is basically a deficiency or survival model of motivation. Thus behaviour can be explained in the following way. We all have a number of basic physiological needs (e.g. for food) which if not met give rise to specific drives (e.g. hunger). These drives give rise to activity (e.g. the search for food) which is aimed at attaining some incentive, goal object or state (e.g. food) which can satisfy the original need. Such a deficiency model, however, is not adequate to explain research evidence[4] which suggests that some activities have an incentive value of their own, e.g. play, exploration, curiosity, manipulation. But if we accept a looser definition of 'need' than the strict physiological one, we do now have the components of a basic motivational model (Figure 3.1) upon which to build our understanding of motivation at work.

Figure 3.1

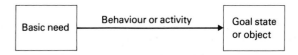

Unfortunately the complexities of human motivation make it impossible to make simple predictions as to which human needs will give rise to what work-related activities in response to what organizationally available goals or incentives. For example:

1. The same goal may be reached by a number of different activities.
2. A single activity may lead to the attainment of a number of different goals.
3. Attainment of a single goal could satisfy a number of different basic needs.

With regard to the behavioural component of the model, we have already seen three types of activity which are of prime interest to the manager. Some way is now required of categorizing basic human needs.

Basic human needs

Any attempt to draw up a list of basic human needs must of necessity be tentative and as yet is unlikely to be universally accepted. One influential list compiled by Murray *et al.*[5] itemizes forty such needs, divided into twelve 'viscerogenic' (physiological) needs and twenty-eight 'psychogenic' (psychological) needs. But in the area of organizational behaviour one classification of human needs and related theory of motivation has probably been more influential than any other. That is the theory presented by Maslow[6] which will now be examined more closely.

Maslow's hierarchy of needs   In Maslow's terms the human being should be seen as a 'perpetually wanting animal'. Based primarily on clinical observations, he maintained that nearly all individuals are motivated by the desire to satisfy certain specific needs which could be classified into five major groups.

1. *Physiological needs:* These are the basic needs of the individual, such as food, water, air, and sleep, which are essential for survival. He would also include other physiological needs which appear to be basic but which do not have an obvious survival function, such as sex and sensory stimulation (touching, smelling, etc.).
2. *Safety needs:* The needs for a generally ordered existence in a relatively stable, threat-free environment.
3. *Love needs:* The needs for affectionate relations with other people, a sense of belongingness and acceptance as a member of a group.
4. *Esteem needs:* All people in our society, claims Maslow, 'have a need or desire for a stable, firmly based, (usually) high evaluation of themselves, for self respect, or self esteem.'[7] There is a basic desire for independence and confidence in the face of the world. These needs also include, however, esteem from other people which represents a desire for prestige, importance and attention.
5. *The need for self-actualization:* The need for self-fulfilment, to become everything that one is capable of becoming, to realise one's full potential for doing or creating.

A second, fundamental aspect of Maslow's theory is that he maintained that there is a set order of priority in which these needs become important to us. In other words they should be thought of as constituting a hierarchy with physiological needs at the bottom and the need for self-actualization at the top. This can be represented diagrammatically as in Figure 3.2.

The significance of the hierarchy is that the behaviour of any person is dominated by the lowest group of needs which remain unsatisfied. Only once a level of needs has been largely satisfied will the activities of the

Figure 3.2

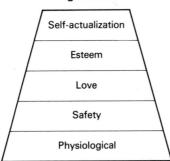

individual be directed towards satisfying the next level up. In other words a person whose love needs remain unsatisfied will not be activated by the desire for self-actualisation. But once needs have been satisfied they cease to play an activating role. As Maslow puts it 'a satisfied need is not a motivator'.[8] In later formulations of the theory[9] he suggests that the last point is not true however of the highest level. For self-actualization needs, increased satisfaction leads to increased need strength.

It is interesting to note at this point that in the early formulations of the theory Maslow suggested that there might be two other sets of needs which he could not fit neatly into the hierarchy of basic needs: but he was reluctant for them to be seen as completely separate from them. These were the cognitive needs (needs for knowing and understanding and for a sense of meaning) and aesthetic needs (the desire for good form, to move towards beauty and away from ugliness). It seems a pity that they should have disappeared from subsequent discussion of the original ideas.

As has been indicated, this theory, originally formulated in a clinical setting, has been highly influential on the work of subsequent students of organizational behaviour. Surprisingly, therefore, there has been relatively little empirical research to test the relevance of the theory in organizational settings. This may, in part, be due to the relatively imprecise nature of the original hypotheses which make it difficult to make sufficiently detailed predictions of behaviour for them to be operational. Lawler and Suttle,[10] however, reviewing the research that has been done by themselves and others, suggest that these 'studies offer little support for the view that the needs of managers in organizations are arranged in a multilevel hierarchy'. But this does not necessarily mean that we must reject all of Maslow's ideas for, as others have said, he

> is important because he directs attention to the point that many motives may direct behaviour, and that people may engage in activities simply because they believe they are valuable and not because of other extrinsic motives.[11]

In addition, the ideas do provide a useful framework for studying the development of what might loosely be termed managerial approaches to motivation.

The development of managerial approaches to motivation

Regardless of the validity of the hierarchy concept in explaining the emergence of an individual's salient needs, it does seem to give an indication of the order in which theories of, or basic assumptions about, man's motives at work have emerged. So, in the early part of this century, the prevailing view of the worker was that of economic man for whom any higher order needs were irrelevant. The thirties and forties saw the development of what became known as the Human Relations school of thought which explained man's behaviour at work primarily in terms of his social needs. The theories which emerged in the sixties and which still underlie much of today's management practice placed much more emphasis on the importance of higher order needs in understanding man's motivation at work. The significance of these developments as an influence on organizational form or structure is discussed more fully in Chapter VII. At this point we shall look at them more closely in terms of motivation.

The name most frequently associated with the early 'carrot and stick' approach is that of F. W. Taylor, the 'father' of scientific management.[12] According to him:

> What the workmen want from their employers more than anything else is high wages and what employers want from their workmen is low labour cost.

This view of man has been labelled by McGregor[13] as 'Theory X' and is, he maintained, based on the following assumptions:

1. 'The average human being has an inherent dislike of work and will avoid it if he can.'
2. 'Because of this human characteristic of dislike of work, most people must be coerced, controlled, directed, threatened with punishment to

get them to put forth adequate effort toward the achievement of organizational objectives.'

3. 'The average human being prefers to be directed, wishes to avoid responsibility, has relatively little ambition, wants security above all.'

The implications of this approach for management practice are close supervision of subordinates, breaking down of tasks to the simplest, most easily learned, repetitive operations and the establishment and enforcement of detail work routines and procedures. Such strategies, together with proper, physical working conditions (it was claimed) would minimize worker inefficiency. They were, however, far from problem free and the underlying theory of motivation proved quite inadequate for explaining all work behaviour.

The subsequent development of theories to compensate for the inadequacies of the traditional model owe much to the 'Hawthorne Studies' carried out over a twelve-year period from 1927 at the Hawthorne Works of the Western Electric Company, Chicago, initiated by Elton Mayo, and described in detail by Roethlisberger and Dickson.[14] Ironically the studies and resulting theories developed initially from attempts to examine the effect of various aspects of the physical working conditions upon production. The surprising findings that output seemed to improve almost regardless of what variations were made to working conditions led to a search for explanations outside the man-machine relationship, and the emergence of a set of assumptions based on the view of man primarily as a social animal, gaining his basic sense of identity through relationships with others. It was assumed that, as a result of industrialization and rationalization, work itself held no meaning, and it was therefore sought in relationships on the job. Peer group pressure was seen as more influential than incentives or management controls. Such assumptions led to greater concern for morale at work, the employment of group rather than individual incentive schemes, the development of company newspapers as means of keeping employees 'informed', and the emergence of strategies aimed at making the workplace a source of social satisfaction. But as Steers and Porter[15] point out:

The basic ingredient that typically was *not* changed was the nature of the required tasks on the job.

Such a view of motivation, however, was still rather simplistic and proved just as inadequate for explaining the variety of behaviour evidenced at work as that which it replaced. Another group of theorists came to the fore in the sixties who, while sharing the Human Relations school's rejection of the traditional, scientific management ideas about motivation, claimed that that school's paternalistic orientation not only indicated a far from complete understanding of the nature of man but was no less manipulative than its predecessor's.

Schein[16] refers to this new group as the Self-Actualizing Man approach, which gives an indication of their basic orientation. For them the manager's task is to make use of the full human potential of his subordinates by providing opportunities for them to achieve self-fulfilment in their work. Typical of this approach are McGregor,[17] Argyris,[18] Likert[19] and Herzberg,[20] all of whom either explicitly or implicitly have extended the ideas of Maslow into management practice.

We have seen that McGregor criticized the traditional management practice that he labelled Theory X. His preference was for the integration of individual and organizational goals based on assumptions he labelled Theory Y:

1. There is no inherent dislike of work itself (although established practice may be seen as distasteful and therefore to be avoided).
2. Man will exercise self-direction and self-control in the service of objectives to which he is committed.
3. The degree of commitment is a function of the rewards seen to result from meeting these objectives. In this context the most significant rewards are the satisfaction of higher order needs. Such rewards are intrinsic to work not externally mediated.
4. If the conditions are right the individual will not only accept but seek responsibility.
5. A high proportion of the population is capable of imagination, ingenuity and creativity in solving organizational problems.
6. Industrialization has meant that such capacities are underutilized.

Such assumptions imply that, if employees appear lazy, indifferent or unco-operative, the causes lie in management's methods of organization and control. This does not represent, however, a plea for 'soft' management and a slackening of discipline. McGregor maintained that

the essential task of management is to arrange organizational conditions and methods of operation so that people can achieve their own goals best by directing their own efforts toward organizational objectives.

Put differently, if he can get high performance targets and get his subordinates to accept them as their own, he is not likely to have to worry much about discipline. McGregor, therefore, followed Drucker[21] in advocating 'management by objectives' in contrast to 'management by control'.

Argyris's approach is similar to McGregor's in that he has claimed that there is an inevitable incompatibility between the way organizations have developed in the service of limited economic goals, and the natural development of a psychologically healthy individual. In other words there are severe human costs which outweigh the advantages of organization structures designed for technical efficiency. This point will be taken further in Chapter VII.

Likert too starts from the same basic assumptions about the nature of man and claims that with effective management

> reliance is not placed solely or fundamentally on the economic motive of buying a man's time and using control and authority as the organizing and co-ordinating principle.

Rather a

> highly motivated, co-operative orientation toward the organization and its objectives is achieved by harnessing effectively all the major motivational forces.[22]

Likert's recommendations as to how this might be achieved rest heavily on assumptions about effective management style which will be discussed more fully in Chapter V when we look at approaches to small-group leadership. In brief, however, he distinguishes four systems of management ranging from exploitive authoritative (system 1) through benevolent authoritative (system 2) and consultative (system 3) to participative (system 4). Inevitably it is System 4 which he favours, recommending group involvement in setting high performance goals and wide-spread participation in the decision-making process.

While such approaches seem to have had a considerable appeal to the practising manager, perhaps because they were very much in accord with the prevailing management values of the sixties (in the United States at least), they do seem still to rely on an overgeneralized view of man. That is, by assuming common motivational responses to management initiatives they have failed to address themselves to the problem of explaining individual differences in effort and performance between employees in the same department and are certainly inadequate for explaining the kinds of results we referred to in the previous chapter arising from the Luton Studies of Goldthorpe et al.[23]

But before we turn to the problem of individual differences ourselves, there is one more contribution to the 'self-actualizing man' approach that needs to be examined more fully. That is the work and ideas of Herzberg known variously as the two-factor theory, the dual-factor theory and the motivation-hygiene theory.

Herzberg's motivation-hygiene theory

Herzberg's theory and supporting research evidence from a survey of two hundred Pittsburgh engineers and accountants was first published in 1959.[24] Since that time the theory and the research have been the source of continuing attention and controversy among managers and academics alike.

The ideas stem from the finding that when men were asked to remember times when they felt exceptionally good about their jobs, they seemed to be referring to quite different events and activities from those they described when asked to remember times when they felt exceptionally bad about their jobs. In other words, job factors were allowed to emerge from descriptions of actual job situations rather than being based on responses to checklists or sets of statements prepared ahead of time by the researchers. The factors that emerged as major determinants of job satisfaction and which were relatively unimportant in connection with dissatisfaction were achievement, advancement, recognition, responsibility and work itself. Dissatisfaction on the other hand seemed to be associated with company policy and administration, supervision, salary, interpersonal relations and working conditions. These factors seemed rarely to be involved in job satisfaction.

From these findings it was concluded that satisfaction and dissatisfaction, rather than being opposites of one another, represented two quite independent dimensions of man's nature. One dimension is primarily concerned with avoiding unpleasantness (the Adam side of man), the other is concerned with seeking personal growth (the Abraham side of man). Satisfaction then, according to Herzberg, will be sought in aspects of job content (achievement, advancement, etc.) that provide opportunity for growth. These he called the motivators. Their absence will not cause dissatisfaction but merely lack of positive satisfaction. Avoidance of dissatisfaction, however, will be sought in aspects of the job context (company policies, working conditions, etc.). Using a medical analogy, he called these hygiene factors. Their presence does not lead to positive satisfaction but simply no dissatisfaction.

Hence Herzberg maintains that, while it is important to get the hygiene factors right, if the manager wants to motivate his employees, he should focus his attention on the job itself and attempt to manipulate the motivator factors. Such an approach implies a programme of 'job enrichment' which will be discussed more fully in the section dealing with job design.

His ideas have had a considerable impact on practising managers, perhaps partly because they offer relatively uncomplicated prescriptions and partly because of his own colourful way of presenting them, but they have been criticized heavily on a number of grounds by fellow behavioural scientists. It is to these criticisms we shall now turn, and which it is convenient to categorize as focusing either on research methodology, findings of further research or the research conclusions.

With regard to methodology it has been suggested that the findings reported by Herzberg are as likely to be a function of the critical incident storytelling method he used, as they are to represent true associations between satisfaction and work characteristics. Vroom[25] explains the point thus:

It is possible that obtained differences between stated sources of satisfaction and dissatisfaction stem from defensive processes within the individual respondent. Persons may be more likely to attribute the causes of satisfaction to their own achievements and accomplishments on the job. On the other hand, they may be more likely to attribute their dissatisfaction not to personal inadequacies or deficiencies but to factors in the work environment.

Wall and Stephenson[26] have taken this particular criticism further by submitting it to empirical examination. They state that their own studies

suggest that the research results upon which Herzberg's theory is based are a function of 'social desirability'.

They go on to say that:

consequently, as a description of the structure of job attitudes, and of the determinants of satisfaction and dissatisfaction the two-factor theory is not tenable.

An additional problem with this methodology is that since the interviews were relatively unstructured the subsequent coding of the responses required some interpretation by the researchers themselves. This interpretation could as much reflect their own preconceptions or hypotheses as the respondents' own view of the situation.

Another methodological criticism has been that despite the centrality of the concept of job satisfaction to the theory it is never made clear what is meant by the term and Ewen[27] claims that since the study contains no measure of overall satisfaction there is no basis for assuming that the so-called motivators and hygiene factors contribute to overall satisfaction or dissatisfaction as claimed.

Still on the theme of lack of precise definition King[28] has claimed that much of the controversy surrounding Herzberg's ideas stem from the fact that there has never really been an explicit statement of the theory itself and as a result it is possible to identify five quite distinct versions of the theory stated or implied by the researchers claiming to examine it. This obviously makes direct comparison of the subsequent studies claiming either to support or refute Herzberg's original findings very difficult. Such studies have been carried out in a number of different countries now, and using subjects from a much wider range of occupations and backgrounds than in the original research. The results continue to be conflicting but an interesting fact does emerge. That is that research which supports the theory tends to use very similar methods to those used in the original study, whereas research which refutes it has tended to use different methods. Such a pattern seems to lend weight to the 'social desirability' criticism.

In their review of the research that has used different methods, House and Wigdor[29] claim that four important conclusions emerge:

1. A given factor can cause job satisfaction for one person and job dissatisfaction for another person and *vice versa*. This will be determined to some extent by the individual's occupational level, age, sex, education, culture, and standing within his group.
2. Any single factor can be the source both of satisfaction and dissatisfaction within the same sample of people.
3. Intrinsic job factors are more important both to satisfaction and to dissatisfaction.
4. Therefore the two-factor theory is an oversimplification of the relationships between motivation and satisfaction, and the sources of job satisfaction and dissatisfaction.

Finally a number of criticisms have focused on the conclusions that Herzberg has himself drawn from the research evidence. For example, it has been questioned whether there is sufficient evidence to suggest that motivators form a distinctive grouping separate from hygiene factors. In fact, House and Wigdor reanalysing evidence presented by Herzberg himself, suggest that:

Although many of the intrinsic aspects of jobs are shown to be more frequently identified by respondents as satisfiers, achievement and recognition are also shown to be very frequently identified as dis-satisfiers.

In fact, achievement and recognition are far more frequently identified as dissatisfiers than working conditions and relations with the superior. Another aspect on which Herzberg's conclusions can be, and have been, criticized is in the implicit assumption that there is a direct relationship between job satisfaction, motivation and performance, which we shall see later is not necessarily the case.

Despite all these criticisms and the reservations about the value of the two-factor theory to which they must inevitably give rise, it must not be overlooked that Herzberg has made a considerable contribution to the study of motivation at work, not least in terms of the discussion and research which his ideas have stimulated. In addition he has succeeded in convincing many managers that intrinsic aspects of job design can potentially have as much influence on work behaviour as contextual factors such as money and fringe benefits.

So far the approaches to motivation at work that have been examined, despite conflicting with each other and offering the manager differing prescriptions, have had one underlying theme in common. That is the assumption that it is possible to formulate principles of motivation and hence recommend procedures that will be applicable to any individual in whatever organizational setting. Lupton[30] has dubbed this 'psychological universalism'. The fault lies not so much in the wrongness of the various approaches but in their simplicity and the failure to acknowledge that what is appropriate in one situation will not necessarily be appropriate in others. This is a point which will recur in this book, particularly when we come to deal with leadership or management style and organizational form or structure. In the context of motivation what is required is an approach which allows for the complexity and variability of man and the complexity and variability of the social, organizational and work settings in which he finds himself. One approach that does explicitly recognize individual differences and personal variability and the impact of class is Achievement-motivation theory.

Achievement motivation

Probably the name most frequently associated with this theory is that of McClelland.[31] His work was initially much influenced by that of Murray who has already been mentioned earlier in the chapter. Unlike Murray, however, his concern has not been with the examination of an entire set of needs but with three needs in particular: the need for achievement (often referred to as n-Ach), the need for power (n-Pow), and the need for affiliation (n-Aff.). More precisely still, much of the attention has been focused upon the first of these which has been defined as 'behaviour towards competition with a standard of excellence'.

McClelland maintains that there are two basic groupings of people: those who are challenged by opportunity and are willing to work hard to achieve a goal and those who do not really care all that much. In other words those with an urge to achieve and those without. His studies have attempted to probe this dichotomy to determine whether n-Ach is accidental, hereditary, or the result of environmental influences. In addition he has been concerned to find out whether it represents a single isolated motive or represents a combination of motives such as the desire to accummulate wealth, power and fame. He has also investigated the possibility of a technique whereby people with low n-Ach can be trained to develop a greater will to achieve.

His research has convinced him that there is a definite human motive distinguishable from others which can be tested for and found in any group. The strength of this motive, however, will vary considerably from one individual to another. This variability, he maintains, is not a function of heredity but differing cultural backgrounds, childhood training, parental attitudes, education and the like. For example, he claims:

> The evidence suggests it is not because they (high-need achievers) are born that way, but because of special training they get in the home from parents who set moderately high achievement goals but who are warm, encouraging and non-authoritarian in helping their children reach these goals.

The evidence accumulated suggests that people with high levels of need for achievement have a number of identifiable characteristics in common:

1. They prefer situations in which they can take personal responsibility for carrying out a task or solving a problem. If this were not so they could get little personal sense of accomplishment from success. It also seems that the satisfaction comes not from public recognition of accomplishment but from having initiated the successful action. But the high n-Ach individual is not a gambler and does not look forward to situations where the outcome depends not on his own abilities and efforts but on chance or other factors beyond his control. As a case in point, one of McClelland's studies at Harvard Business School involved an exercise where students had to choose one of two options. In each option they had a chance of one in three of succeeding. For one option they could roll a die, and if it valued say a one or a three (out of six possibilities) they won. The other option was to work on a difficult business problem which they knew only one out of three people had been able to solve in the time allowed. Under these conditions, the students with high n-Ach regularly chose to work on the business problem, even though they knew the odds of success were statistically the same as rolling the die.

2. The individual with high n-Ach has the tendency to set moderate achievement goals and to take calculated risks in reaching them. By adopting this strategy he has the greatest probability of getting the achievement satisfaction he wants. If he were to take an easy problem

he would succeed but get little satisfaction from the success. In other words, he will not work harder under all probabilities of winning but only when there is some challenge involved, i.e. some chance of losing. On the other hand, he will not select an exceptionally difficult task since, being unlikely to succeed, he will be unlikely to gain any satisfaction. This obviously has implications for target setting as a management activity. But it also means that such individuals tend to have a high need for variety in their work and to innovate because repetition tends to increase the probability of success to the point where the task becomes easy and no longer challenging.

3. The third major characteristic of these people is that they want concrete feedback on how well they are doing. Without this feedback they are unable to derive satisfaction from their own activities.

Such characteristics seem very much akin to the traditional 'entrepreneurial spirit'. This was particularly significant for McClelland and his associates[32] who were concerned with the problem of how to accelerate economic growth in underdeveloped countries. Following Weber's thesis[33] it was maintained that such economic growth is to a large extent a function of the level of entrepreneurial activity. Courses were developed and run for Indian businessmen and negro businessmen in Washington D.C. aimed at helping them to understand their own motives, enhance their self-esteem and strengthen their need for achievement. The follow up studies indicate that such courses were successful in that the participants subsequently significantly increased their business activity.

These factors seem to be particularly relevant to the man who runs his own business and therefore has the independence to act (see Chapter X), but what of the manager in the large organization? McClelland himself in more recent work[34] suggests the picture may be quite different:

For one thing, because they focus on personal improvement, on doing things better by themselves, achievement-motivated people want to do things themselves. For another, they want concrete short-term feedback on their performance so that they can tell how well they are doing. Yet a manager, particularly one of or in a large complex organization, cannot perform all the tasks necessary for success by himself or herself. He must manage others so that they will do things for the organization. Also feedback on his subordinate's performance may be a lot vaguer and more delayed than it would be if he were doing everything himself.

This can give some insight into the problems frequently associated with the highly successful salesman, for whom the high n-Ach characteristics are very appropriate, who because of his performance is promoted to a managerial position for which he is unsuited.

These recent researches, furthermore, suggest that need for affiliation is even less appropriate for the effective manager. The general conclusions are that he should possess a high need for power, that is, influencing people, and this need for power ought to be greater than his need for being liked by people. This rather alarming finding is, however, qualified by an additional measure—the degree of inhibition. The effective manager scores high on inhibition as well as power, which indicates that the power motivation is not directed towards personal aggrandizement but toward the institution for which he works and is exercised on behalf of other people. This has been termed the 'socialized face of power'.

Expectancy theory and the motivational process

Referring back to our basic model of motivation (Figure 3.1), it can be seen that the components of that model and its relevance to organizations have been expanded by the research and theory that have been discussed so far. We have seen some of the basic needs that may activate an individual in an organization. We have seen some of the behaviour that is required for organizational effectiveness. And we have seen some of the aspects of organizational and managerial practice that may act as an incentive or have some impact on need satisfaction. So far, however, we have not examined any approaches which specifically deal with the way in which the various components of the model might interact. In other words, the emphasis has been more on the content of motivation rather than the motivational process. One increasingly popular attempt to understand motivation in terms of process is known as expectancy theory.

The development of this theory into its current form owes much to the early 'cognitive' approaches of Lewin and Tolman. The foundation of the cognitive view of motivation is that individuals are seen as thinking, reasoning beings who have beliefs and expectations about future events in their lives. This includes expectations about the outcomes of their own behaviour. It is also assumed that they will have preferences amongst these possible outcomes.

For Lewin[35] behaviour takes place within a field of differing forces upon the individual. These forces may be internal or external to the individual. Some will be driving him towards a given goal and some will act as barriers impeding his progress. Behaviour then depends on the nature of these forces and the attractiveness (referred to as valence) of the particular goal. The important point to make, however, is that the force field represents the way the individual perceives reality and not a deterministic model of forces in 'objective' reality. This point is fundamental to the whole expectancy theory approach. Tolman[36] saw behaviour as influenced by a 'belief-value' matrix that specified for each individual the value he placed on particular outcomes of activity and his beliefs that those outcomes can be attained.

Influenced by these writers Georgopoulos, Mahoney and Jones[37] adopted what they called a 'path-goal' approach to the study of differing levels of productivity within organizations. Their approach is based on the following assumptions: individual productivity is among other things a function of one's motivation to produce at a given level. In turn such motivation depends upon (a) the particular needs of the individual as reflected in the goals towards which he is moving and (b) his perception regarding the relative usefulness of productivity behaviour as an instrumentality, or as a path to the attainment of these goals. The path will be chosen if his need(s) is sufficiently high, or his goal(s) is relatively salient and if no other more effective and economical paths are available to him. But even if the individual is motivated to produce at a high level it is not certain that he will become a high producer. This would be the case only if there were no restraining forces, if no barriers blocked the desired path. Such factors acting as limiting conditions may hinder the translation of motivation to produce into actual productive behaviour of a given level.

More recently Vroom[38] has presented a process theory of work motivation, the basic variables in which are expectancies, valences, instrumentality and force (terminology showing the influence of earlier cognitive theories).

Valence refers to the strength of an individual's preference for a particular outcome from his own effort or activity. Presumably, outcomes gain their valence as a function of the extent to which the individual sees them to be related to his own needs, but Vroom does not deal concretely with this point. He does however allow for outcomes to have a negative valence, i.e. for the individual to prefer not attaining them to attaining them. In this way it is possible to incorporate avoidance as a driving force in behaviour. In addition, he does point out that many outcomes can be positively or negatively valent for an individual without themselves being anticipated as satisfying or dissatisfying. Their valence derives not so much from any intrinsic properties but from whatever other outcomes they may be thought to lead to. In other words, their valence is a result of their perceived 'instrumentality'. The obvious example for most of us of an outcome with positive instrumental valence is money. Money is seldom seen to have much intrinsic value but may have high valence as a result of the other satisfying outcomes to which it may lead.

Expectancy is defined as a belief concerning the likelihood that a particular act will be followed by a particular outcome. The degree of belief can vary between zero (complete lack of belief that it will follow) and one (complete certainty that it will). For example, an individual may believe that if he purchases a premium bond he has virtually no chance of winning (zero expectancy): but he may believe that by placing a bet on a certain horse in the Grand National he is bound to win (expectancy of one). Note, however, that, just as valence refers to the perceived or expected value of an outcome, not its real or eventual value, so with expectancy it is the perception of the individual that is important not objective reality. The concept has been referred to by others as 'subjective probability'.

Finally Vroom maintains that the various expectancies and valences interact with one another to produce a force on the individual to perform a certain act and that individuals choose from alternative acts the one corresponding to the strongest positive (or possibly weakest negative) force.

Vroom's theory has had a great influence on subsequent writers but it does leave some questions unanswered. In particular, it does not deal with the problem of translating motivation to perform an act (force) into the actual performance of that act.

Current formulations of the theory

Figure 3.3 represents in diagrammatic form a theoretical model based largely on that formulated by Porter and Lawler[39] but also incorporating subsequent modifications by Lawler[40] and Campbell *et al.*[41] It is hoped that it will make more easy to understand the following discussion of the components of the model and their interrelationship.

Box 1 corresponds roughly to what Vroom termed 'force'. It is compounded in the same way from 'valence' and expectancy.

Valence is the attractiveness of possible outcomes to individuals. A given potential reward is differently desired by different individuals. (Porter and Lawler on the one hand mention that the model does not deal with how rewards acquire value and on the other hand, by implication, commit themselves to Maslow's hierarchical model.) In fact Lawler[42] is quite explicit.

I would like to argue that the reward value of outcomes stems from their ability to satisfy one or more needs. Specifically relevant here is the list of needs suggested by Maslow.

Expectancy in this model, unlike Vroom's, is sub-divided. That is, the overall probability that rewards depend on effort is a product of the probability that rewards depend on performance (Box 1B) and the probability that performance depends on effort (Box 1A). For example, an

Figure 3.3 Theoretical model showing determinants of effort, performance and satisfaction

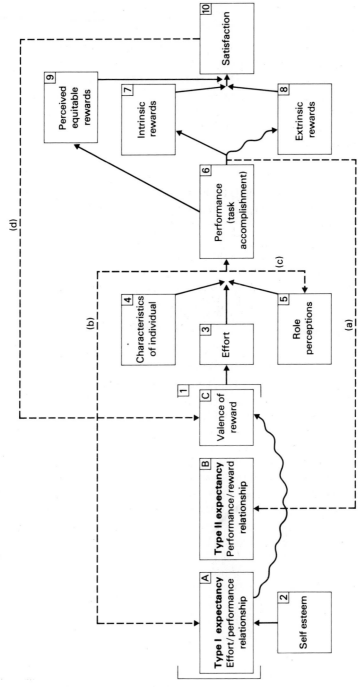

individual may believe that a particular reward that he values, say promotion, in no way depends on his effective performance but is determined solely on grounds of seniority. In such a case he would have a Type II expectancy of zero. On the other hand he may perceive promotion as directly related to performance but still his expectancy that rewards depend upon effort may be low, because he feels that no amount of additional effort on his part will improve his performance, either because of situational factors beyond his control, or because he does not think he has the abilities to perform the job well enough to deserve the reward. That is his Type I expectancy is zero. Lawler[43] suggests that this is determined in part by the individual's self-esteem (Box 2). In addition, following Achievement motivation theory, it might be suggested that for some people there will be a relationship between this Type 1 expectancy and the valance of the outcome or reward (indicated by the wavy line). In other words, a high n-Ach person, as we have seen, will be more attracted to tasks in which he has some chance of failing. In the context of this model the implication is that the likelihood of achievement satisfaction is greater where the perceived relationship between effort and task accomplishment is less than perfect.

The force upon an individual to exert effort (Box 3) is the product of Expectancies 1 and 2 and the valence of the reward. This model, however, goes further than Vroom did in making a clear distinction between effort and effective performance or task accomplishment (Box 6). Effort essentially is how hard the individual is trying, how much energy he is expending in a given situation. But unfortunately the amount of effort an individual puts into a task does not necessarily correlate with how successfully that task is carried out. In some senses then effort is the key factor in that the strength of motivation should show up more directly in the amount of effort expended than in the performance results attained. This can be so for a number of reasons.

Firstly the personal characteristics of the individual (Box 4) can set limits to his ability to perform effectively. Intelligence, skill, personality can all influence an individual's performance in addition to his effort.

In addition there are frequently variations or differences in role perceptions (Box 5). An individual will have beliefs and expectations regarding the kind of activities and behaviour he should engage in to perform his task effectively. If, however, these perceptions do not correspond to those held by his boss, it is possible that he could be expending a lot of effort without doing the task properly (at least in the eyes of his boss). Thus, just as personal characteristics may limit an individual's capacity for translating effort into effective performance, so accuracy of role perceptions will limit the amount of effort that is relevant to effective performance. This latter point will be explored in more detail in Chapter VI.

It can be seen then that performance is by no means directly related to effort. Furthermore, this model does shed some light on the controversial relationship between performance and satisfaction. Brown[44] says:

> The present consensus of opinion is that, on the whole, there is evidence for a low but fairly consistent relationship between satisfaction and performance. It is, however, not clear why this relationship exists. Did satisfaction with the job cause the performance? Or did performance cause satisfaction?

This model allows us to examine the effect that rewards and perceptions of equity can have in moderating that relationship and also suggests the direction of causality.

Extrinsic rewards (Box 8) are those which are controlled by the organization such as pay, promotion, status, security, etc. The connection between these rewards is indicated on the diagram by a wavy line because it is likely to be relatively weak or at least indirect, with the exception perhaps of the simpler incentive payment systems.

The connection, however, between performance and intrinsic rewards (Box 7) is likely to be more direct and is therefore indicated by a straight line. These rewards, such as feelings of accomplishing something worthwhile, a sense of achievement and the feelings of making full use of and developing one's skills and abilities, are seen as more certain outcomes of performance because they are internally mediated. They are the rewards the individual gives himself.

But satisfaction (Box 10) will not result from the receipt of rewards alone. This will be determined by the gap between the rewards actually received and perceived equitable rewards (Box 9). By perceived equitable rewards we mean the level or amount of rewards that an individual feels he *should* have or is fair as a result of a given level of performance. It can also refer to the rewards an individual feels should be associated with certain positions within the organization. The line on the diagram connecting performance and perceived equitable rewards (Box 6 and Box 9) is an acknowledgement of the influence that an individual's own rating of how well he has done his job will have on what he will regard as a fair reward. So satisfaction is only in part determined by the level of rewards actually received. High performance will only lead to high levels of satisfaction if it decreases the gap between what is received and what is seen as fair. Furthermore, a low performer, if his expected rewards are also low, might be equally or even more satisfied than a given high performer. This effect of perceived equity on performance and satisfaction has been developed further and examined extensively by Adams.[45]

The theory then suggests that satisfaction is primarily a dependent variable not a casual one.

An additional advantage of this model is that it does regard motivation as a dynamic process. In other words it does incorporate learning from observed and actual experience in similar situations in the past. The way in which this learning may feed back and influence various aspects of the model is indicated on the diagram by the broken lines. Thus the way in which an organization rewards (or does not reward) an individual for his performance will effect his perceptions of the connection between rewards and performance. (Feedback (a).) Similarly the success (or otherwise) with which effort is in fact translated into performance will effect the individual's perceptions of the connection between effort and performance. (Feedback (b).) It may also effect the subsequent accuracy of his role perceptions. (Feedback (c).) It is also suggested that when an individual feels satisfied after having received rewards, this will have an effect on the future valences of those rewards. (Feedback (d).)

Having outlined the main features of the expectancy theory, we shall now examine its validity in terms of the research evidence available.

Vroom, having constructed his conceptual model (outlined earlier), 'sought to relate the large number of concepts found in the literature of applied psychology, to the basic concepts in the model'. In other words, he attempted to 'fit' his model retrospectively to extensive past research findings, in particular with regard to Occupational Choice, Job Satisfaction, and Job Performance. He found that there was considerable correspondence between the hypothesis derived from his basic model and the information which was at that time available. (He did admit that with regard to occupational choice there was little evidence that was directly relevant to the model.) He did however state that

> The evidence in no sense *proves* the propositions, but it does suggest that they constitute a fruitful point of departure in our efforts to find principles and generalizations concerning work and motivation.

This point can be expanded by reference to research specifically designed to test the model(s).

In a study to test their path-goal theory, carried out on over 600 workers in a household appliances factory, Georgopoulos, Mahoney and Jones[46] found that

> If a worker sees high (or low) productivity as a path to the attainment of his personal goals he will tend to be a high (or low) producer. The

relationship was more pronounced among workers who have a high need with respect to a given goal.

They did, however, show some reservations with regard to their own results, by pointing out that when a different multiple correlation technique was applied, it was indicated that only a modest portion of the variance in productivity was explained in path-goal terms.

Galbraith and Cummings[47] sought to test Vroom's model. Studying 32 workers in a plant manufacturing heavy equipment, they measured by individual questionnaires, the valence of a set of job related outcomes such as pay, support and consideration from supervisor, promotion, etc. Similar measures were obtained of workers' conceptions of the extent to which effective job performance was instrumental to the attainment of each of these outcomes. While the overall results provided considerable support for the model, the interaction between valence and instrumentality was most marked in the case of support and consideration from supervisors. Thus the actual output of these workers tended to be the highest when they valued the support of their superior and at the same time believed that his support was contingent on their performance.

Porter and Lawler,[48] in a study of over 400 managers in 7 organizations, testing their own model, found that managers who saw pay closely tied to performance received higher effort and performance ratings. Furthermore, the strongest relationship between performance/reward probability and measures of effort existed for those managers who attached greatest importance to pay as a reward, showing as predicted, valence and effort-reward probability are interactive. Their findings also showed an interactive effect of effort and role perceptions to produce performance. (Abilities were not given much attention). The findings also suggested that the relationship between performance and satisfaction with pay holds only for those managers for whom performance is directly related to their actual pay.

Goodman, Rose and Furcon[49] compared four approaches to assessing motivational antecedents of work performance of a number of scientists and engineers in a government research laboratory. The four approaches were:

(i) Direction of Motivational Orientation (whether they were concerned with advance of science or status in the organization).
(ii) Source of motivational stimulation (preferred sources—internal or external).
(iii) Job dedication (intensity of work motivation).
(iv) An expectancy model.

They found that predictions from the expectancy model were the only ones to show any correlation with performance.

Kesselman et al.[50] conclude from their own test of the Porter-Lawler model that the findings clearly support the general theory and the linkages predictable from the theory. They also confirm the impact of role perceptions. But the point is also made that the climate or setting and the nature of the position (job duties and opportunities) do have a marked influence upon the relative importance of certain variables in the theory.

Parker and Dyer[51] make the point more emphatically:

First, expectancy theory models may, by themselves, have limited potential as a practical means of predicting work-related behaviour. With the inclusion of additional situational and psychological components in the model, however, practically useful behavioural predictions may be attained.

They go on to suggest that there will inevitably be problems in identifying which variables are appropriate in particular settings and to point out the dangers of including so many that the meaning of any results will be obscured.

These points, however, seem wholly consistent with the model outlined in this chapter, which makes a clear distinction between force upon an individual to perform an act and the actual, effective performance of that act, which will be the result of a number of factors, only one of which will be individual motivation.

All of this implies that expectancy theory has much to offer but there is still a great need for conceptual and methodological refinement, not least in the area of determining the impact upon work-behaviour of variables other than individual expectancies and reward valences. Even at this stage of development, however, the theory does have a number of practical implications. For example, attempts to measure and/or enhance satisfaction at work are likely to have little direct effect on their performance (although they may still be very influential on absenteeism and turnover). In addition there is a need to consider the appropriateness of rewards in that what is seen to be rewarding by one individual may not be by another. In other words, individualized rewards systems should be considered, perhaps along the lines suggested by Lawler as a 'cafeteria-style'.[52] Obviously attempts must also be made to establish clear links between effort, performance and rewards *in the eyes of the individual*. Finally, greater attention needs to be paid to the non-motivational factors which can effect performance including adequacy of facilities and procedures, individual abilities, differing role perceptions and role conflicts (see Chapter VII), group pressures on the individual (see Chapter V), organizational climate and so on.

The role of money and job design

So far this chapter has examined a number of theories that have emerged from attempts to gain further understanding of motivation at work. We have seen that the various approaches have focused on different aspects of the motivational model and in particular have placed emphases on different organizationally available sources of individual rewards, and more recently have distinguished between extrinsic and intrinsic rewards. We shall conclude the chapter by looking briefly at the roles played by money, as the major extrinsic reward, and job design as a source of intrinsic reward.

Money The first point to be made with regard to the motivational significance of money emerges clearly from what has already been said in this and the preceding chapter. That is, attempts to make statements about the importance of financial rewards which will be applicable to all situations are unrealistic. There will inevitably be a wide range of individual differences in orientation, depending in part on perceptions, personal characteristics and circumstances, and cultural factors. It is possible, however, on the basis of the theories discussed, to suggest a number of roles that money might play in the motivational process. It is not intended that these roles should be seen as mutually exclusive.

Firstly, while it is assumed that money has no intrinsic value, it can be seen as having acquired value as a result of its perceived instrumentality in obtaining other valued objects or states. In other words, although not directly related to any of the basic human needs described earlier, it could be seen as a means of attaining satisfaction of any of them.

As perhaps the most tangible of rewards, money can be an important means of comparison of personal rewards with the rewards received (or believed to be received) by others. This comparability or equity aspect of pay has become institutionalized in our industrial relations system as one of the major bases of collective bargaining.

The precise measuring-stick attribute of money also has other implications. It may perform the role of indicating to the individual his own level of accomplishment. This may be particularly important to the high n-Ach person who requires concrete feedback on how well he is doing. In this context, it would seem that increases in salary can still have an important role to play even at high income/high tax levels where the increase in take-home pay is minimal.

It has also been suggested by McClelland[53] that money may function as a symbol 'guaranteeing' a contract between two parties (employer and employee) which in fact involves more than the simple exchange of labour for money.

Following Herzberg, it may well be that for some people, at least, money serves not as a positive source of satisfaction or motivation but rather as a means of avoiding or reducing dissatisfaction.

Finally it has been suggested that as a result of socialization or conditioning money may have an important reinforcement effect in its own right. In other words, by repeated association with goal objects which are valued, it has acquired value of its own. If this is the case, then reinforcement theory would imply that different patterns or schedules of reinforcement have significantly different effects on behaviour.[54] For example, it seems that reinforcement at fixed intervals, such as would be the case with annual increments, particularly on a set scale, does little to encourage high levels of performance.

It seems unlikely that there will ever be a single universally acceptable theory regarding money. Meanwhile, to quote Opsahl and Dunnette:[55]

> Much remains to be learned before we will understand very well what meaning money has for different persons, how it effects their job behaviours, which motives it serves, and how its effectiveness may come about.

Job Design

> Job design means specification of the contents, methods and relationships of jobs in order to satisfy technological and organizational requirements as well as the social and personal requirements of the job holder.[56]

Cooper[57] points out that this implies two distinct aspects of work: job content, and job relationships. We have seen how early managerial approaches to job content concentrated on attempts to gain greater technical efficiency by simplifying the tasks required from employees. Current approaches seem more concerned with how job content can be made a source of intrinsic reward (and it is to this we shall turn our attention now). We shall also see in Chapter VII how approaches to the organization of work relationships have varied from emphasis on technical efficiency to consideration of the social-psychological implications.

As has been mentioned earlier, by far the most influential contribution to redesigning job content to increase intrinsic rewards has been that made by Herzberg and his followers. Building on the two-factor theory, their emphasis has been to concentrate on the motivator factors in work. This has meant a programme of 'job enrichment'. The term is distinguished from the older alternative 'job enlargement'. The latter, according to Herzberg, implies expanding the job horizontally: that is giving the employee a greater range of tasks or activities of the same kind, without requiring any difference in the type or level of skill. Job enrichment, however, implies expanding the job vertically to require a greater repertoire of skills and thus, it is assumed, providing greater opportunity for psychological growth. Herzberg[58] has suggested seven guiding principles for vertical expansion:

1. Remove some controls while retaining accountability.
2. Increase the accountability of individuals for own work.
3. Give a person a complete natural unit of work.
4. Grant additional authority to an employee in his activity; job freedom.
5. Make periodic reports directly available to the worker himself rather than to the supervisor.
6. Introduce new and more difficult tasks not previously handled.
7. Assign individuals specific or specialized tasks, enabling them to become experts.

The research evidence available on such approaches to job enrichment does suggest that it can have a positive effect on reduced turnover and absenteeism, job satisfaction, and quality of production. There is little evidence supporting improvements in productivity or level of output and such programmes usually involve increased costs in training time and occasionally retooling. Additionally, like the theory upon which it is based, this approach to job design is universalistic. In other words, it does not cater for individual differences in orientation to work and hence responsiveness to enriched jobs. In the light of what has gone before, it is not surprising that there is considerable evidence suggesting that differences between people do moderate their reactions to the increased complexity and challenge advocated by the job enrichers.

Recent attempts to gain a fuller understanding of the circumstances under which jobs will be intrinsically motivating have, therefore, included not only job characteristics but also individual attributes and the psychological states mediating between the job and the personal and organizational outcomes. The model presented and tested by Hackman and Oldham[59] represents such an approach.

They suggested that five core job dimensions 'potentially' prompt three significant psychological states which 'potentially' lead to a number of beneficial personal and work outcomes. But the strength of the link between these major elements of the model is influenced by individual differences. Reviewing research in the area they conclude that the most important difference is in the strength of individual growth needs. This was, however, seen as related to various background characteristics of the individual such as educational level, sex, age, place of work and place of residence.

The job dimensions contributing to its overall motivating potential are: skill variety, task identity (degree to which it involves doing a 'whole' piece of work), and task significance (degree of impact on the lives or work of others), these three potentially leading to experienced meaningfulness of work; autonomy, potentially leading to experienced responsibility; and feedback, potentially leading to knowledge of results. These dimensions then combine in the following way to provide a motivating potential score (MPS).

$$MPS = \left[\frac{\text{Skill Variety} + \text{Task Identity} + \text{Task Significance}}{3} \right] \times \text{Autonomy} \times \text{Feedback}$$

The model demonstrating how the motivating potential does or does not get translated into desired outcomes can be represented diagrammatically as in Figure 3.4.

Figure 3.4 The job characteristics model of work motivation (courtesy of Hackman, J. R. and Oldham, G. R., 1976)

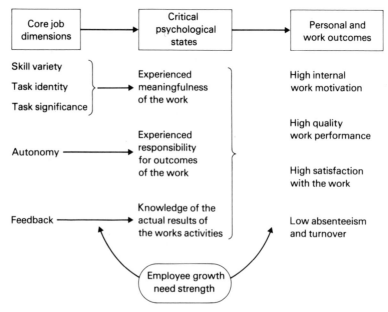

The implications are that those interested in a programme of job enrichment should proceed with caution. It does not represent a universal remedy to the problems of work design. The costs may be high and the benefits arising may well be less than expected or hoped for.

REFERENCES

1 VROOM, V. H., *Work and Motivation*, Wiley, 1964.
2 KATZ, D., 'The motivational basis of organizational behaviour', *Behavioural Science*, **9**, pp. 131–46, 1964.
3 CANNON, W. B., *Wisdom of the Body*, Norton, 1932.
4 HILGARD, E. R., ATKINSON, R. C. and ATKINSON, R. L., *Introduction to Psychology*, Harcourt Brace Jovanvich, 1971.
5 MURRAY, H. A. *et al., Explorations in Personality*, Oxford University Press, 1938.
6 MASLOW, A. H., 'A theory of human motivation', *Psychological Review*, **50**, pp. 370–96, 1943.
7 MASLOW, A. H., *op. cit.*
8 MASLOW, A. H., *op. cit.*
9 MASLOW, A. H., *Toward a Psychology of Being*, 2nd ed. Van Nostrand, 1968.
10 LAWLER, E. E. and SUTTLE, J. L., 'A causal correlational test of the need hierarchy concept', *Organisational Behaviour and Human Performance*, **7**, pp. 265–87, 1972.
11 BLACKLER, F. H. M. and WILLIAMS, A. R. T., 'People's motives at work', in WARR, P., *Psychology at Work*, Penguin, 1971.
12 TAYLOR, F. W., *Scientific Management*, Harper & Row, 1947.
13 McGREGOR, D., *The Human Side of Enterprise*, McGraw-Hill, 1960.
14 ROETHLISBERGER, F. and DICKSON, W. J., *Management and the Worker*, Harvard University Press, 1939.
15 STEERS, R. M. and PORTER, L. W., *Motivation and Work Behaviour*. McGraw-Hill, 1975.
16 SCHEIN, E., *Organisational Psychology*, Prentice-Hall, 1972.
17 McGREGOR, D., *op. cit.*
18 ARGYRIS, C., *Integrating the Individual and the Organisation*, Wiley, 1964.
19 LIKERT, R., *New Patterns of Management*, McGraw-Hill, 1961.
20 HERZBERG, F., *Work and the Nature of Man*, World, 1966.
21 DRUCKER, P. F., *The Practice of Management*, Harper, 1954.
22 LIKERT, R., *op. cit.*
23 GOLDTHORPE, J. H. *et al., The Affluent Worker: Industrial Attitudes and Behaviour*, Cambridge University Press, 1968.
24 HERZBERG, F., *The Motivation to Work*, Wiley, 1959.
25 VROOM, V. H., *op. cit.*
26 WALL, T. D. and STEPHENSON, G. M., 'Herzberg's two-factor theory of job attitudes: a critical evaluation and some fresh evidence', *Industrial Relations Journal*, December 1970.

27 EWEN, R. B., 'Some determinants of job satisfaction: a study of the generality of Herzberg's theory', *Journal of Applied Psychology*, **48**, 1964.

28 KING, N., 'Clarification and evaluation of the two-factor theory of job satisfaction', *Psychological Bulletin*, **70**, 1974.

29 HOUSE, R. J. and WIGDOR, L. A., 'Herzberg's dual-factor theory of job satisfaction and motivation: a review of the evidence and a criticism', *Personnel Psychology*, No. **20**, 1967.

30 LUPTON, T., *Management and the Social Sciences*, Penguin, 1971.

31 McCLELLAND, D. C., *The Achieving Society*, Van Nostrand, 1961.

32 McCLELLAND, D. C. and WINTER, D. G., *Motivating Economic Achievement*, Free Press, 1969.

33 WEBER, M., *The Protestant Ethic and the Spirit of Capitalism*, Scribner, 1930.

34 McCLELLAND, D. C. and BURNHAM, D. H., 'Power is the great motivator', *Harvard Business Review*, March/April 1976.

35 LEWIN, K., *Field Theory and Social Science*, Harper, 1951.

36 TOLMAN, E. C., *Purposive Behaviour in Animals and Men*, Appleton-Century, 1932.

37 GEORGOPOULOS, B. S., MAHONY, G. M. and JONES, N. W., 'A path-goal approach to productivity', *Journal of Applied Psychology*, **41**, 1957.

38 VROOM, V. H., *op. cit.*

39 PORTER, L. W. and LAWLER, E. E, *Managerial Attitudes and Performance*, Irwin, 1968.

40 LAWLER, E. E., 'Job attitudes and employee motivation: theory, research and practice', *Personnel Psychology*, **23**, 1970.

41 CAMPBELL, J. P., DUNNETTE, M. D., LAWLER, E. E. and WEICK, K. E., *Managerial Behaviour, Performance and Effectiveness*, McGraw-Hill, 1970.

42 LAWLER, E. E., 'Job design and employee motivation', *Personnel Psychology*, **22**, 1969.

43 LAWLER, E. E., *op. cit.*

44 BROWN, H., 'The individual in the organisation', in *Organisational Control: interaction, roles and rules*, The Open University, 1974.

45 ADAMS, J. S., 'Injustice in social exchange', in BERKOWITZ (Ed.), *Advances in Experimental Social Psychology*, Academic Press, 1965.

46 GEORGOPOULOS, B. S., *et. al.*, *op. cit.*

47 GALBRAITH, J. and CUMMINGS, L. L., 'An empirical investigation of the motivational determinants of task performance', *Organisational Behaviour and Human Performance*, **2**, 1967.

48 PORTER, L. W. and LAWLER, E. E., *op. cit.*

49 GOODMAN, P. S., ROSE, J. H. and FURCON, J. E., 'Comparison of motivational antecedents of the work performance of scientists and engineers', *Journal of Applied Psychology*, **54**, 1970.

50 KESSELMAN, G. A., HAGAN, E. L. and WHERRY, R. J., 'A factor-analytic test of the Porter-Lawler expectancy model of work motivation', *Personnel Psychology*, **27**, 1974.

51 PARKER, D. F. and DYER, L., 'Expectancy theory as a within-person behavioural choice model: an empirical test of some conceptual and methodological

refinements', *Organizational Behaviour and Human Performance*, **17**, 1976.

52 LAWLER, E. E., *Pay and Organizational Effectiveness*, McGraw-Hill, 1971.

53 McCLELLAND, D. C., 'Money as a motivator: some research insights', *The McKinsey Quarterly*, Fall, 1967.

54 HILGARD, E. R., ATKINSON, R. C. and ATKINSON, R. L., *op. cit.*

55 OPSAHL, R. L. and DUNNETTE, M. D., 'The role of financial compensation in industrial motivation', *Psychological Bulletin*, **66**, 1966.

56 DAVIS, L. E., 'The design of jobs', *Industrial Relations*, **6**, 1966.

57 COOPER, R., *Job Motivation and Job Design*, IPM, 1974.

58 HERZBERG, F., 'One more time: how do you motivate employees?', *Harvard Business Review*, **46**, 1968.

59 HACKMAN, J. R., and OLDHAM, G. R., 'Motivation through the design of work: test of a theory', *Organisational Behaviour and Human Performance*, **16**, 1976.

IV

INTERACTION WITH OTHERS

Very few people in organizations work in total isolation. Organizations are, after all, made up of people. These people come together to exchange information, discuss progress, solve problems, give instructions, and so on. In some situations there is a requirement to make explicit judgements about others as in selection procedures, performance appraisals, promotion boards or disciplinary interviews. And of course people also come together for the pleasure of each others company. For the manager in particular, a large part of his job involves interacting with others. Indeed one British study suggests that on average a manager spends 80 per cent of his time in conversations of one sort or another.[1]

In this and the next two chapters we shall be exploring more fully the implications of interacting with other people at work. Chapter V will look at the dynamics of small groups and Chapter VI will look at the concept of role and its impact on the expectations of and responses to the behaviour of others. This chapter will, in part, serve as a foundation for the next two by examining what might be thought of as the basic element of social behaviour—the interaction of one person with another.

Social skills and interpersonal competence

Following the example of Argyle[2] many writers have likened social interaction to basic manual or motor skills. The key elements of a motor skill are the selective perception of signals from the environment, a translation of the perceived information into appropriate plans of action, specific motor responses, feedback and corrective action, and appropriate timing or rhythm. So, for example, a car driver pays more attention to the road, other cars, road signs, and speedometer than to the scenery, the architecture, or the upholstery. On the basis of such signals he makes decisions about steering, changing gear, applying the brakes and so on. In time much of this translation process becomes unconscious and automatic. The result is a pattern of co-ordinated movements to drive the car. But the driver needs constant feedback of information with regard to the effect of his actions so that he can correct oversteering, change down again if the engine is straining, brake harder if the car is not stopping quickly enough and so on. Finally, all these things need to be carried out smoothly and at the appropriate time to ensure a safe and comfortable ride.

Social interaction, too, is a skilled activity involving perception and interpretation of signals from the other person, decisions about appropriate responses, verbal and non-verbal responses, feedback and opportunity for corrective action. As with motor skills many of the processes are carried out unconsciously and automatically. Also as with motor skills people can vary in the degree of competence with which they perform these activities. So some people are regarded as more socially skilled or having a greater degree of 'interpersonal competence'[3] than others. Social interaction, however, obviously differs from a motor skill in its dynamic nature. In other words, the key element of the environment, the other person, is also perceiving, interpreting, acting and responding. Figure 4.1 represents the basic elements of interaction diagrammatically.

Figure 4.1

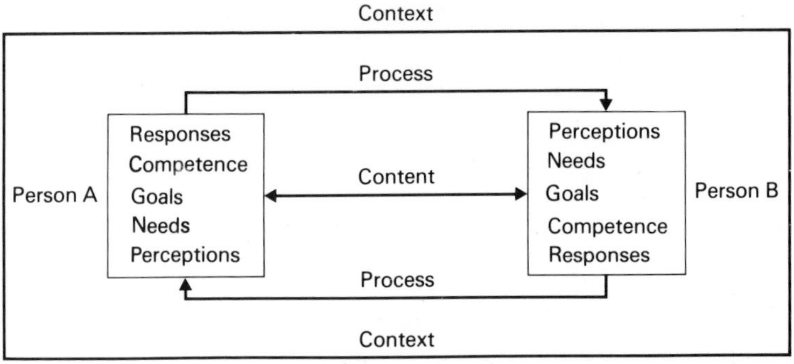

It can be seen that a distinction is made between the content of interaction and the process of interaction. Essentially it is the distinction between the *what* and the *how*. It is a recognition of the fact that when people are working with others their actions are influenced not only by the flow of information related to the task in hand, (content) but also by the judgements about and feelings toward the other person and the way he behaves (process). In practice, of course, the distinction is not a clear cut one. But it does allow us to highlight the difference between a manager's technical competence, as an accountant, an operations expert, or a marketer, and his interpersonal competence. Both are obviously equally important but it is the latter which has been the major concern of behavioural scientists. In this chapter, therefore, we shall be looking at the process of interaction rather than the content.

Let us start by examining the nature of interpersonal competence more closely. Bennis *et al.*[4] suggest there are five major elements:

1. *Capacity to receive and send information and feelings reliably.*
   In this they include not only the ability to listen and perceive accurately, but also a 'heightened alertness to salient interpersonal events'.
2. *Capacity to evoke the expression of feelings.*
   They say that anyone can listen passively, but some listeners can evoke the expressions of thoughts, beliefs or feelings normally held back, while others seem to inhibit such expression.
3. *Capacity to process information and feelings reliably and creatively.*
   This is the ability to conceptualize all the elements of the interaction process and arrive at accurate undistorted diagnoses.
4. *Capacity to implement a course of action.*
   Social sensitivity and awareness are an important part of interpersonal competence but without behavioural flexibility they can have a negative effect. As Massarik and Wechsler say:

   > Seeing too much, if not buttressed by an appropriate range of available behaviours, can indeed prove a threat to self and others and thereby reduce ultimate social effectiveness.[5]

5. *Capacity to learn in each of the above areas.*
   This involves the constant observation, analysis and interpretation of one's own interpersonal experience.

Argyris[6] has suggested that some organizational climates inhibit rather than foster the development of such skills. These are typified by what he terms 'pyramidal' values. Such values maintain that the importan human relationships are those concerned with getting the job done, that effectiveness increases as behaviour is rational and logical and decreases as emotionality increases, and that rewards and punishments should serve to reinforce rational, non-emotional behaviour. The consequences of such values, Argyris maintains, are that task-oriented behaviour will be emphasised, idea behaviour will tend to be more frequent than feeling behaviour, and, since individuals are primarily rewarded for their contribution to organizational objectives and are controlled through scarce rewards and competition, they will tend to *sell* their own ideas at the expense of others.

The context of interaction

Already then it can be seen that an understanding of the interaction process will also include an awareness of the context within which the interaction takes place. In organizations, for example, the role relationships between people will influence the way in which they communicate with each other. Thus Hall,[7] surveying a thousand managers ranging from company presidents to just above first-line supervisors, found that there were significant differences in the extent to which they used candour and risk-taking self-disclosure, and solicited feedback from others. These differences were a function of the role relationships in a given situation. Thus self-disclosure decreased as relative formal status compared with the others decreased. That is, the greatest use of candour was with subordinates, less with colleagues and least of all with superiors. The extent to which feedback was solicited also varied as a function of role differences. This was highest in relationships with colleagues, lowest with subordinates, and intermediate with superiors. In general, these managers reported that their least open and effective relationships were with their superiors.

On a similar theme, Lawler et al.[8] report that superiors tend to attach much less significance to superior-subordinate interactions than do subordinates. Subordinates tend to over-interpret and place too much importance on everything that is said.

Not only the organizational but also the physical context can have a marked impact on the amount and quality of social contact that takes place. Steele[9] has reviewed the significance of physical setting for organizational effectiveness, and maintains that the arrangement of facilities, the location of people relative to one another and to activities, and the amount of mobility the setting allows, can all have a major impact. We shall be looking more closely at some of these effects in the next chapter.

In a way, related to the impact of physical settings, it is fairly widely accepted that:

Individuals and groups typically assume a propriety orientation toward certain geographical areas which they defend against invasion.[10]

This orientation is quite separate from any formal rights of ownership they may have. The territory is simply occupied, either permanently or intermittently, by an individual who then acts as though it belongs to him. The smooth functioning of a relationship is dependent upon the extent to which such territorial rights are respected. There are some ways of behaving which although permissible on the individual's own or perhaps 'neutral' territory are inappropriate on another's. Indeed uninvited entry can bring about a definite negative reaction. So, for example, Whyte[11] found in studying restaurants that kitchen workers established such territorial rights over their kitchen area. Open attempts were made to block low status invaders. Although not subject to open resistance, the presence of high status invaders usually had a disruptive effect on relationships. Handy[12] has also extended the territorial analogy to psychological areas of influence or responsibility in organizations, suggesting individuals will jealously protect these too from invasion.

Having recognized the impact of context on interaction let us now look at the interaction process itself a little more closely.

Person perception and the interaction process

We saw earlier that face-to-face interaction could be regarded as a dynamic process of perception, diagnosis and action engaged in by two people with varying degrees of competence. Figure 4.2 represents a more detailed elaboration of that process. It only focuses on one of the parties to the interaction, but it must obviously be remembered that the points to be made hold true for both parties. To help in understanding the main elements of the process and their interrelationship, they have been represented in the form of a flow diagram. This is not intended to imply, however, that when we encounter others we always consciously go through a logical sequence of searching for information, making judgements and deciding upon action according to certain rules of behaviour. On the contrary, much of our everyday social interaction (some would say too much) takes place without any conscious awareness of the processes involved.

Sources of information   The diagram indicates that when we react to another person we often do so on the basis of more information than that person presents to us directly, whether intentionally or unintentionally. For example, if we have met the person before, we are likely to have a memory of what kind of person he is and expectations about how he is likely to behave; this will influence the way we deal with him. Such a memory store is cumulative so that new information is available as a result of the interaction itself. This means that even when meeting someone for the first time our reactions can be influenced by impressions formed early in the encounter. Interesting evidence of this is provided by Springbett[13] who found that the outcome of the great majority of selection interviews was determined in the first few minutes. Interviewers seemed to make an early judgement on the basis of first impressions and then either look for information that confirmed it or even just act out the ritual for the

Figure 4.2 Person perception and the interaction process

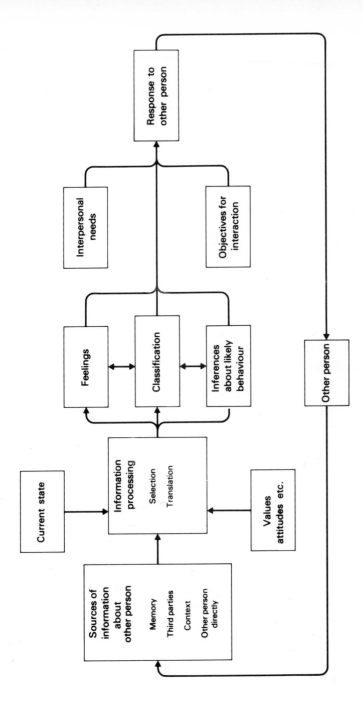

'appropriate' amount of time. This 'store' of information will, of course, also be fed by the comments and reports about the other person made by third parties. The impressions we gain can be influenced by the kind of person we have been told to expect. Kelley,[14] for example, told half a class that a new teacher was rather cold and half that he was very warm. Those that expected him to be warm, afterwards described him as such. Those that expected him to be cold not only subsequently described him as such but also participated much less in the class discussion.

Obviously, however, the major source of information about a person is that person himself. Much of the research into how we react to others has concentrated on the non-verbal signals or sources of information, but this should not cause us to overlook the content of what the other person says about himself. One simple way of gaining information about a person is to ask him. At least the information in this form is explicit and less ambiguous than much non-verbal behaviour. Indeed there are dangers in not taking such information at face-value as Giedt[15] discovered in his study of psychiatric interviews. Inaccurate judgements tended to be associated with overinterpretation of what the client said. Against this there are, of course, a number of problems. Foremost of these is the 'social desirability' effect already mentioned in the previous chapter. There is a tendency for people to present themselves in the best possible light. In addition there is a considerable amount of research that suggests that how people say they will behave in a given situation does not tally with how in fact they do behave when that situation arises.[16]

In talking about non-verbal signals from the other person it is worth highlighting two distinctions. The first, suggested by Cook,[17] is that between static information, which does not change during the encounter, and dynamic information which does. Included in the first category would be such things as face, physique, voice, clothes, etc. In the second would be physical orientation and distance, posture, gestures, facial expression, eye movements, and non-verbal aspects of speech (tone, fluency etc.). The second distinction is that suggested by Gahagan[18] between non-verbal behaviour which is *communicative* and that which is simply *informative*. When someone is speaking we can usually assume that he does so intentionally, to communicate. Some non-verbal signals are intended to communicate. This may be some specific meaning, like the size of the fish that got away, or an indication of anger—shaking the fist, or assent—nodding the head, or contempt—the footballer's gesture to the referee. Goffman[19] also suggests that people give out non-verbal signals as a part of 'impression management': that is in the attempt to create a certain image of themselves in the eyes of others. In addition to such communicative behaviour, however, there is a wealth of information which is not under the conscious control of the other person and which potentially can tell us much about him. This information, however, is highly ambiguous and so it should be mentioned that there are differences between the amount it is used, the manner in which it is typically interpreted and the validity of such interpretations.

Cook, for example, reviewing the literature on static information,[20] suggests that people are quite willing to make judgements about an individual's personality on the basis of face and physique; indeed there is often a fair degree of consistency in such judgements. Despite that, there is very little evidence to suggest that such judgements have any validity. The story is similar with regard to judgements based on a person's voice.

The significance of dynamic signals goes beyond either conveying meaning or making judgements about the person. Dynamic signals can also play an important part in the regulation of the interaction itself. The way a person physically orientates himself to the other person can give an indication of the kind of encounter expected or intended; typically, side by side for co-operation, and face to face for competition.[21] Eye movements and the direction of gaze seem important in the expression of the attitude of one person towards another, but here the evidence is confusing. Looking at someone a lot can be an indication of liking but it can also be an expression of dominance. Obviously other signals need to be taken into consideration, accompanying facial expression, for example.[22] Eye movements also seem to play an important part in the flow of a conversation. Typically the talker looks away when he starts talking and intermittently looks back to the listener to *check* that he is still listening. At this stage, the presence or absence of direct gaze or head nods, from the listener can make him say more or less, respectively. As the speaker comes to the end of what he is saying he tends to look at the listener more continuously, as if handing over to him. The absence of such signals can have a disruptive effect.[23]

Dynamic non-verbal signals are a major source of information (often the only source) about a person's current emotional state. Facial expression, body movements, and voice tone all give us clues as to what the other person is feeling. Of these, facial expression is often assumed to be the most important. Indeed it seems that people can fairly accurately identify a number of emotional states portrayed facially by actors. However, research using such an approach has been criticized in that it is more an indication of ability to recognize sterotyped expressions of the *communicative* type than genuine sensitivity to current state. This is significant in that the face is under a greater degree of control than many other sources of non-verbal information. Therefore, in cultures in which it is the 'done thing' to control emotional expression (the British culture for example) the facial expression may be misleading. Eckman and Friesen[24] suggest in fact that 'the face is likely to be the major non-verbal liar'. But in such cases they also suggest there is likely to be emotional 'leakage' via other body movements, in particular from the feet and the hands. Unfortunately, it seems that most people are less attentive to such informative behaviour: which brings us to the next aspect of the process. Given such a wealth of potential information about the other person, how is it used and indeed how much of it is used, for as has just been implied, we do not necessarily 'pick up' all the information available.

Processing the information   The answers to such questions are influenced to some extent by the individual's own current emotional state, his motives at the time, and also his more enduring characteristics, personality, attitudes, values and so on. That is, the way we experience another person is not only determined by the characteristics of that person but also by factors within ourselves. Our model of the interaction process suggests then that an individual does not simply respond directly to the information available but he processes it and gives it meaning. But there is a limit to our processing capacity. Some of the information is filtered out. In other words, perception is selective. This means, of course, that the same situation may well be seen quite differently by different people. Dearborn and Simon[25] give an example of this selective perception at work in an organizational context. They presented a case study to a number of middle managers drawn from different functional areas of the company; sales, production, accounting and miscellaneous. The managers were asked to identify the most important problem facing the company depicted in the case. Despite being encouraged to take a 'company-wide view', it was found that the great majority of them identified the major problem as being related to their own particular sphere of activity. An additional example of this selective aspect of perception was given earlier with regard to the employment interview. Thus it seemed that only information that confirmed initial impressions was attended to.

Already then we can see that there is potential for misunderstanding between people, but in addition to the *selective* element of perception, there is an *interpretive* element. The information received is translated and given meaning, resulting in a number of judgements about the other person. Central to this judgement process is the way we use the information to identify the other person as a certain type or to attribute certain characteristics to him. In other words, we make it easier for ourselves to respond to the other person by classifying him in some way. We may notice the young trainee frequently asking awkward but pertinent questions and conclude that he is intelligent. Another may blush whenever spoken to, from which we may assume that he is shy. A third may be labelled unreliable because he has been late for a number of appointments. In this way we make judgements about aspects of an individual's personality. In addition we may identify the other person as occupying a certain role or holding certain beliefs on the basis of the information we notice. The man with the pin-stripe suit, bowler hat and brief case arriving on the 8.30 train may be classified as a city business man. The young man with long hair and a beard who tries to sell him a copy of an underground newspaper may be classified as an anarchist.

Obviously, any or all of these judgements could be inaccurate. They are highly significant, however, in terms of the subsequent inferences or assumptions we may make about other aspects of the individual's personality, attitudes and behaviour about which we may have no information. Before exploring this further, it is worth pointing out that people vary considerably in the way they classify others. For example, one person may typically use quite different dimensions or categories for thinking about or describing people than would another. Zalkind and Costello,[26] viewing research in the area, suggest that when forming impressions of people, the more sociable an individual is, the more likely he is to evaluate in terms of sociability and, the more authoritarian, the more likely to view others in terms of power and less likely in terms of personality characteristics. Little[27] has also found that there is a greater tendency for women to use more psychological or personality terms when describing people whereas men tend to describe others in terms of role, achievement and physical characteristics. Not only does the content of the classifying system vary from person to person but also the complexity. That is, some people use more categories and recognize more distinctions between them than do others. This is significant as it seems that more complex people are better able to integrate conflicting information about others, whereas less complex people tend to see things more in terms of 'black and white'.

The judgement process, however, does not stop at classification. Our response to another person is influenced by the kind of inferences we make on the basis of such classification. Thus it has been suggested that we all have our own *implicit personality theory* or basic assumptions about which characteristics go together and what the behavioural implications are. This implies, of course, a general readiness to infer some characteristics with no direct evidence at all. We may, for example, classify someone as ambitious and from this assume he will also be aggressive, hard-working, inconsiderate and dishonest and we respond to him accordingly. Just as the dimensions we use to classify people vary, so it seems do the assumed linkages. So for another person, ambition may be associated with sociability, co-operativeness, and reliability. Two managers discussing a candidate for promotion may both agree that he is ambitious but find they disagree about what this means about his behaviour at work.

In addition to implicit personality theories, there are strong tendencies to attribute characteristics to an individual on the basis of their ethnic origins, group membership or occupation. Such *stereotypes* may be personal or they may be more widely held. It cannot be assumed however that the more widely held a stereotype the more accurate it will be. Many a well known fact proves to be fiction. Indeed any statement of the characteristics of the members of a given group are likely to be inaccurate for some of them.

Haire[28] gives an interesting example of how such stereotyping might apply in union/management relationships. Given photographs and a written description of 'Mr. B.', a middle-aged, reasonably dressed man, with no particular expression on his face, managers ascribed quite different characteristics to him, if they were told he was a manager, from those ascribed by others who were told he was secretary-treasurer of his union. The former described him as conscientious, dependable, conservative, industrious and sincere, while the latter described him as active, argumentative, aggressive, opinionated, outspoken and persistent. Union negotiators, presented with the same information, tended to describe Mr. B in favourable terms if they thought he was a union official and less favourable if they thought he was a manager.

In addition to the inevitable inaccuracies involved in stereotyping, a number of other recurrent sources of error or distortion have been identified in the process of person perception. One such source of error which has received a considerable amount of attention, particularly with regard to its implications for staff appraisal schemes, has been termed the *halo effect*. Blum and Naylor[29] define this as:

> a tendency to let our assessment of an individual on one trait influence our evaluation of that person on other specific traits.

Thus, if we rate someone favourably on some dimension which we regard as important, then there is a tendency to rate him favourably on other dimensions regardless of how they apply to him in fact. Other distortions can occur as a result of assumed similarity, assumed liking, assumed intentionality, and projection. There seems to be a tendency to assume, particularly where there is a lack of reliable information, that other people are like ourselves. This is even more the case if we like the person. We tend to assume he likes us and shares our views and so on. Furthermore, there is a tendency to assume that people always intend to do what they do, and intend it to have the consequences it has. And indeed the more serious the outcome the more likely we are to claim that it was intended.[30] Finally, it has been suggested that we often *project* on to other people characteristics of our own which we find difficult to accept. Zalkind and Costello[31] give as an example the manager who, frightened by rumours of organizational changes, sees his subordinates as more frightened than they really are; or the foreman who, lacking insight into his own incapacity to delegate, sees his own superiors as failing to delegate to him. Not surprisingly, in view of such potential for *internal* distortion, it has been suggested that the greater an individual's self-insight, the more likely he is to perceive others accurately.[32]

A further important component of the process of responding to another person has been implied by what has gone before but has not been dealt with directly; that is our emotional or feelings reaction to that person. Such reactions, be they positive or negative, are inevitable. Thus, in addition to making the kind of classifying and inferential judgements we have referred to, we will like, dislike, respect, fear, admire, or sympathize with the other person. What is more, there can be no doubt that such feelings responses can colour our judgements in many ways, whether we recognize those feelings or not. True objectivity, then, in person perception is illusory.

Needs and objectives   But our interaction with the other person, the way we respond to him, is not determined by our perceptions alone. As we see from Figure 4.2 there are additional factors to be considered. Amongst these will be our own interpersonal needs. These influence our propensity to respond to people in some ways rather than in others. Some people will typically behave in a domineering manner, others will be submissive, some will display friendliness, while others may be more inclined to coolness and so on. Krech *et al.*[33] suggest twelve basic dimensions or 'primary interpersonal response traits' on which people can vary. It is the various combinations of these traits which determine an individual's basic response style.

Schutz[34] has developed and tested a simpler way of looking at what he calls an individual's 'fundamental interpersonal relations orientation' (FIRO). His theory maintains that the way an individual relates to other people is influenced by the relative strength of three basic interpersonal needs:

1. *Need for inclusion*   This is the need to maintain a satisfactory relationship with others with regard to the amount of interaction and degree of association.
2. *Need for control*   Refers to the decision-making process between people. It is the need for satisfactory relationships with regard to power and influence.

3. *Need for affection*　　Refers to the degree of closeness and intimacy needed in relationships with others.

It is maintained that we not only vary in the extent of our need for other people to express inclusion, control and affection towards us, but also vary in our need to include, control and to be affectionate towards other people. In other words, how we like to behave towards other people is independent of how we would like them to behave towards us. For example, we may have a high need to include others, to involve them in our own activities and to encourage them to participate. At the same time we may have a low need to be included, and may care little whether people ask us to join in their activities.

One particular significance of individual differences in orientation is that in some encounters the orientations of the two individuals will be incompatible. Compatible interaction is likely to be easier and more productive than incompatible interaction. Two people can be compatible or incompatible with regard to the general level of the three need areas. Some people prefer a great deal of exchange of inclusion, control or affection behaviour, others prefer neither to receive nor to express each of these. Where there is similarity in the general level of exchange required, there is said to be *interchange compatibility*.

Two people, however, may be similar in the general level of exchange needed, but they may differ in their need to initiate or originate that exchange. In this case, *originator compatability* derives from complementary needs, not similar ones. In other words, an individual who has a high need to control others will be compatible with someone who needs to be controlled but incompatible with someone with a similar need to control others. Interactions with the latter are likely to be effected by a power struggle. The implications of compatibility and incompatibility for effective group functioning are taken further in the next chapter.

Finally, we must not overlook that the way a person responds to another will be influenced by his original goals or objectives for the interaction. In some situations, the objective is for the interaction to fulfil itself. In love and friendship interaction provides its own incentive. In other situations the objective might be to change the attitudes, beliefs or behaviour of the other person, as in bargaining, selling or disciplining, for example. The objective might be to convey information or give instructions, or to obtain information as in interviewing. It might be to supervise the activity of another or to co-operate with another on a mutual task.

Clearly the nature of the interaction will be influenced by the objectives of the parties to it. Equally, however, those objectives may be modified or changed as a result of the interaction itself. Thus the boss may call in his secretary with the intention of reprimanding her for her inefficiency, and end by inviting her out for lunch. It is possible that this was her original goal for the interaction, so highlighting the possibility of conflicting objectives in interaction. We shall also see that there is potential for deceit in interaction: that is, behaving as though the objective were one outcome but in fact aiming at another. This is the basis of the confidence trick and also of many of the 'games people play' in organizations.

Interaction This last point brings us to an increasingly popular approach to analysing the way we actually respond to other people. The approach is known as *transactional analysis.* It was originally developed by Berne[35] but has more recently been applied to organizational settings by Jongeward[36] and by Carby and Thakur.[37] The essence of transactional analysis is that our behaviour towards others can originate in any of three basic *ego-states* which are present in all of us. These have been labelled the parent ego-state (P), the adult ego-state (A), and the child ego-state (C). These are said to be stored information about actual experiences in early life, and will therefore be unique to each of us. Thus the Parent derives from the model(s) given us by our own parents (or parent substitutes). It may result in behaviour which is punitive, judgemental, and critical, or in behaviour which is caring, protective, and nurturing. Just as the Parent represents stored patterns of behaviour modelled on significant experiences in our early life, so the Child represents stored patterns of behaviour based on feelings experienced within ourselves early in life. It is evidenced in behaviour which is emotionally expressive such as anger, fear, panic and loving, or in carefree playfulness, curiosity and creativity. The Adult represents the developed ability to process information on the basis of past experience. It is evidenced in planning, problem-solving, making decisions, assessing probabilities, and may also include an internal awareness or monitoring of the influence on behaviour exerted by each of the ego-states. The theory maintains that no ego-state is necessarily better than any other. It is assumed, however, that since the Adult involves the monitoring component, the more developed it is the more likely that the 'appropriate' ego state will be brought into play in any transaction.

Interaction, then, can be understood in terms of which ego-state in one person is transacting with which ego-state in the other. As we see in Figure 4.3, there are nine possible transactions, represented by lines, between the three ego-states in each individual, represented by circles. It is maintained that communication between two people will proceed smoothly only so long as transactions are complementary; that is, the response from one person is appropriate to, or parallels the initial statement or act (stimulus) from the other person. Thus an Adult to Adult stimulus is met by an Adult-

Figure 4.3   (Based on Berne, E.)[38]

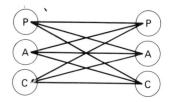

Adult response—'What was the original budget figure for this project?' is met by 'I think it was a hundred thousand pounds.' Communication will, however, break down if *crossed transactions* occur. Thus an Adult-Adult stimulus—'What was the original budget figure for this project?' is met by a Parent-Child response—'You should know that for yourself', or a Child-Parent response—'Why are you always trying to catch me out?' Figure 4.4, (a) represents the first transaction diagrammatically, (b) the second, and (c) the third.

Figure 4.4

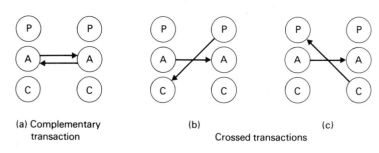

(a) Complementary   (b)   (c)
transaction   Crossed transactions

A third, more complex form of transaction is recognized and termed an *ulterior transaction*. Its complexity lies in the fact that more than two ego-states are operating at the same time. Berne[39] states that salesmen are particularly adept at this kind of transaction and gives as example the salesman who says to his customer, 'This one is better, but you can't afford it.' Her reply is, 'That's the one I'll take.' At the overt, social level the salesman, as Adult, states two facts, and at face value the woman's response is an Adult decision to make a purchase. At the ulterior, psychological level the salesman is taunting the customer's Child and her implicit response is 'I'll show you that I'm as good as any of your other customers.' Figure 4.5 represents this transaction diagrammatically.

The significance of the ulterior transaction is that it forms the basis of the many games people play in social interaction. A game is defined as:

An ongoing series of complementary ulterior transactions progressing to a well-defined, predictable outcome.[40] *(payoff to game initiator).*

Figure 4.5 An ulterior transaction

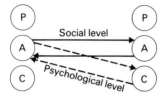

A game, therefore, will proceed smoothly and will superficially appear plausible. However, it will always be typified by an ulterior motive and, if followed through to its conclusion, will result in a *pay-off* at the psychological level to the individual who started it, as was the case for the salesman in the previous example. It is possible to identify many more sophisticated games which are common within organizations. For example *empire-building* involves setting up activities and operations superficially for the good of the organization but the real pay-off is increased personal prestige. Similarly, the individual who is always first in to the office and last one to leave and perhaps works weekends, superficially is displaying commitment to his job, but the real pay-off is in getting his bosses' attention. Another common organizational game is 'Why don't you—Yes but'. This typically involves an individual presenting a problem to his colleagues for comment. They will respond with suggested solutions all of which will be rebuffed by some good reason why the solutions would not work. The game is won when the suggestions dry up. At the social level an Adult is seeking a solution to a problem but at the psychological level a Child is seeking reassurance for feelings of inadequacy.

This brief look at transactional analysis highlights another important aspect of social interaction—its ongoing, dynamic nature. The way we act towards another person will influence the way that person responds to us which will in turn have an effect on the way we subsequently behave towards him. This is indicated in Figure 4.2 by the feed-back loop, via the other person, into information about that person. The quality and quantity of that feedback, however, can be greatly influenced by the climate we create for the interaction. We have already seen from Hall's[41] study that subordinates tend to be less open with their superiors than anybody else in the organization and that superiors seek feedback from their subordinates less than from others. Studies by Read[42] and by O'Reilly and Roberts[43] give us an indication of why this may be so. They found a clear relationship between the amount and quality of information flow between superiors and subordinates and the degree of trust between them. Low trust leads to poor information flow. Low trust is typical of what Gibb[44] refers to as 'defensive climates'. In such climates he maintains that communication is much more likely to be distorted than in 'supportive' climates. These climates tend to be self-perpetuating. Defensive behaviours elicit defensive responses and vice versa. Categories of behaviour he suggests as characteristic of defensive interaction are evaluation, control, strategy, neutrality, superiority and certainty. Supportive interaction, on the other hand, is characterized by description, problem orientation, spontaneity, empathy, equality and provisionalism.

If we refer back to our original motor skill analogy of social interaction, we can see how important adequate feedback is for effective performance. Leavitt[45] has also demonstrated how important it is for effective communication between people. Clearly then the kind of climate a manager's behaviour encourages will have a significant influence on his own interpersonal effectiveness. And, since interaction with others represents, as we have seen, a major component of managerial activity, this obviously has implications for his effectiveness as a manager.

REFERENCES

1 BURNS, T., 'The directions of activity and communication in a departmental executive group', *Human Relations*, **7**, pp. 73–97, 1965.

2 ARGYLE, M., *The Psychology of Interpersonal Behaviour*, Penguin, 1972.

3 ARGYRIS, C., *Interpersonal Competence and Organisational Effectiveness*, Dorsey, 1962.

4 BENNIS, W. G., BERLEW, D. E., SCHEIN, E. H., and STEELE, F. I., *Interpersonal Dynamics*, Dorsey, 1973.

5 MASSARIK, F. and WECHSLER, I. R., 'Empathy revisited: the process of understanding people', *California Management Review*, **1**, pp. 36–46, 1959.

6 ARGYRIS, C., *op. cit.*

7 HALL, J., 'Interpersonal style and the communication dilemma: managerial implications of the Johari awareness model', *Human Relations*, pp. 381–99, 1974.

8 LAWLER, E. E., PORTER, L. W., and TENENBAUM, A., 'Managers' attitudes to interaction episodes', *Journal of Applied Psychology*, **52**, pp. 432–9, 1968.

9 STEELE, F. I., *Physical Setting and Organisational Development*, Addison-Wesley, 1973.

10 SHAW, M. E., *Group Dynamics: the psychology of small group behaviour*, McGraw-Hill, 1976.

11 WHYTE, W. F., 'The social structure of the restaurant', *American Journal of Sociology*, **54**, pp. 302–8, 1949.

12 HANDY, C. B., *Understanding Organisations*, Penguin, 1976.

13 SPRINGBETT, B. M., 'Factors effecting the final decision in the employment interview', *Canadian Journal of Psychology*, **12**, pp. 13–22, 1958.

14 KELLEY, H. H., 'The warm-cold variable in first impressions of persons', *Journal of Personality*, **18**, pp. 431–9, 1950.

15 GIEDT, F. H., 'Comparison of visual content and auditory cues in interviewing', *Journal of Consulting Psychology*, **19**, pp. 407–16, 1955.

16 WICKER, A. W., 'Attitudes versus actions: the relationship of verbal and overt behavioural responses to attitude objects', *Journal of Social Issues*, **25**, pp. 41–78, 1969.

17 COOK, M., *Interpersonal Perception*, Penguin, 1971.

18 GAHAGAN, J., *Interpersonal and Group Behaviour*, Methuen, 1975.

19 GOFFMAN, E., *The Presentation of Self in Everyday Life*, Penguin, 1971.

20 COOK, M., *op. cit.*

21 SOMMER, R., *Personal Space: the Behavioural Basis of Design*, Prentice-Hall, 1969.

22 BURNS, T., 'Non-verbal communication', *Discovery*, **25**, pp. 30–7, 1964.

23 KENDON, A., 'Some functions of gaze-direction in social interaction', *Acta Psychologica*, **26**, pp. 22–47, 1967.

24 ECKMAN, P. and FRIESEN, W., 'Non-verbal leakage and clues to deception', *Psychiatry*, **32**, pp. 88–105, 1969.

25 DEARBORN, D. C. and SIMON, H. A., 'Selective perception: a note on the departmental identifications of executives', *Sociometry*, **21**, pp. 140–4, 1958.

26 ZALKIND, S. S., and COSTELLO, T. W., 'Perception: implications for administration', *Administrative Science Quarterly*, **7**, pp. 218–35, 1962.

27 LITTLE, B., 'Studies of psychospecialists', *Psychological Reports*, 1969.

28 HAIRE, M., 'Role perceptions in labour-management relations: an experimental approach', Industrial Labour Relations Review, **8**, pp. 204–16, 1955.

29 BLUM, M. L. and NAYLOR, J. C., *Industrial Psychology*, Harper & Row, 1968.

30 WALSTER, E., 'The assignment of responsibility for an accident', *Journal of Personality and Social Psychology*, **5**, pp. 508–16, 1966.

31 ZALKIND, S. S. and COSTELLO, T. W., *op. cit.*

32 ZALKIND, S. S. and COSTELLO, T. W., *op. cit.*

33 KRECH, D., CRUTCHFIELD, R. S. and BALLACHEY, E. L., *Individual in Society*, McGraw-Hill, 1962.

34 SCHUTZ, W. C., *The Interpersonal Underworld*, Science and Behaviour Books (Reprint edition), 1966.

35 BERNE, E., *Games People Play*, Penguin, 1968.

36 JONGEWARD, D., *Everybody Wins: transactional analysis applied to organisations*, Addison-Wesley, 1974.

37 CARBY, K. and THAKUR, M., *Transactional Analysis at Work*, IPM, 1976.

38 BERNE, E., *op. cit.*

39 BERNE, E., *ibid.*

40 BERNE, E., *ibid.*

41 HALL, J., *op. cit.*

42 READ, W., 'Upward communication in industrial hierarchies', *Human Relations*, **15**, pp. 3–16, 1962.

43 O'REILLY, C. A. and ROBERTS, K. H., 'Information filtration in organisations: three experiments', *Organisational Behaviour and Human Performance*, **11**, pp. 253–65, 1974.

44 GIBB, J. R., 'Defensive communication', *Journal of Communication*, **11**, pp. 141–8, 1961.

45 LEAVITT, H. J., *Managerial Psychology*, University of Chicago Press, 1972.

V

WORKING IN GROUPS

For many writers on organizational behaviour, work organizations appear as 'goal-orientated systems . . . made up of numerous overlapping face-to-face groups'.[1] Whether or not this is the best way of conceiving of them will be explored more fully in Chapter VII. There is little doubt, however, that the small group is an important unit of analysis for anyone interested in increasing their understanding of the human aspects of management. Despite the wide variety of opinion and feeling among managers as to the value of carrying out tasks in groups, in any organization much of the work at all levels takes place in the small group context. This chapter, therefore, will be examining the implications of group processes for the individual and the organization, both in terms of work effectiveness and employee satisfaction.

Before going further, however, it will be useful to examine just what we mean by the term *group*. At one level this may seem a rather needless activity. The term, after all, is used frequently and widely without too much apparent misunderstanding, but as Shaw[2] points out

> There is no single definition that is generally accepted by all (or even most) students of small group behaviour.

One of the issues associated with the problem of definition is the extent to which the group can be thought of as 'real', that is having some objective existence apart from the individual members in which it consists.

Golembiewski,[3] reviewing the debate in the area, recognizes a range of different standpoints. At one end of the range are those explanations which regard groups as having mental characteristics of their own analogous to those of individuals. Thus the group becomes a unit of study in its own right with a 'group mind' quite separate from the minds of the individuals of which it is comprised.

At the other end of the range is the assertion that there can be no study of groups which is not essentially a study of individuals. The individual represents the only reality and the group is merely an aggregate of individuals. The whole can never be more than the sum of its parts. Thus only the behaviour of individuals, whether alone or together, justifies investigation.

Between these two extremes there are approaches which acknowledge that people behave as if groups were real. In other words, they have an existence in the perceptions of their members and observers. They are subjectively real, and as such can influence the behaviour of individuals, but the individual remains the prime focus of study.

Finally there are approaches which claim that for purposes of analysis the group may be regarded as real. It has a conceptual reality in its social processes and structure of relationships which can legitimately be studied without reference to the characteristics of its members.

In this chapter, while not subscribing to the 'group mind' approach, we shall be focusing not only on the behaviour and experience of the individual, but also on structures and processes at a group level. To this end we shall adopt the definition of a group suggested by Schein[4] as being:

Any number of people who (1) interact with one another, (2) are psychologically aware of one another, and (3) perceive themselves to be a group.

Thus we are not concerned with mere aggregates such as a queue in the works canteen or a number of people who happen to enter the lift together. Nor would we include whole organizations or large departments which, despite possibly having some share sense of belonging to the same unit, do not all interact with one another and are probably not all aware of each other.

What kinds of grouping then are we concerned with? It is common for the distinction to be drawn between formal and informal groups within organizations. Formal groups are created to carry out some specific task or meet some organizationally required goal. Some aspects of their structure, procedural rules and membership are likely to be explicitly stated. They may be relatively permanent in nature, such as a management team, or a particular work unit on the factory floor. They may also be temporary such as a committee of enquiry or a project team. Informal groups, on the other hand, are not explicitly set up by management but arise spontaneously, possibly on the basis of friendship, or some common interest which may or may not be work related. In practice, of course, the distinction is not an absolute one. The formation of informal groups may be enhanced or inhibited by the formally prescribed relationships between people and as Glen[5] points out:

The categories of formal and informal groups . . . are often found in the same situation, as any formally constituted group of people will tend to develop informal relationships and groupings within it in the course of its normal day to day activities.

If groups are both set up to serve organizational purposes and arise unplanned out of the interactions of the members of the organization we might reasonably assume that they potentially perform a number of functions not only for the organization but also for the individual. It is to these functions we shall now turn.

Groups are used to perform a number of formal organizational functions. Handy[6] presents these under ten major headings: the distribution of work; the management and control of work; problem-solving and decision-making; information processing; information and idea collection; testing and ratifying decisions; co-ordination and liaison; increased commitment and involvement; negotiation or conflict resolution; inquest or inquiry into the past. We can see from this list that groups can be and are used to carry out most management tasks. We shall see, however, that the effectiveness of the group and indeed the nature of the group processes will vary from task to task and situation to situation. But what of the individual group member? What does he stand to gain from his membership?

The first answer to this question is obviously organizationally related, that is assistance in getting a job done. Some collaborative tasks cannot be performed by the individual alone. On others, however, we shall see that perhaps individuals would be more productive working alone. But the individual has needs other than task ones and group membership can be a very important source of satisfaction of these needs. In Chapter III we saw that individuals have varying degrees of need for affiliation and in Chapter IV inclusion and affection were suggested as important interpersonal needs. It is clear that, almost by definition, association with others in a group activity, be it formal or informal, is capable of satisfying such needs. Warr and Wall[7] also suggest that contact with others, such as occurs in work groups, 'is essential as a stimulus to mental activity or behaviour'.

The same authors following on from the work of Festinger[8] suggest that the opportunities for social comparison provided by group membership are an important influence on the individual. The theory maintains that we all have a need to compare our opinions and abilities with others. Obviously there is a preference for hard, objective information but this is not always available, particularly in social situations. Such situations are more likely to be ambiguous. The discomfort associated with this ambiguity can be reduced by the process of social comparison. In other words, by comparing our own beliefs with those of others we can gain a clearer definition of our social reality. For example, the young apprentice in his first week at work may not be clear as to the most appropriate way to approach the foreman. He may quickly learn from the behaviour and expressed opinion of his workmates that 'he's a right "so and so" and should be steered clear of'. One aspect of his social reality will have been made less ambiguous. The significance of this process will be discussed again in connection with influence of group norms on individual behaviour.

A related psychological function of group membership is the opportunity for establishing or testing a sense of self-identity. We shall see in the next chapter how important the roles we play with regard to other people are in influencing our beliefs and feelings about ourselves.

Group membership can also provide a sense of security and greater influence over our environment, particularly our social environment—the assumption being that a number of people of like interest will be better able to achieve their own ends if they band together than if they continue to operate separately. It has been suggested that organizations should be thought of as a coalition of such interest groups which will inevitably to some degree be in conflict with one another. This is a theme which is taken further in Chapter VIII.

Finally, of course, our study of motivation theory would suggest that an individual may be attracted to join a group not only as a way of getting a particular job done or of directly satisfying some basic need, but rather because he perceives it as instrumental to the attainment of some goal outside of the group and its activities. For example, a student may join a union committee not because he is particularly interested in the declared goals of that group but because he believes it will enhance his job prospects if he can disclose the fact on his application forms.

So we can see that potentially the small group in an organizational setting is a rich source of individual satisfaction. An awareness of the social-psychological functions of group membership is as important for an adequate understanding of work group behaviour as is a knowledge of the formal task requirements. In other words, as we saw in the previous chapter, the process is as important as the content. Before going on to look more closely at the various aspects of group process it will be of value to clarify the ways in which group performance does differ from individual performance.

Group and individual performance

The first interesting fact arising from research evidence is that the mere presence of other people, whether they be a passive audience or performing a similar task, seems to have a significant effect on the performance of the individual. The evidence, however, is inconsistent as to whether such a presence is enhancing or inhibiting. Reviewing the work done on the subject, Zajonc[9] suggested that this inconsistency could be explained by regarding the presence of others as having an arousing effect. Such an arousal can enhance performance on simple tasks which involve a little in the way of new behaviour. On more complex tasks, however, in which the required behaviour is less familiar, it can have adverse effects.

Already then we can see that a comparison between individual and group performance does not allow us to draw any simple conclusions as to the one being better than the other. As has already become clear in previous chapters, and will become more obvious throughout the rest of the book, what is the 'best' policy for the management of human resources will vary from situation to situation. This is certainly the case with regard to the decision as to whether to use groups or whether to pool the efforts of individuals working separately. Some of the research into this area confirms 'common sense' but some of the findings are slightly more surprising.

It may come as no surprise that groups often, although not always, take more time to complete a task than would individuals working alone. (This, of course, assumes the task is the kind that can be performed by a single individual.) This tends to be the case even if measuring in terms of total time elapsed, but if we talk in terms of man-hours involved then groups may be regarded as even less efficient. This is an important point to remember if the manager's prime concern is to keep costs to a minimum. If, however, time is less important than quality or accuracy of problem solutions, then the picture is different. Reviewing the research Shaw[10] states:

> The evidence thus strongly supports the conclusion that groups produce more and better solutions to problems than do individuals.

But obviously an expert individual may still do better than a group of less competent people. On the whole, however, there is likely to be more information available in a group and there is also a greater chance of mistakes or errors being recognized and corrected.

Another related area in which the picture is still far from clear is in the comparison of group creativity compared with individual creativity. The technique introduced by Osborn[11] known as *brainstorming* has had its supporters and critics amongst managers and academics alike. Basically, it is a method of group participation claimed to generate new and radical ideas, such as new products a company might invest in or new uses for an old declining product. The basic procedure involves the group members expressing as many ideas as possible, the more farfetched the better. No idea may be evaluated or criticized until all ideas have been expressed. Participants are encouraged to present ideas which elaborate on the previously expressed ideas of others. On the basis of their own research, however, both Taylor *et al.*[12] and Dunnette *et al.*[13] dispute the claims made for the technique. They claim that individuals working alone under brainstorming rules produce far more ideas than if working as a group, possibly because people working together are more likely to adopt the same set or approach to a problem than if they are working separately. Krech et al.[14] use such evidence to suggest that:

> sometimes group membership inhibits man, constricts his creativity, and prevents self-fulfilment.

But Shaw[15] points out that in both the studies quoted the time available was limited and it is possible that the groups were cut off in the middle of the process. He claims that there is evidence showing:

> That with longer work periods groups produce more under brainstorming instructions than do individuals. Groups continue to produce ideas indefinitely, whereas individuals run dry.

Whether or not groups are more creative then is still a question for debate, but what is clear is that both individuals and groups produce far more ideas if critical evaluation is held in abeyance until all ideas have been expressed.

One area in which research suggests that 'conventional wisdom' may be misguided is risk-taking. Many people seem to believe that decisions made in groups, committees for example, tend to be rather conservative, but according to Kogan and Wallach[16] this is not borne out by the evidence. Their claim is that decisions made after group discussion will usually be more risky than individual decisions on the same problems. This may possibly be accounted for by some diffusion of the sense of responsibility for the decision or perhaps because in our society there is value placed upon some degree of risk-taking.

But the use of groups does not only have implications for the making of decisions but also for their implementation:

> People are more likely to carry out a decision that they have had a hand in making than one that has been imposed. If effective implementation is critical, therefore, it is important to involve the implementers as much as possible.[17]

Whatever the relative value of groups or individuals in different situations, there does seem to be considerable agreement that groups can be used more effectively with an understanding of the dynamic processes involved when a number of people are acting together, so we shall now examine some of these.

Figure 5.1 represents a framework for analysing groups. It shows that group phenomena can be understood in terms of the interaction of three

Figure 5.1 A framework for analysing groups

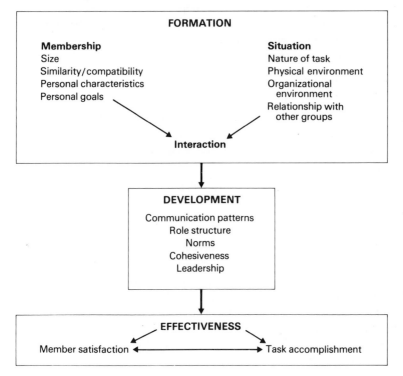

major groups of variables: formation variables, i.e. the way the group is composed and the context within which it is operating; development variables, i.e. factors emerging from the interaction of a given membership in a given situation; and effectiveness variables, i.e. the extent to which the group does adequately fulfil the kind of organizational and individual functions mentioned earlier in the chapter.

It might reasonably be assumed that the manager will be interested in the way that the first two types of variable effect the last. What follows, therefore, is an examination of the behavioural science research and theory that has attempted to shed light on these interrelationships. It should be remembered, however, that effectiveness is multidimensional. So, following, the advice of Krech *et al*:

When measuring the effectiveness of a group we must always ask ourselves, 'group effectiveness for whom?'[18]

We have already seen that individuals may value group membership for a range of different reasons. So in terms of individual satisfaction it is possible that a given group will be effective for some members and not for others. Furthermore, with formal groups it is possible for management criteria for effectiveness to exist which make no explicit reference to the satisfaction or otherwise of individual members.

Group Formation

Membership Variables   Whether or not a group will be effective depends to a fair extent on its composition, not only in terms of its size but also in terms of the characteristics of its members. Such things will not only influence the way an individual behaves but also the way in which others respond to him.

First let us consider the impact of group size. Not surprisingly the relationship between size and task effectiveness is not a straight-forward one. It is not possible to make generalizations about whether small or large groups are 'better'. The effect seems to be a result of the interaction of two factors which work in opposite directions. On the one hand the larger the group the greater the likely range of resources in terms of skills, knowledge, ideas and so on. On the other hand, the more people working together the more difficult it becomes to organize them. In addition, we shall see that increase in size has an inhibiting effect on some people. Which of these factors is the more influential depends to a large extent on the nature of the task engaged on by the group. Thelen,[19] by way of compromise, suggested that the optimum size of a group would be the smallest possible that contains all the skills required for the accomplishment of its task. Such a prescription is acceptable, but not particularly useful, in that it does not distinguish between different kinds of task. If we make a distinction between additive tasks (on which the end result is primarily a combination of individual outputs) and conjunctive tasks (on which everyone in the group must accomplish the task together) then the research evidence becomes easier to understand. We find that on additive tasks, group performance increases with increased size, but interestingly not at the same rate. In other words, there is a diminishing degree of improvement for every additional member. On conjunctive tasks, however, group effectiveness can be expected to decrease with increasing size.[20] Obviously the problems of getting organized become more critical on such tasks, as indeed may other member reactions.

Perhaps one of the most significant impacts of size is on member participation. Some members feel a greater sense of threat and inhibition about participating in larger groups than in smaller groups.[21] This means that not only does the absolute amount of participation decrease but perhaps more significantly the distribution of participation becomes less even. Thus Bales *et al.*,[22] found that the larger the group, the larger the gap in amount of participation between the most active member and the others in the group. Krech *et al.*[23] see this as a particularly negative thing:

> The constraints upon participation which persons may experience in large groups will tend to stifle critical evaluation of the ideas presented by the more self-assertive, dominant members. The productivity of creative groups may suffer because of the silence of the majority.

This is an important point to remember for any manager who finds himself the chairman of a large committee.

Whatever the impact of group size on task effectiveness, its effect on member satisfaction seems to be clear, whether measured by how they report their own feelings or by indirect measures such as absenteeism and turnover. Most people much prefer to work in small groups.[24]

Not only the number of group members but also the degree of similarity between them can be of importance. Intuitively one might assume that the more diverse task-related skills and abilities members have, the more productive they would be, and this is substantiated by the research evidence.[25] But with regard to other characteristics the picture is not quite so clear. There appears to be a strong case for the proposition that homogeneity on values, attitudes and interests leads to the formation of more stable, enduring groups and to greater member satisfaction. There is some evidence, however, suggesting that in terms of problem solving effectiveness, member heterogeneity is preferable.[26] At this stage it is not possible to make generalizable statements in favour of heterogeneity.

> It may be the case that homogeneity in certain characteristics facilitates group effectiveness, and that heterogeneity in other characteristics may be facilitating.[27]

This leads us to an alternative but related way of examining group composition: that is in terms of compatability of member characteristics. Probably the most comprehensive attempt to explore this dimension has been carried out by Schutz.[28] He was interested in the impact of compatibility of group members in terms of their 'fundamental interpersonal relations orientations', discussed in the previous chapter, the assumption being that time and energy are more likely to be wasted on interpersonal problems in incompatible groups. The evidence seems to support the proposition that compatible groups are both more task effective and lead to greater member satisfaction. There is still a great need, however, for further research to establish just which are the crucial characteristics upon which compatibility should be sought.

It seems obvious, from the foregoing, that any manager responsible for the composition of a group for the accomplishment of some task or other in the organization would be well advised to consider other factors in addition to individual skills and abilities in deciding who should be a member of that group, given the nature of the task.

Before leaving the examination of membership variables, it is probably worth highlighting the point made earlier, that for some individuals the main attraction of group membership is its perceived instrumentality for achieving goals other than group goals. This is likely to have an impact on the way they behave in the group and could well hinder group effectiveness. It has been suggested[29] that individuals bring 'hidden agendas' into the group activities which they try to work through below the surface of the explicit group task. Such activities are likely to hinder the progress of the group on the formal task while they remain hidden.

Situational variables   No group exists or operates within a vacuum. The context of its operations are likely to influence its subsequent development and effectiveness.

We have already seen that the nature of the task interacts with membership variables to influence effectiveness. We shall also see that it has a great influence on leadership effectiveness. Sayles[30] concluded from his study of some 300 shop floor work groups that the nature of the task and the organizational setting had a major impact on the level and quality of grievance activity engaged in by these groups and on their internal structure. He distinguished four types of group which displayed characteristic behaviour over a period of time even when the personnel changed.

Groups he labelled 'apathetic' lacked any clear or accepted leadership, were subject to internal disunity and friction, and engaged in relatively little grievance activity. They were usually employed on low paid and unskilled tasks. Each member usually performed a different job utilizing different equipment.

'Erratic' groups typically occurred in situations where the members had identical or near-identical tasks to perform. Such groups often had highly centralized leadership. They were easily inflamed but with quick conversion back to good relations with management. They were often highly active in the organizational aspects of their union.

'Strategic' groups had a high degree of internal unity, used continuous, well-planned pressure tactics in furtherance of their interests, and the departments they worked in were often acknowledged as trouble spots in the firm. Members of such groups were often the heart of the local union. Such groups were typically engaged in highly skilled operations, on which the individuals judgement played a large part in making time-study, and tolerance standards difficult to apply. The jobs were often key ones in the plant and were generally held by senior workers at the top of the promotional ladder.

The final type of group Sayles termed 'conservative'. Members of such groups often worked as individuals with unique mobile skills and were, therefore, often widely distributed throughout the plant, for example maintenance men. They were usually the highest status and highest paid. These groups usually had high internal unity. Their use of pressure tactics was very restrained and usually employed to redress a very specific grievance. Their relationships with management were generally good and their involvement in union activities was not particularly high.

Sayles found the explanation for such consistent differences in work-group behaviour and structure, in the way social relations, the division of labour, and the nature of technology were employed on the different tasks. Thus the degree of independence among workers, the number and similarity of jobs concentrated in any one location, the indispensability of any part for the whole, the promotional ladders and status relationships, the nature of skills required and the plant layout, were all concluded in some way to influence the nature of groups that were formed.

The impact of organizational setting is not limited to shop-floor work groups. Most organizations have either implicit or explicit rules governing the behaviour of their employees with regard to where, when, and how they work, the procedures to be adopted and methods and channels of communication. All of these are potential influences on the formation, development and effectiveness of groups. We shall be looking later at the way groups develop their own working rules or norms which may or may not be in line with those officially laid down.

In this context it will be useful to examine the effect of limiting communication to set channels. It has often been assumed by those responsible for planning the structure of organizations that there is a logical way of arranging communications channels for maximum efficiency. Most frequently the conclusion has been that flow up and down a hierarchy is the most efficient (see Chapter VII). Such conclusions, however, may be questioned on the basis of a considerable amount of laboratory research that has been carried out on communication networks in small groups, notably by Leavitt[31] and Shaw[32] This research has aimed to explore the effect of imposed communication networks on such things as problem-solving effectiveness, member satisfaction, and leadership emergence. Typically it has involved a group of subjects faced with a problem to solve, but who can only communicate with each other in writing and, according to the particular network being studied, not everyone can communicate with everyone else. Thus in Figure 5.2 we can

Figure 5.2

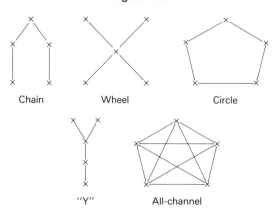

Chain   Wheel   Circle

"Y"   All-channel

see some of the different networks that have been studied by representing the permitted communication channels by lines, and each person by a cross. It can be seen that the networks can vary in their degree of centralization, the wheel, for example, being highly centralized (one person being more closely connected to all the others than the rest) and the circle and all-channel networks being decentralized (nobody has any greater access to information than anybody else) although obviously the all-channel net has greater interconnectedness. The 'Y' and chain are in between.

The findings from such research have been consistent. On simple problems centralized networks are most efficient but on complex problems decentralized networks are better. A leader is much more likely to emerge in a centralized network. The greater the degree of interconnectedness the higher the general level of satisfaction in the group. The more central an individual's position in the network, the higher is likely to be his personal satisfaction.

Shaw[33] suggests that the findings can be explained by two concepts—independence and saturation. Independence is valued in our society and the greater an individual's access to information, the greater the sense of independence and so the greater his satisfaction. On complex tasks the central member of a centralized network is more likely to become overloaded (saturated) by information and processing demands so that the whole network becomes less efficient. In other words, the system suffers from the role overload of the central figure (see Chapter VI).

But such experiments are obviously rather artificial. Do they have relevance to the work organization? Smith points out:

Clearly they are not like the small group in which communication is face to face and everyone can hear everyone else. They are rather more like situations which arise in large organizations. People in different parts of the organization are in touch with one another only indirectly, or, if directly, then often only be relatively impersonal media such as telephone and memorandum, which are not necessarily shared by others. Members of organizations can communicate with one another in more personal and direct ways, but quite often they do not have sufficient time to do so. . . . The provision or absence of communication links in large organizations is a key aspect of the control exercised by higher management.[34]

Such patterns of communication will obviously be influenced by the physical setting. We have already seen that Sayles' considered plant layout and distribution of individuals effected the nature and activities of work groups. The effect of the physical environment seems to be mediated via the communications it facilitates and inhibits. Thus, for example, proximity seems, not surprisingly, to be an important influence upon who will form a group with whom.

Even when the members of a group are all together in a single room and so potentially can all communicate with each other, the physical setting can still be influential. The seating arrangement, for example, may influence both the flow of communication and the emergence of a leader. Thus people sitting opposite each other tend to interact with each other more frequently than with people in other positions.[35] And there is evidence to suggest that not only do people who perceive themselves as having high status in the group choose the most favourable seating position (e.g. the head of a table), but perhaps more significantly, people who sit in such positions tend to be regarded by the rest of the group as having a higher status and are reacted to accordingly.[36]

The internal development of the group can also be significantly effected by the nature of its relationship with other groups. Thus, for example, the impact of intergroup competition has been shown to be fairly consistent by the research of such people as Sherif[37] and Blake et al.[38] Usually the group becomes more cohesive and the pressures towards conformity increase. There is a move away from concern for meeting the social needs of the individuals towards concentration on task activities. Related to this the group tends to become more organized or clearly structured and more tolerant of autocratic leadership. Winning or losing in such situations can also have a significant effect. The winning group tends to retain its cohesiveness but lose its task orientation, whereas the opposite tends to be true for the losing group. More will be said about the management of conflict situations in Chapter VIII.

So we have seen that the nature and outcome of group activity may be influenced by factors which were in existence from the time of formation, both in terms of the nature of the membership and of the situation within which they were acting. Before examining the development aspects of groups we must first look at what is in effect the starting point of that development, i.e. the interaction between the group members.

Interaction   We have seen then that direction of communication or patterns of interaction are an important group variable. Equally important is the nature or quality of that interaction. Numerous attempts have been made to find a meaningful way of categorizing the various behaviours displayed by individuals in a group context. Some have been developed primarily as research tools, others have been developed primarily as aids to interactive skills training.

We saw earlier in this chapter that groups can be thought of as potentially serving two major functions—accomplishing formally prescribed tasks and satisfying various needs of the members. It has been suggested that, for a group to continue to be effective some equilibrium between those two functions must be maintained.[39] It is common, therefore, for categorizing systems to differentiate between those behaviours which seem to be performing task functions and those performing 'socio-emotional' functions. The latter term was coined by Bales who developed what has probably been one of the most influential systems. He called it 'interaction process analysis'.[40] The twelve categories comprising the system are claimed to be mutually exclusive, and any verbal or non-verbal contribution of a group member can be classified by a trained observer using the system. These are the categories:

A. SOCIO-EMOTIONAL: POSITIVE
> 1. *Shows solidarity*, raises others status, gives help, reward.
> 2. *Shows tension release*, jokes, laughs, shows satisfaction.
> 3. *Agrees*, shows passive acceptance, understands, concurs, complies.

B. TASK: ATTEMPTED ANSWERS
> 4. *Gives suggestion*, direction, implying autonomy for others.
> 5. *Gives opinion*, evaluation, analysis, expresses feeling, wish.
> 6. *Gives orientation*, information, repeats, clarifies, confirms.

C. TASK: QUESTIONS
> 7. *Asks for orientation*, information, repetition, confirmation.
> 8. *Asks for opinion*, evaluation, analysis, expression of feeling.
> 9. *Asks for suggestion*, direction, possible ways of action.

D. SOCIO-EMOTIONAL: NEGATIVE

    10. *Disagrees*, shows passive rejection, formality, withholds help.

    11. *Shows tension*, asks for help, withdraws out of field.

    12. *Shows antagonism*, deflates others status, defends or asserts self.

Bales maintained that there are a number of problems to be coped with both in the task area of activity and in the socio-emotional area. Behaviour can be further understood in terms of which of these problems it is related to. Thus in the task area, categories 6 and 7 are related to problems of orientation, 5 and 8 to problems of evaluation, and 4 and 9 to problems of control. In the socio-emotional area categories 3 and 10 are related to problems of decision, 2 and 11 to problems of tension management, and 1 and 12 to problems of integration. Such problems are likely to crop up at different times in the group's life and, therefore, the related behaviours are likely to predominate at different times. Also the type of behaviour on individual displays in a given group will influence the kind of role or roles he is seen as fulfilling. These are both points which we will take further in the discussion of group development.

Development of a group

The concept of development recognizes that, once a group has formed, then through time its processes and the relationships between its members will become qualitatively different, and a structure of roles and norms will emerge.

Phases of development   A number of behavioural scientists, operating in widely differing situations, have observed that groups seem to pass through a set sequence of stages or phases of development, in each stage the dominant concern of the group being different from that in the preceding one. Thus Bales for example maintains that problem solving groups tend to follow the pattern of orientation, evaluation and control. Tuckman[41] reviewing the literature was able to formulate a model which represented the changes which take place in both the social and the task aspects of group behaviour. The model appeared:

> to hold up under widely varied conditions of group composition, duration of group life and specific group task.

He suggests that groups pass through four main stages in a set sequence. Each stage is characterized by dominant task issue and a dominant social issue. Thus:

Stage 1: he termed *forming*. On the task dimension this is a period of orientation. Group members try to establish just what the parameters of the task are, how they should go about accomplishing it, what information and resources they will need and so on.

On the social dimension this is a period of testing and dependence. Members try to discover what kinds of interpersonal behaviour are appropriate. There is a tendency to look to the leader or some powerful group member for guidance in this new situation.

Stage 2: Storming is characterized on the social dimension by internal conflict. There is often polarization around key interpersonal issues. Members seem to be expressing their own individuality and attempting to resist group influence.

With regard to the task, this stage is typified by emotional responses to the demands it seems to be making on the individual, particularly where the individual experiences a discrepancy between these demands and his own orientation.

Stage 3: Norming. The group develops cohesion. Members perceive themselves to be part of a genuine 'group' which they wish to maintain and perpetuate. New standards and new roles emerge and are accepted. The emphasis is on harmony at all costs. Potentially conflict producing aspects of the task are avoided.

The task activities are typified by an open exchange of ideas and opinions. There is a willingness to listen to and accept the views of others.

Stage 4: Performing. The group has established a flexible and functional structure of interrelated roles. The interpersonal aspects of the group's activity have been sorted out, and now group energy can be channelled into the task.

The task dimension sees the emergence of solutions to problems and constructive attempts at successful task completion. The task and social dimensions seem effectively to have come together in this phase.

The model implies that groups must progress through the various stages before they can reach effective performance. Some groups obviously exist for a much shorter time than others. Tuckman suggests that the length of life of a troup determines the rate at which these various stages are passed through. It may well be, however, that time determines how adequately the key issues of each phase are dealt with. We can take this point a bit further by reintroducing the concept of 'hidden agendas'. In other words, issues which are not truly resolved may be driven underground. If then we regard group development not as linear, as Tuckman implies, but rather as spiral, we can explain the phenomenon that many managers will have come across—the re-emergence of problems which seemed long ago resolved. With this modification Tuckman's model can provide useful insights into the complexities of group development and also act as a background to the particular aspects we are going to consider now.

Communication and the structure of roles   We have already seen that different communication patterns within the group can have differing effects on satisfaction and performance according to the nature of the task. In some circumstances these patterns are predetermined but we have also seen that they can emerge from the inter-action. Such emergent patterns may be influenced by a number of things: seating arrangement and physical layout; individual differences in propensity to participate; existing status and role differences. There is in fact a dynamic relationship between role structure and communication patterns. We have already seen, for example, that the emergence of the leader role is influenced by the flow of communication.

But, through time, there is a tendency for groups to become differentiated on other dimensions in addition to that of leader-follower. Even within the leader role, it has been suggested that there will nearly always be differentiation between task-leader and socio-emotional leader.[42] Although we shall be exploring the concept of *role* more fully in Chapter VI, we must look at it here in terms of its significance for group functioning, for it is the differentiation of the group members into identifiable roles that is usually thought of as the development of group structure.

The particular role, or roles, that an individual plays in a given group will be influenced by a number of things: his position in the communication network; the kind of behaviour he typically displays with that particular group of people; his personality and abilities, and so on. It is important to mention at this stage that the role an individual develops in one group may be quite different from that he plays in other groups. The role structure is worked out, sometimes explicitly, often implicitly, between the particular group members in their particular situation. So, for example, Bales points out:

> The behaviour of the person, including what he says and how he says it, in the particular group, as seen through the perceptions and evaluations of all the members including himself, and the resulting expectations of him may be called his group role. His group role is not the same as his personality. His personality consists of his relatively enduring characteristics as a total being. You see only his interpersonal behaviour which may reflect only one side of his personality, elicited by this

particular group, its structure and his role in it, the expectations others have of him.[43]

The part played, then, by expectations in the emergent structure is an important one. As the group gains a history, it becomes more clear to its members what kind of behaviour can be expected from each individual. The unexpected is discouraged and the roles become more clearly defined and more stable. The relative status of any particular role is likely to vary according to its relevance to the dominant group issue at any time.

The particular role structure of any group will, for the reasons we have seen, be peculiar to that group, but a number of writers have attempted to itemize the kind of roles they may develop. Thus Bales[44] has recently extended interaction process anlaysis to formulate a list of 27 typical group roles. The identification of each role is however rather complex, based on various combinations of the major behavioural categories of his original theory.

A simpler system of classifying group roles, which has subsequently proved popular particularly in management training spheres, was developed by Benne and Sheats.[45] Recognizing, as Bales did, the need for some equilibrium between the task and social demands of group activity, they distinguished between task-oriented roles and those they referrred to as oriented towards group maintenance. In addition, they suggested that some roles seem functional to the group neither in terms of task accomplishment nor in terms of group maintenance. They therefore referred to these as self-orientated. Here are some examples from each of their three categories.

A. SOME TASK-ORIENTATED ROLES

Initiator-contributor: suggests new ideas or changes in the way of doing things.

Information giver: offers relevant facts or relates personal experience which is pertinent to the problem.

Co-ordinator: shows or clarifies the relationships between various ideas and tries to pull suggestions together.

Evaluator: supplies standards of accomplishment and measures group progress.

B. SOME MAINTENANCE-ORIENTATED ROLES

Encourager: praises and supports the contributions of others, indicating warmth and solidarity.

Harmonizer: mediates differences between others and attempts to reconcile disagreements.

'*Gate-Keeper*': keeps the communication channels open, making sure that those who want to contribute can do so, and also limits over-talkative members.

Group observer and commentator: calls attention to group process, offering suggestions about problems they may be having in functioning.

C. SOME SELF-ORIENTATED ROLES

Aggressor: deflates others by expressing disapproval of their ideas, opinions or feelings or by attacking the group as a whole.

Blocker: is negativistic, and stubborn resistant, keeps on returning to issues that the group has already rejected.

Playboy: makes a show of his lack of involvement in the group by nonchalance, horse-play and raising irrelevant mundane issues.

Help-seeker: attempts to elicit sympathy responses from all or certain group members by expressing insecurity or confusion.

Depreciates self beyond reasonable limits.

Obviously this is just a sample of the many roles that may be played in a group, and as Benne and Sheats point out, one member may perform several different roles during the life of that group.

Group norms   In addition to role structure, another characteristic aspect of group development is the emergence of group norms. These are shared rules or standards which designate what is acceptable and what is unacceptable in terms of group member behaviour, attitudes and beliefs. In a working context they may apply to quantity and quality of production, methods of work, interpersonal behaviour, attitudes to other groups or individuals, language, clothing or anything else that is regarded by the group members as relevant to their existence as a group. There is also usually an accepted set of rewards and punishments associated with compliance or non-compliance with these norms.

This process of normative influence has been of considerable interest to behavioural scientists and has given rise to a wide range of research in both laboratory and natural settings. Probably the most widely known field studies of group norms are the Hawthorne Studies[46] mentioned in the chapter on motivation. It was observed that the group had developed clearly defined norms about what represented a fair day's work for a fair day's pay. The standard was set at a level which, although acceptable to management, was well below what was possible. There were sanctions against producing too far above this level (being a 'rate-buster') or producing too far below it (being a 'chiseler'). The pressures exerted upon offenders to conform to the standard ranged from use of derogatory names, through ostracism, to the practice of 'binging' (giving a hard blow on the upper arm). The group also applied social pressure to the inspectors and group supervisor to get them to conform to what was acceptable behaviour for those in authority.

Lupton[47] was also interested in the effect of group norms on levels of output. And indeed he found in one of the factories he studied that work groups were involved in an elaborate 'fiddle' aimed at regulating their output and stabilizing their earnings. However, he found that, in another factory, no such restrictive norm existed. He concluded that the differences could in part be understood in terms of internal differences. But he considered that the different social and economic environments of the two factories were of prime importance. These, he implied, meant that the workers brought different attitudes to productivity into the factory with them. In other words, following the implications of Chapter II, the group norms of production were significantly influenced by the different orientations to work.

Behavioural norms are not necessarily task related. Thus Roy[48] gives an interesting account of group norms which seem to be more oriented towards group maintenance. His observations were of a small work group of which he became a participant. The group was engaged in extremely simple and repetitive work of operating a punch press during a twelve-hour day. He noticed that what at first seemed disconnected and rather pointless horseplay and banter, in fact could be seen as a patterned set of rituals which were an important part of the culture which the group had developed for itself. Thus, for example, the long boring day was interrupted almost hourly by 'the daily repetition in an ordered series of informal interactions'. The first such interruption each day was 'peach time' when one worker provided a pair of peaches for his mates to eat. These were always received by complaints about the quality. Peach time was followed by 'banana time'. These occasions centred around a banana brought in by the same worker who supplied the peaches only this time intended for his own consumption. Each morning another worker would steal the banana, call out 'Banana time!' and eat it while the owner made futile protests. In the time Roy was with the group the first worker never managed to eat his own banana but continued to bring one for lunch every day. Similar ritualized interactions surrounded window time, pickup time, fish time and cake time. Roy concluded that such activities served not only to mark off the time but also to give it content and hurry it along. In this way the boredom of the work became easier to endure. In addition they served to reinforce the 'system of roles which formed a sort of pecking hierarchy'.

Probably the best known attempts to study the impact of social influence in small groups in a laboratory setting are the researches carried out by Sherif[49] and by Asch.[50] In the Sherif experiments subjects were placed in a darkened room and asked to estimate how much and in what direction a single visible point of light moved. (In fact the light did not move but a common phenomenon known as *autokinetic effect* occurs under these conditions whereby it appears to.) It was found that individual estimates made alone varied considerably more than when made in a group where the judgements of others could be heard. In the group there was a tendency for estimates to converge on a norm. The Asch studies were slightly different. Subjects were asked which of three lines on a card was the same length as a fourth presented along with them. The task was so simple that if asked alone the subjects very rarely made a mistake. However, when subjects were placed individually in a group of people all of whom, unbeknown to the subjects, were confederates of the researcher, the findings were different. In this situation, when the confederates unanimously made a patently wrong choice a surprisingly high proportion of the subjects went along with it, despite the evidence of their own eyes. Even those that stuck to their own opinion showed signs of discomfort. These two studies seem to highlight two quite different kinds of group influence on the individual. In the former, the individual is in a highly ambiguous situation in which he himself is unsure. That ambiguity is reduced by information from the others. In the latter, there is no ambiguity. The individual is succumbing to the immediate social pressure to conform to the expectations of the others. There is an additional significance to the difference in that the effects of the former type of situation seem to be relatively enduring whereas the effects of the latter seem to be confined to that situation alone.

It should be noted, however, that pressure to conform is not exerted evenly amongst group members. Thus Hollander[51] suggests individuals can build up an 'idiosyncrasy credit' which permits deviance from group norms in certain circumstances. This idiosyncrasy credit is related to status and the extent to which the individual has earlier conformed to the expected behaviour.

There is also some evidence to suggest that individuals differ in their susceptibility to social influence. Thus individuals high on intelligence, assertiveness, self-esteem and low on anxiety and authoritarianism seem less prone to conformity than others. (In this context independence should be distinguished from counterconformity or rebelliousness. The latter is paradoxically as determined by group norms as conformity in that it always involves doing the opposite.)

Cohesiveness   Another element of group development that has received a considerable amount of attention from behavioural scientists is cohesiveness. This is essentially the attractiveness of the group to its members—the extent to which they would make sacrifices to maintain its existence. Following on from the last section, it is not surprising to discover that as cohesiveness increases so does the general level of conformity to group norms. The social rewards available for conformity are, by definition, more highly valued. Similarly group members tend to be more satisfied. This is in part reflected by lower absenteeism and turnover. In addition

> highly cohesive groups provide a source of security for members which serves to reduce anxiety and heighten self-esteem.[52]

The relationship, however, between cohesiveness and productivity is not a direct one. In other words, contrary to some assumptions, high cohesiveness does not necessarily lead to high productivity. The mediating factor seems to be the group's own production norms. Thus highly cohesive groups seem to be more effective at achieving whatever goals their members establish for themselves, but as we have seen, these will not necessarily be in line with those set by management.[53] In Chapter VII the *socio-technical* approach to organization design is discussed, which attempts to harness the benefits of group cohesiveness to technical efficiency.

Leadership   The final aspect of group development we shall look at is leadership effectiveness. In many ways this may be regarded as one of the most fundamental aspects of management. Indeed one recent contributor to this area of study suggests:

> Almost everything in organizational life is either a function of leadership or is, at least, associated with it.[54]

The problem, however, facing researchers has been where to look for the key elements in effective leadership. Are they to be found in the characteristics and abilities of the individual occupying the role? Is it a question of some activities or styles of behaviour being more effective than others? Or should we be looking at the interaction between different styles and different situations? These three questions are in effect representative of the three major approaches adopted by behavioural scientists in the study of leadership, which can be referred to as the trait approach, the best style approach, and the contingency or situational approach.

We have already seen that certain situational factors seem to influence who will emerge as a leader in an informal situation. It also seems that certain characteristics of individuals are associated with emergent leadership. Thus Fineman and Warr[55] summarising the research suggest:

People who take the lead are likely to differ somewhat from other group members. In general they are likely to be rather more intelligent, self-confident, adjusted, dominant, and extroverted than non-leaders.

There is also a considerable amount of research correlating individual traits with leadership effectiveness, in particular relative intelligence, sociability, self-confidence, perseverance, and even physical superiority. Such findings are fairly consistent across a whole range of different settings, which would at first seem very promising. Unfortunately, as Porter et al.[56] point out:

> The magnitude of the correlations . . . is so low (e.g. on the order of ·10 to ·20) that their usefulness in either selecting individuals for positions of leadership or as the basis for a more general theory of leadership effectiveness is extremely limited.

In the light of this fact it is not surprising that the trend has been away from the trait approach to the study of leadership. Much of the research now concentrates one way or another on aspects of the leaders style.

An early and very influential study adopting the style approach was carried out by Lewin et al.[57] They looked at the impact of three different leader styles, autocratic, democratic, and laissez-faire, on groups of schoolboys engaged on hobby activities. In general the autocratic 'climates' were typified either by high hostility and aggression or by complete apathy. Democratic 'climates' were much more popular with the boys. As far as productivity was concerned there seemed to be no significant differences in quantity but the quality of democratic groups was considered much superior. Although the nature of the subjects and the setting limit the applicability of these findings in industrial organizations, they are none-the-less highly significant in that they set the scene for much subsequent research and theory.

In examining these subsequent contributions it is worth mentioning the difference highlighted by Stogdill[58] between the 'propagandists' and the 'researchers', and thus recognize that statements about 'best style' have tended to rest as much on value preferences as on research evidence.

The two most extensive research programmes adopting this approach have centred on Michigan University[59] and Ohio State University.[60] The Michigan studies have concentrated on establishing differences between the supervisors of high-producing groups and those of low-producing groups. The research settings have ranged from insurance companies, through research laboratories, to railway maintenance gangs. It was found that the typical high-producing supervisor was seen as 'employee-centred' whereas the supervisor of a low-producing group was typically seen as 'production-centred'. Such findings gave rise to a theory of leadership which saw supervisory style varying along a single dimension from production to employee-centred. There was assumed to be a direct relationship between style and subordinate performance. The more employee-centred the supervisor, the higher will be subordinate production. Unfortunately most of the evidence is purely correlational and as such provides no guide to the direction of causality. Likert maintains that supervisor behaviour causes performance but it could just as easily be the other way round. Where experimental methods have been used there is no consistent link between style and performance.

The Ohio Studies were more thorough in classifying leader behaviour. From their early researches they identified two main aspects of leader style:

consideration—the extent to which he is considerate of his subordinates' feelings, trusts and respects their ideas and shows personal relationships with them;

initiating structure—the degree to which the leader himself defines and organizes the work and determines who does what.

Although similar in nature to the Michigan styles a major difference is that they are seen as independent dimensions rather than opposite ends of a single continuum. So conceivably a manager could be high or low on both at the same time. High consideration was found to be related with employee morale as indicated by such measures as turnover and grievance rate. But once again, the direction of causality is not clearly established. There do not appear to be any consistent relationships with individual or group performance.

Despite these inconclusive findings the 'propagandists' still continue to advocate (and offer training courses for) best managerial styles. Thus the Blake and Mouton[61] theory known as the 'managerial grid' has received a fair degree of support. Like the Ohio researchers they identify two independent dimensions of leadership: concern for people and concern for production, each of which they measure on a scale of 1 to 9. According to them the ideal manager is extremely concerned with both. They refer to him as a '9,9' manager. On the basis of these assertions they have developed a management development package which they offer to industry; this aims in its early stages to help managers to identify their existing style and to move towards a 9,9, style.

It is interesting to note that in a recent publication the Ohio team not only tries to adapt its own research to take into consideration the impact of situational factors on leadership effectiveness, but also explicitly dissociates itself from the Blake and Mouton assumptions.[62]

Just as in other areas of organizational behaviour, so in leadership theory, there is a move away from generalized prescriptions and the search for the one best way. Much greater emphasis is now being placed on the relationship between leadership effectiveness and various aspects of the situation. The most notable example of this 'contingency' approach is the work carried out by Fiedler.[63]

Fiedler's model arose out of a considerable number of studies carried out in a wide variety of settings. The main contention is that:

> The group's performance will be contingent upon the appropriate matching of leadership style and the degree of favourableness of the group situation for the leader.

To arrive at this conclusion it was obviously necessary to find ways of measuring both style and situation. The measures actually adopted have been the subject of a fair amount of criticism and debate, but this should not be allowed to detract from the important implications of the general model.

Fiedler maintains that people can be differentiated according to whether they are primarily 'relationship-motivated' or 'task-motivated'. This differentiation is reflected in the way they score on a questionnaire measure he developed. People are asked to think of the individual with whom they can work least well and then rank that particular person on a series of scales each ranging from an unfavourable to a favourable judgement. This provides a least preferred co-worker score (LPC). High LPC scorers, i.e. those who describe their least preferred co-worker in relatively favourable terms are said to be relationship motivated. Low LPC scorers are said to be task-motivated. According to Fiedler:[64]

> Current evidence suggests that the LPC scores and the personality attributes they reflect are almost as stable as most other personality measures. . . . Changes do occur, but in the absence of major upsets in the individual's life, they tend to be gradual and relatively small.

The feature that distinguishes this model from its predecessors is the explicit attempt to categorize and measure influential aspects of the situation. Fiedler chose three dimensions upon which situations could be thought of as favourable or unfavourable:

leader-member relations—the extent to which he is, or feels, accepted and supported by group members;

task structure—the extent to which it is clear-cut and programmed with regard to goals, procedures and measures of progress;

position power—the extent to which the organization provides him with the power to reward and punish and so obtain compliance from subordinates. If each of these dimensions is thought of as either favourable or unfavourable it is possible to combine them to yield eight different overall situational descriptions ranging from highly favourable to highly unfavourable. This is demonstrated on Figure 5.3 which also summarizes the major findings from the extensive research programme. In other words,

Figure 5.3   The performance of relationship and task—motivated leaders in different situational—favourableness conditions (courtesy of Fielder, F. E.)[65]

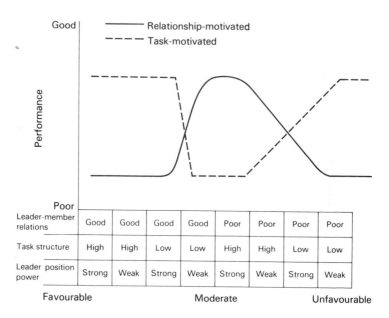

Leader-member relations	Good	Good	Good	Good	Poor	Poor	Poor	Poor
Task structure	High	High	Low	Low	High	High	Low	Low
Leader position power	Strong	Weak	Strong	Weak	Strong	Weak	Strong	Weak

Favourable	Moderate	Unfavourable

in very favourable or very unfavourable situations, task-motivated leaders (as measured by LPC score) seem to be most effective, whereas in moderately favourable situations relationship-motivated leaders seem to be most effective.

As has been said Fiedler's methods have been criticized. In particular the utility of the LPC measure has been questioned, and indeed he himself has revised or at least elaborated on the original assumptions about behaviour that could be based on LPC scores.[66] In addition it has been suggested that the three situational dimensions, chosen it seems fairly arbitrarily, although likely in themselves to be important, are inadequate to reflect the complexity of real life situations. Such criticisms may be well founded but none the less the contingency model is important as a stimulus to look at leadership effectiveness from a new point of view and to recognize that it is not accurate to speak of a good or bad leader, but rather that an individual will perform well in one situation and not in another. His performance depends as much upon the situation to which the organization assigns him as it does on his own particular orientation. An outstanding research team leader will not necessarily make a good production manager.

Fiedler goes further by suggesting that as a person's style is a reflection of a stable personality characteristic, it would be easier to engineer the situation to suit the man than to attempt to change the man himself. He questions, therefore, whether any current approach to management training can be expected to bring about across-the-board organizational improvement. Furthermore, as a manager gains experience in a particular job, the level of uncertainty associated with it will possibly reduce. The situation can in a sense be said to become more favourable. This would imply that some leaders would be more effective in the long-run, but not in the short-run, whereas others may shine as newcomers but their effectiveness will reduce through time. This obviously has implications for selection and job-rotation policies.

Others have suggested that style may not be so fixed as Fiedler implies. Thus Reddin's[67] '3-D Theory', although similar in many ways to the contingency model, implies that adaptability is an important aspect of managerial effectiveness. Reddin does not as yet, however, have any empirical foundation for his model.

Obviously there is still a need for refinement of the ideas and further research but the situational approach does represent a major step forward in the understanding of the manager's role as leader.

REFERENCES

1 SMITH, P. B., *Groups within Organizations*, Harper & Row, 1973.
2 SHAW, M. E., *Group Dynamics: the psychology of small group behaviour*, McGraw-Hill, 1976.
3 GOLEMBIEWSKI, R. T., *The Small Group*, University of Chicago Press, 1962.
4 SCHEIN, E. H., *Organisational Psychology*, Prentice Hall, 1972.
5 GLEN, F., *The Social Psychology of Organisations*, Methuen, 1975.
6 HANDY, C. B., *Understanding Organisations*, Penguin Books, 1976.
7 WARR, P. and WALL, T., *Work and Well-being*, Penguin Books, 1975.
8 FESTINGER, L., 'A theory of social comparison processes', *Human Relations*, 7, pp. 117–40, 1954.
9 ZAJONC, R. B., *Social Psychology: an experimental approach*, Wadsworth, 1960.
10 SHAW, M. E., *op. cit.*
11 OSBORN, A. F., *Applied Imagination*, Scribner, 1957.
12 TAYLOR, D. W., BERRY, P. C. and BLOCK, C. H., 'Does group participation when using

brainstorming facilitate or inhibit creative thinking', *Administrative Science Quarterly*, **3**, pp. 23–47, 1958.

13 DUNNETTE, M. D., CAMPBELL, J. and JAASTAD, K., 'The effect of group participation on brainstorming effectiveness for two industrial samples', *Journal of Applied Psychology*, **47**, pp. 30–7, 1963.

14 KRECH, D., CRUTCHFIELD, R. S. and BALLACHEY, E. L., *Individual in Society*, McGraw-Hill, 1962.

15 SHAW, M. E., *op. cit.*

16 KOGAN, N. and WALLACH, M. A., 'Risk-taking as a function of the situation, the person and the group', in NEWCOMB, T. M. (Ed.), *New Directions in Psychology III*, Holt, Rinehart & Winston, 1967.

17 SCHEIN, E. H., *op. cit.*

18 KRECH, D., CRUTCHFIELD, R. S. and BALLACHEY, E. L., *op. cit.*

19 THELEN, H. A., 'Group dynamics in instruction: principles of least group size', *School Review*, **57**, pp. 139–48, 1949.

20 STEINER, I. D., *Group processes and productivity*, Academic Press, 1972.

21 GIBB, C. A., 'The effects of group size and of threat reduction upon certainty in a problem-solving situation', *American Psychologist*, **6**, p. 324, 1951.

22 BALES, R. F., STRODTBECK, F. L., MILLS, T. M. and ROSEBOROUGH, M. E., 'Channels of communication in small groups', *American Sociological Review*, **16**, pp. 461–8, 1951.

23 KRECH, D., CRUTCHFIELD, R. S. and BALLACHEY, E. L., *op. cit.*

24 PORTER, L. W. and LAWLER, E. E., 'Properties of organisation structure in relation to job attitudes and job behaviour', *Psychological Bulletin*, **64**, pp. 23–51, 1965.

25 SHAW, M. E., *op. cit.*

26 HOFFMAN, L. R. and MAIER, N. R. F., 'Quality and acceptance of problem solutions by members of homogeneous and heterogeneous groups', *Journal of Abnormal and Social Psychology*, **62**, 401–7, 1961.

27 KRECH, D., CRUTCHFIELD, R. S. and BALLAHEY, E. L., *op. cit.*

28 SCHUTZ, W. C., *The Interpersonal Underworld*, Science and Behaviour Books (Reprint edition), 1966.

29 PFEIFFER, J. W. and JONES., *The 1974 Handbook for Group Facilitators*, University Associates, 1974.

30 SAYLES, L. R., *The Behaviour of Industrial Work Groups*, Wiley, 1958.

31 LEAVITT, H. J., 'Some effects of certain communication patterns on group performance', *Journal of Abnormal and Social Psychology*, **46**, pp. 38–50, 1951.

32 SHAW, M. E., 'Communication networks', in BERKOWITZ, L. (Ed.), *Advances in Experimental Social Psychology*, Vol. **1**, Academic Press, 1964.

33 SHAW, M. E., *ibid.*

34 SMITH, P. B., *op. cit.*

35 STEINZOR, B., 'The spatial factor in face to face discussion groups', *Journal of Abnormal and Social Psychology*, **45**, 552–5, 1950.

36 SOMMER, R., *Personal Space: the behavioural bases of design*, Prentice Hall, 1969.

37 SHERIF, M., *Group Conflict and Cooperation*, Routledge & Kegan Paul, 1966.

38 BLAKE, R. R., SHEPARD and MOUTON, J. S., *Managing Intergroup Conflict in Industry*, Gulf, 1964.

39 BALES, R. F., 'The equilibrium problem in small groups', in PARSONS, T., BALES, R. F. and SHILS, E. A., *Working Papers in the Theory of Action*, Free Press, 1953.

40 BALES, R. F., *op. cit.*

41 TUCKMAN, B. W., 'Development sequence in small groups', *Psychological Bulletin*, **63**, pp. 384–99, 1965.

42 BALES, R. F. and SLATER, P. E., 'Role differentiation in small groups', in PARSONS, I. and BALES, R. F. (Eds.), *Family Socialisation and Interaction Process*, Free Press, 1955.

43 BALES, R. F., *Personality and Interpersonal Behaviour*, Holt, Rinehart & Winston, 1970.

44 BALES, R. F., *ibid.*

45 BENNE, K. D. and SHEATS, P., 'Functional roles of group members', *Journal of Social Issues*, **4**, p. 2, 1948.

46 ROETHLISBERGER, F. J. and DICKSON, W. J., *Management and the Worker*, Harvard University Press, 1939.

47 LUPTON, T., *On the Shop Floor*, Pergamon, 1963.

48 ROY, D. F., 'Banana time: job satisfaction and informal interaction', *Human Organization*, **18**, pp. 156–68, 1960.

49 SHERIF, M., *The Psychology of Social Norms*, Harper, 1936.

50 ASCH, J., *Social Psychology*, Prentice Hall, 1952.

51 HOLLANDER, E. P., 'Conformity, status and idiosyncracy credit', *Psychological Review*, **65**, pp. 117–27, 1958.

52 CARTWRIGHT, D., 'The nature of group cohesiveness', in CARTWRIGHT, D. and ZANDER, A., *Group Dynamics* 3rd ed. Tavistock, 1968.

53 SEASHORE, S. E., *Group cohesiveness in the industrial work group*, Institute for Social Research, University of Michigan.

54 HOLLANDER, E. P., 'Processes of leadership emergence', *Journal of Contemporary Business*, Autumn 1974.

55 FINEMAN, S. and WARR, P., 'Managers: their effectiveness and training', in WARR, P., *Psychology at Work*, Penguin, 1971.

56 PORTER, L. W., LAWLER, E. E. and HACKMAN, J. R., *Behaviour in Organisations*, McGraw-Hill, 1975.

57 LEWIN, K., LIPPITT, R. and WHITE, R. K., 'Patterns of aggressive behaviour in experimentally created "social climates"', *Journal of Social Psychology*, **10**, pp. 271–99, 1939.

58 STOGDILL, R. M., 'Historical trends in leadership theory and research', *Journal of Contemporary Business*, Autumn 1974.

59 LIKERT, R., *New Patterns of Management*, McGraw-Hill, 1961.

60 FLEISHMAN, E. A. and HARRIS, E. F., 'Patterns of leadership behaviour related to employee grievances and turnover', *Personnel Psychology*, **15**, pp. 43–56, 1962.

61 BLAKE, R. R. and MOUTON, J. S., *The Managerial Grid*, Gulf, 1964.

62 KERR, S., SCHREISHEIM, C. A., MURPHY, C. J. and STOGDILL, R. M., 'Toward a contingency theory of leadership based upon the consideration and initiating

structure literature', *Organisational Behaviour & Human Performance*,**12**, pp. 62–82, 1974.

63 FIEDLER, F. E., *A Theory of Leadership Effectiveness*, McGraw-Hill, 1967.

64 FIEDLER, F. E., 'The Contingency model—new directions for leadership utilisation', *Journal of Contemporary Business*, Autumn 1974.

65 FIEDLER, F. E., *ibid.*

66 FIEDLER, F. E., 'Personality, motivational systems, and the behaviour of high and low LPC persons', *Human Relations*, **25**, pp. 391–412, 1972.

67 REDDIN, W. J., *Managerial Effectiveness*. McGraw-Hill, 1970.

VI

WORK ROLES

A disturbing feature of the literature in the field of management is that the reader encounters difficulty in reconciling the notions of individual autonomy and organizational order. The work of the Classical Theorists (see Chapter VII) tends to be highly prescriptive for the most part and all too often the individual is disregarded. In Systems Theory, conformity and harmony are stressed, and problems associated with organizational stress and conflict are likely to be neglected. The Human Relations School tends to focus on an acceptance of a universal set of needs, after the fashion of Maslow and Herzberg, and is somewhat limited in its explanatory powers as a result. Even Social Action Theorists (Chapter II) have sometimes devoted more attention to conformity in organizations than to explaining conflict and its consequences. Further, the Social Action approach to organizational analysis is often limited in its ability to link the individual with the wider organization.

It can be said that a pre-condition of organizational effectiveness is the existence of reasonably predictable behaviour patterns within the organization concerned. In turn, this predictability or social order within organizations is dependent upon the existence of a network of power and authority to preside over the allocation and use of organizational resources (see Chapter VIII). However, managerial authority is unlikely to be obeyed unless it is seen as being in some measure legitimate and this legitimation is won by means of reward systems fitting, in some measure, the motivations of those participating within the organization (see Chapters II and III).

Thus, we can say that a measure of organizational structure is obtained via the distribution of power and authority, and commitment to organizational objectives is obtained via the operation of reward systems. However, the essential link between individuals participating in the organization and the attainment of managerial objectives is what may be called the 'role structure' of the organization. Any social organization functions as a result of participants assuming or being allocated to roles and interacting in terms of those roles.

A role may be thought of as a set of rights and norms, duties and responsibilities, designed to mobilise human effort in a predictable manner. Thinking in these terms, we can visualize the personnel practices of selection and induction as processes of role allocation and role familiarization. Job descriptions can be thought of as role descriptions, and processes such as counselling and performance appraisal as being concerned with role performance.

Whilst the examination and analysis of organizational behaviour in terms of role concepts may have appeal in terms of conceptual tidiness, the exercise would be of relatively little use to the manager, or indeed the social scientist, if it did not provide a means for greater understanding of behaviour within organizations. It is the intention of this chapter to define and describe the main terms used in the study of what may be called 'role theory' and then to demonstrate the ways in which role theory has proved useful in the exploration and analysis of organizational problems.

Role theory

Role theory is not a theory in the sense that a physical scientist may use the term. That is, it does not predict a dependent relationship between two distinct variables, e.g. gas pressure and volume. Rather, role theory is a model or framework involving a battery of concepts based on an appreciation of the usefulness of the concept *role* as a point of articulation between the individual and his wider social environment. Further, in analysing the individual's relationship with his environment, it has been found useful to develop other concepts associated with roles, for example, *role performance, role conflict, role strain, role ambiguity*, etc.

Writers on role theory frequently distinguish between the terms *role and position* (or *status*).[1] Father, mother, manager, engineer, accountant, etc., are examples of positions (or statuses). It could be said though that the concept of 'position' is a rather static or empty one. In itself it leads us to nothing more than a knowledge of the label or title, e.g. manager, attached to a particular position. It is only when a position has rights and norms, duties and responsibilities, attached to it, and is acted out in terms of these, that it takes on social significance and becomes a social 'role'. Further, a knowledge of the position a person holds does not always tell us all we might like to know about the role.

To elaborate this point slightly, the *position* of 'wife' is common to virtually all known societies but the *role* of wife in primitive societies differs markedly from the role of wife in our own society because of variations in norms, values and expectations. Similarly, the role of policeman in, say, Chile, differs greatly from the role associated with the same position here.

Finally, the role of manager in Japanese industry,[2] with its emphasis on paternalism, differs in many ways from our own understanding of the role of manager.

Thus, an individual *occupies* a position but *performs* a role and the rights and norms associated with the role act to define how individuals should behave. Because of differences in the rights and norms associated with different roles, certain kinds of behaviour become acceptable or unacceptable. For instance, the norms governing a doctor's relationship with a female patient are not those associated with the position of husband. Similarly, the significance of the act of killing can vary greatly depending on the position of the actor. In the case of a public executioner, or a combat soldier, it is seen as constituting a legitimate act of public duty. In the case of a burglar, killing constitutes murder and an act inviting harsh punishment.

Further, it may be that a single individual who performs two different roles will find that a particular kind of behaviour is acceptable in the context of one of these roles but not the other. For example, a manager may maintain highly impersonal relationships with his subordinates. However, a similar approach towards relationships in the home, in the context of his position as husband or father, is likely to prove unacceptable because the relevant norms and expectations here are contravened.

However, whilst it is unlikely that a manager would attempt to organize relations in his home along the lines he uses to get results at work, it is equally unlikely that he will be able to completely separate his work-life from his non-work-life. A successful manager may find that he needs to work long hours, travel away from home on business, and possibly move home every few years if his employer wishes to transfer him from subsidiary to subsidiary in order to broaden his experience and usefulness to the company. This is not likely to be without consequences for his domestic life as conflicts arise between the competing demands of work-life and home-life.

The Pahls, in *Managers and their Wives*,[3] have examined this situation in some detail and claim that:

> . . . a husband's attitude to his work affects, and may be affected by, the couple's marital relationship. Indeed his attitude to the balancing of his home and work roles may be crucial in determining their marital happiness. . . . In the long-term sense, of course, most wives value their husband's work effort for the security and financial reward it brings to them and their family. Day-to-day attitudes, however, may be different, more ambivalent and antagonistic. Just as a husband can claim 'I do all my work for my wife' and then work so hard that he hardly ever sees

her; so a wife may value her husband's contribution to the family budget while yet grudging the time he spends earning it.[4]

In examining the relations between managers and their wives, the Pahls posit two extreme role positions which a wife may adopt in respect to her husband's work: those of *pusher* and *drop-out*. The pusher is one who supports the general competitive values of our society and encourages her husband to strive for advancement in his job. In strict contrast to this 'power behind the throne' role is the so-called drop-out wife who is more concerned to foster home-centred, close patterns of family interaction and involvement likely to serve as a source of moderation to the more aggressive values of ambition and success prevalent in her husband's work environment.[5] These stereotyped roles, open to the manager's wife do, however, focus very much on the demands of the work situation. If we turn the situation around and view the husband's family role as more important than his work role, it might now be said that the pusher wife (above) was the real drop-out whilst the drop-out (above) is now the pusher attempting to make her husband succeed in his role as a family man.

Role-set

Merton[6] has used the term 'role-set' to refer to the complement of role relationships in which an individual may be involved by virtue of occupying a single position or status. Use of this theoretical formulation can act to sensitize us to the variety of relationships which follow on from the occupancy of a single position. For instance, the role of medical student involves relationships not only with lecturers but also with other medical students, physicians, nurses, social workers, patients and medical technicians. Similarly, a manager will have role relationships with not only his subordinates but also with other managers (peers), superiors, and possibly staff specialists, trade unions, customers, suppliers and salesmen.

The notion of role-set can be particularly useful in the development of training schemes.[7] This is particularly so when the position under training is one which links with a large number of other positions and where the quality of inter-personal skills in these relationships is important. If it is accepted that an important element of such positions involves adjustment to or consideration of the expectations of others, then it follows that management and supervisory training programmes should benefit here. Jaques[8] has taken the view that work can be broken into its prescribed elements (clear, measureable, unambiguous) and its discretionary elements (unclear, ambiguous, requiring judgement). As the authority ladder of an organization is ascended, so the discretionary element of jobs typically increases, and so does the potential pay-off for role-set training.

It could be said that many of the techniques used by modern business schools contain elements of role-set training. For instance, negotiating exercises based on industrial relations situations often result in participants taking on roles as union negotiators although their real life experiences have previously been strictly limited to the confines of their managerial responsibilities. Role-play exercises based around issues such as the disciplinary interview provide similar opportunities. Here, interviewer and interviewee typically play out their designated situations and subsequently reverse roles. This exercise gives each of the participants a 'feel' for both roles. Case-study exercises, similarly, require participants to adopt unaccustomed stances in attempts to analyse organizational problems. Finally, T-Group or sensitivity training sessions (see Chapter IV) give individuals an opportunity to analyse group processes and to see themselves as others see them.

However, these are essentially 'off-the-job' training techniques and perhaps the greatest potential benefits to be derived from role-set training come from 'in-company' training. Here, the trainee and those involved in his role-set relationships have the opportunity to come together. The 'trainee' may be a green recruit or an established member of the organization undergoing re-training or refresher training. Such training, though somewhat expensive in terms of organizational resources, is potentially useful not only to the trainee but also to the other parties involved when they come to realize the nature of the problems and anxieties which the trainee encounters in his relationships with them.

Role-set training as an aid to coping with role conflict   Role conflict[9] may result from two sources. First, an individual may occupy two positions simultaneously involving roles which are in conflict. Examples of this situation are the housewife career woman, the military chaplain[10] or, from the field of industry, the manager or supervisor who is also a union member at the time of a strike involving his own union. With this form of conflict, however, the employing organization has control over only one of the sources of conflict. It can do little to influence the career woman's treatment of her role as housewife, the way in which the military chaplain interprets his religious beliefs in the context of a military situation, or the way in which the trade unionist manager orders his priorities in a strike situation.

However, that is not to say that managements cannot, indeed they often do, adapt their selection procedures in an attempt to avoid the consequences of such conflicts. Thus, an army would be likely to resist attempts to install, as a military chaplain, a man well known for his pacifist views. In addition, promotion procedures are likely to operate to sanction candidates who, when faced with conflict situations such as the above, fail to resolve them in a manner acceptable to the employing organization. A career woman whose work suffered as a result of her domestic obligations, or a manager who supported a union directive to strike, would be unlikely to receive sympathetic treatment from a subsequent promotion board.

A second source of possible role conflict may arise when a person occupies a single position but is subjected to two or more sets of conflicting role-set expectations. A much cited example of this form of role conflict in industry concerns the position of the foreman, 'the man in the middle'. Workers' views of the foreman often include expectations of him to protect their interests in the face of what they perceive as unfair management demands. Management, on the other hand, expect the foreman to ensure that management directives are carried out and productivity maximized. It may therefore be difficult in some circumstances for the foreman to meet both sets of demands.[11]

Other examples of conflicting role-set expectations of this kind are those involving the quality control inspector in industry and the salesman. The quality inspector is committed to the maintenance of quality standards for his firm's product. Sub-standard products released on to the market would impair his firm's reputation and reflect adversely on the inspection department. However, any product rejected by inspection is an indictment against production departments and can result in reprimands for production supervisors and possibly loss of earnings or bonuses for production workers. Thus, at one and the same time, the inspector is subjected to expectations involving, firstly, the maintenance of product quality and the reputation of the firm and, secondly, expectations from production departments whose own standing within the firm may be at risk.

A similar situation can arise in the case of the salesman. For instance, in a fast-moving science-based industry such as electronics, a salesman may be reliant on established customers not only for one-off sales but also for repeat orders for both existing and new equipment. Because of the fast rate of technical advance in the industry, customers may in turn rely on salesmen from supplier firms as a source of technical intelligence on new developments. A situation may then arise where the salesman is expected by his firm to sell a somewhat out-dated product when an improved version is only months away from full production. If he advises his customers to delay their orders and await the arrival of the new product, this may conflict with the expectations of his employers. If, on the other hand, he continues to canvas orders for the old product whilst remaining silent about the new one, he is likely subsequently to lose the confidence of customers.

A role-set training pattern can be useful both in pointing up the very existence of such problems in the first instance and in subsequently developing remedies based on the firm's priorities. Another problem which could be dealt with in a role-set based training programme is that of the traditional conflict between sales departments and production. Salesmen often feel obliged to give customers unrealistic promises of quick delivery dates in order to win orders. Conflict then arises if production departments fail to meet these dates and appear inefficient as a result. Again, the salesman is subjected to two sets of conflicting expectations and, all too often, has no relevant training to help him deal with the situation.

Other solutions to role conflict situations

The classic role-conflict situation referred to in social science and management literature is that experienced by the foreman or supervisor, mentioned above. Thurley and Wirdenius, claim:

> The traditional term 'foreman' is an occupational title of a role which was largely self-defined according to experience and belief among foremen in the particular trades concerned. The term 'supervisor' is a general organizational title indicating a role defined by that organization. In many industries, this has been a purely negative type of definition, with more and more functions reserved for qualified specialists.[12]

Thus, there exists a high degree of uncertainty in these roles and strategies for dealing with the diversified demands made upon them are not always apparent. Thurley and Wirdenius go on to say:

> Problem solving, search processes, the playing for time, the 'cooling' of difficult situations all require self-confidence, adequate skills, and a sense of detachment from pressures, which can only be built on role security. If supervisors do not know who they are and what they are doing, then it is difficult for them to deal with the unexpected.[13]

Merton[14] has identified several factors which may help the actor in a role conflict situation. The first three factors require no special activity on the actor's part whereas the last three require positive action:

1. Institutional patterns may exist to protect the actor's autonomy, e.g. the foreman's relations with workers on the one hand and higher management on the other may be isolated from each other and dealt with separately.

2. The pressure groups in the actor's role-set may have varying degrees of interest in his activity. The group with the weakest interest can be subordinated to the interests of the group with the strongest interest, e.g., the foreman with a non-organized workforce may devote more attention to satisfying managements' expectations of him.
3. The actor may have a degree of autonomy by virtue of competing groups in his role-set neutralizing each other. Weak groups may form coalitions to counter strong groups, e.g. some of the foreman's subordinates with anti-trade-union sympathies may identify with management in order to weaken an otherwise strong and militant union group.
4. The actor may be able to set forces competing to influence his role performance against each other thereby reducing their influence upon his behaviour. For instance, a foreman being pressurized by a health and safety officer to enforce the use of protective clothing, which reduces the earnings of workers on piecework, may attempt to win a measure of autonomy by encouraging the two other parties to meet directly.
5. The actor may form a protective coalition to increase his influence over groups in his role-set. Thus, the foreman, unprotected by union representation or by his superior management, may join with other foremen for protection.
6. Finally, the actor may go on the offensive and attempt to eliminate troublesome elements influencing his role performance, e.g. the foreman may attempt to build up a list of misdemeanours against a militant shop-steward as a basis for his dismissal.

Role ambiguity

It has been said that role ambiguity exists where there is a:

... discrepancy between the information available to the person (role holder) and that which is required for adequate performance of his role.[15]

Another attempt at a definition claims:

Role ambiguity results when there is some uncertainty in the minds, either of the focal person or of the members of his role-set, as to precisely what his role is at any given time. ... If his conception of his role is unclear, or if his conception of his role differs from that of others in his role-set, there will be a degree of ambiguity.[16]

Job descriptions are never complete role definitions and this is probably increasingly the case the more high-ranking the role. Interesting examples here are the Chairman of a nationalized industry or the Governor of a prison. The Chairman of a nationalized industry tends to be judged by two main criteria of success, i.e. balance sheet and service to the public. However, the two criteria are often contradictory. Both British Rail and the Post Office could improve their balance sheet performance by means of pruning, or abandoning altogether, services to rural and other outlying areas. But, this would result in severe public criticism from organized pressure groups. On the other hand, financial losses often meet with ridicule from the media and politicians. There can hardly have been a nationalized industry Chairman who did not crave either a clear role definition or, alternatively, sufficient independence to determine his own role definition with the assurance that it would be accepted by others.

A criticism sometimes levelled against role theory in general is that many of the key terms and concepts associated with it have not yet been sufficiently rigorously refined and clarified to provide universally agreed meanings. The term 'role ambiguity' could be regarded as a case in point for there appears to be an overlap in the way the terms 'role conflict' and 'role ambiguity' are often used. If the example of the position of the foreman earlier in this chapter is taken to represent a case of role conflict, then this overlapping of terms is well demonstrated. The foreman is subjected to differing expectations as to his role performance from different members of his role-set. Thus it can be said that there is likely to exist uncertainty in the minds of members of his role-set as to precisely what his role is at any given time. Further, it is probably fair to say that this uncertainty is related to vagueness in the basic job description and so doubts about the true nature of the rights and norms attaching to the role exist also in the mind of the foreman himself. Thus, the situation of the foreman fits the definition of role ambiguity yet is also offered as a classic example of role conflict.

Further, the example of role ambiguity of the Chairmanship of a nationalized industry could likewise be described as an example of role conflict if the ambiguity associated with the role is seen as resulting from conflicting pressures in the actors role-set relationships pushing for economic viability *and the* provision of a comprehensive service. The role of prison Governor has similar ambiguities; he may find that certain role-set pressures encourage him to perceive his role as that of running a purely custodial institution, whereas competing pressures may stress a more therapeutic interpretation of the role, involving re-socialization and re-habilitation of prisoners into the wider community.

Another ingredient in our treatment of the study of work roles in this chapter, is a consideration of the way in which the person occupying a position, and performing the role concerned, *himself* perceives his role and attempts to introduce his own values and priorities. Here, the terms 'role-taking', 'role-making', 'latent social identity' and 'role strain' are useful.

Role-taking and role-making in organizations

Role theory probably offers greater scope and potential for understanding individual behaviour in an organizational context than any alternative approach. However, the potential for breaking free of the limitations of other theoretical approaches for analysing and understanding organizational life has not always been realized. More recent developments in the field give room for optimism. It has taken some time to break free from the early influence of Linton[17] who tended to see roles as being virtually totally defined by external forces to a high degree of concreteness and consistency. His idea of man seems to be that of a puppet, with rigid role definitions or job descriptions controlling the strings. Such an approach leaves us saddled with immutable self-regulating systems, and leaves little room for an understanding of either conflict or change within organizations.

Alternative approaches towards an understanding of role behaviour and role performance have been more useful but still often tend to under-emphasize the importance of the individual occupying a role. However, Turner has said:

Conformity to perceived expectations is but one special way in which an actor's role-playing may be related to the role of relevant others. From this viewpoint, role behaviour in formal organizations becomes a working compromise between the formalized role prescriptions and the more flexible operation of the role-taking process.[18]

Turner argues that the actor takes on a role (role-taking) and fills out that role (role-making) by probing and exploring the less prescribed areas of the role and interpreting even the prescribed elements in the light of his own values and goals. This occurs through a process of interaction and monitoring of the responses of members of his role-set. Thus, Turner stresses the element of *interaction* in role relationships and role performance. The role of manager, for instance, has no meaning except in relation to the roles of those who are managed. Further, whilst many elements of a manager-subordinate relationship are mutually understood, others remain flexible, to be agreed or established through exploration, discussion, consensus or conflict.

Turner discusses the *internal* and *external* validation of roles. Internal validation of a role, he says, involves successful anticipation of the behaviour of relevant others inasmuch as it is relevant to the actors' own role performance. External validation, on the other hand, relates to the actors behaviour being seen as legitimate by others whose opinions have relevance for the role in question. Finally, if the actor develops a perception or definition of his role which accords strongly with the view which others have of the same role, then the role is said to be *consensually* validated.

Roles then, have no meaning or significance other than in a social context. Social roles never exist in a completely defined form, and the more obvious core elements of a role are assumed by the role holder (by a process of role-taking) and thereafter embroidered and elaborated through interaction with others (role-making). Turner's use of the concept of internal validation highlights the importance of the individual in any role performance, while the notion of external validation here focuses on the key element used in many previous definitions of the term role itself and concerns conformity to the expectations of relevant others.

A role is internally validated then when the actor is able to anticipate accurately the behaviour and expectations of relevant others relative to his own role. However, this does not automatically imply his agreement with, or acceptance of, the content of his role as defined by others. It is possible that a role holder may understand the expectations of others but disagree with them and, in turn, those whose expectations are being contradicted may not then view his behaviour as acceptable. For instance, scientists in industry (see later) may not agree with the definition their employers have of their role and especially the research tasks they are given. Thus two different definitions exist for the same role, each supported by the attitudes, values and norms of the party concerned.

Here, from the viewpoint of the actor, we could see the role *as he would construct it* as having internal validation and the role as his employers would construct it as having external validation. Various alternatives may now arise. If the respective definitions of the role closely correspond, then we could say there exists consensual validation. If they do not correspond, there are three possibilities:

1. the role definition having internal validation may govern role performance,
2. the role definition having external validation may govern role performance, or
3. conflict and/or compromise by negotiation may result.

Here we have expanded the meaning of internal validation from that adopted by Turner in order to focus more on the individual actor. The internally validated role is no longer simply that defined externally and understood by the actor, but that defined by the actor himself. This is not to say the actor defines his role in a purely haphazard or whimsical manner for such a conceptualization would not lend itself to rigorous analysis. The actor is influenced by external social forces but still believes his own role definition superior to that of other members in his role-set.

The 'me' and the 'I'

Mead,[19] in his influential writings on role theory, has stressed the exclusively social nature of human attitudes and behaviour. This standpoint is well summed up by Robert E. Park:

> Man is not born human. It is only slowly and laboriously, in fruitful contact, co-operation, and conflict with his fellows, that he attains the distinctive qualities of human nature.[20]

Mead attempted to distinguish an element of freedom for the individual in his role relationships by distinguishing between what he called the 'me' and the 'I'. The individual's self-definition as a player of any particular role is the 'me' and he has a 'me' in each role. His perception of himself as a whole (including all his roles) is his 'I' or 'self-conception'. Rose, in his interpretation of Mead, has written:

> Once defined, the self-conception takes on characteristics and attributes which are not necessarily part of its constituent roles.[21]

The 'me's' are the individual's parts of his relationships with others—the sets of attributes of others which he himself assumes. The 'I' then is the creative self which is aware of, and can react to, the aspect of self arising out of the individual's 'me's'.

Using this approach, the individual emerges as something more than a mere amalgamation of the parts of himself which are in turn, parts of his relationships with others. In short, the individual cannot be reduced down to a series of 'me's'. If each 'me' is seen as a piece of a jig-saw puzzle with a definite boundary and separate existence in its own right, then it could be said that, when the pieces are put together, a personality emerges in its own right, and has a significance over and above the constituent parts. Or again, an individual only has a social existence through his relationships with others but he has a self-awareness which is separate from his 'me's' and allows him to establish a relationship to himself.

The 'I' then represents the spontaneous dimension of human experience and involves a purely personal aspect. However, if Mead meant the actor's 'I' to be completely independent of social and cultural expectations, then it is difficult to imagine what he could have been referring to, and it is probably more useful to think of them as being linked. As Rose puts it:

The 'I', while personal, is by no means independent of cultural expectations since it is built on the individual's 'me's', and since the individual always sees himself in relation to the community.[22]

An individual may be observed to adopt a more optimistic view of his world and his position within it on Fridays than on Mondays, even though the number and quality of his role relationships (his full complement of 'me's') has not altered. This, however, does not imply that the individual's view of the world and his position within it varies on a random basis. Similarly, people are more likely to grant favours when in certain moods than in others. Again, this does not mean that behaviour is random in nature and without explanatory roots. The tendency is rather for our mood to be influenced by some very recent area of role-play activity and our wider universe of values and beliefs. However, the individual possesses the awareness and self-control (the 'I') to understand and, if necessary, correct for the influences of one role on another ('me's').

It could further be said that, when an individual attempts to cope with a situation of role conflict, it is the 'I' rather than the 'me' which acts because 'me's' act essentially within the context of roles, and conflict resolution, unless coped with institutionally, (i.e. by permanent social practices designed to minimize its impact) requires a personal and subjective decision or stance. Typical responses to role conflict situations of the type met by, say, a cleric in a segregationalist state or by an army chaplain (above) are: rationalization ('someone has to do it, so why not me?', or 'it's all in a job of work'); repression ('I see no conflict'); negativism ('I prefer not to talk about such things'), or possibly an ordering of priorities or compartmentalization ('one thing at a time.')

A further example that can be cited here is the disciplinary interview. Mead says that social control is achieved through the expression of the 'me' over the 'I'. The 'I' uses the 'me' in order to act in conformity with others. However, the 'I' may reject the option of conformity to expectations. The interviewee, in a disciplinary interview may find his situation humiliating. However, the self-aware 'I' draws from his 'me's' a definition of appropriate behaviour—that is to apologise for his wrong-doings and give an assurance that they will not be repeated. Such behaviour, he knows, is likely to prove acceptable to the interviewer.

The creative aspect of the interviewee's self, the 'I', may feel no remorse for the mis-deeds in question. But, he may still adopt the pattern of behaviour which his 'me's' tell him will be appropriate in gaining him forgiveness—deference. On the other hand, he may decide to tell the interviewer to 'stuff his job'. This 'I' dominated behaviour, is unlikely to be purely whimsical. Rather, it is likely to be based upon a consideration, albeit a somewhat rapid one, of the market demands for his skills, alternative employment opportunities, and the fillip for his self-respect which his action is likely to provide.

Labelling and the self-fulfilling prophecy

If individuals engage in forms of behaviour which correspond to aspects of stereotypes, there is a possibility that they may be 'labelled' in terms of those stereotypes. This may happen even though perhaps only a single aspect of the stereotype in question is visible in the behaviour of a person being labelled.

Salaman has written:

> The point about labelling a person as a particular type is that it is possible for the act of labelling itself to cause us to behave in such a way that our predictions . . . will come true.[23]

This is particularly true where the person applying the labels is in a position to make the label stick. A study by Rosenthal and Jacobson demonstrates this point.[24] Researching in a school, they selected pupils at random and informed their teachers that they had been identified, using a Harvard University test, as pupils likely to make rapid progress over the next year. This prophecy in fact came true because the quality of interaction between the teachers and pupils concerned improved.

Similarly, in the work situation, if a subordinate is pre-judged by his or her superior, a prophecy is likely to be fulfilled. A manager who labels one of his trainees as 'bright and likely to go places' is likely to devote more energy to the trainee in question since he sees this as a worthwhile investment. Further, the encouragement that the trainee receives in the process is likely to lead him to try harder than he might do otherwise. In the opposite way, a person labelled ungenerously (and perhaps unfairly) is likely to do badly.

A second source of reinforcement for the self-fulfilling prophecy is what we may call selective perception. That is, if we expect a person to perform well, we may disregard his bad performances and exaggerate good ones. In short, we may see what we expect to see. This point is made somewhat amusingly in an Open University publication.[25] The caption to a Victorian society drawing room scene goes as follows:

INTERLOCUTOR: Who's that showy Woman who Talks and Laughs so loud, and digs People in the Ribs?

INTERLOCUTRIX: Oh, that's the Duchess of Bayswater. She was a Lady Gwendolen Beaumanoir, you know!

INTERLOCUTOR (*with warmth*): Ah! to be sure! That accounts for her high-bred Ease, her aristocratic Simplicity of Manner, her natural and straightforward. . . .

INTERLOCUTRIX (*putting up her eye-glass*): By the bye, pardon me! I have unintentionally misinformed you; it's Mrs. Judkins. She's the Widow of an Alderman, and her Father was a Cheesemonger in the New Cut.

INTERLOCUTOR: Dear me!—Ah!—Hum!—er—Hum!—Ha! That *quite* alters the case! How she goes on to be sure! I wonder she's admitted into decent society!

(N.B. It *was* the Duchess, after all).

Cases of premature labelling in the workplace situation are probably known to most readers of this book. The dangers and consequences are obvious and the practice should be avoided whenever possible although, inevitably, we tend to label without thinking.

Manifest and latent social roles

The work of Alvin Gouldner,[26] on role theory has been influential in the analysis of behaviour in the workplace and, in fact, will be used later in Chapter X to examine the attitudes and behaviour of the small businessman. Important in Gouldner's work on role theory is his use of the concepts of manifest and latent social roles and social identities. Again, as a starting point, he uses the terms 'social position' and 'social role'. However, in doing so, he introduces the idea of *social identity*. A social position, he says, is an assigned social identity defined in terms of culturally prescribed categories, e.g. negro, teacher, and assigned by members of his group. A social role is the shared set of expectations directed towards people who are assigned to a particular social identity.

In any situation, a person will have a variety of social identities. A student, for instance, in a classroom situation will find his identity of 'student' to be most relevant to his immediate situation. This identity, which is consensually regarded as relevant to the situation by other group members, is termed a *manifest* social identity. On the other hand, other identities may be 'introduced' into the classroom situation, e.g. identities based upon sex, age-group, membership of ethnic groups, or various attitudes and ideologies. These are unlikely to be regarded by the group as consensually relevant and legitimate and are therefore termed *latent* social identities. This is not to say that all latent identities are considered illegitimate. For instance, a manager may intrude an identity based on his previous experience as a shop-floor worker. This is likely to win co-operation, and is unlikely to be regarded as illegitimate by the workers concerned.

This 'intrusion' of a latent identity may have two sources. In fact Gouldner says:

> Just as others can be oriented towards an individual's latent identities, so, too, can the individual himself be oriented to his own latent identities.[27]

For instance, if we think of the situation of a manager interviewing candidates for the position of secretary, the manifest identities relevant to the situation are those of 'manager' and 'secretary'. Accordingly, the manager should assess only the qualities of respective candidates relevant to his requirements of them in an organizational context, e.g. shorthand and typing speeds, past experience and responsibilities, personal manner, etc. However, there is always a possibility that sexual identities will be intruded into the situation. Looking at the situation from the viewpoint of the interviewee, she herself can intrude her latent sexual identity in the fashion of revealing clothing, flattery of her interviewer, and the use of charm designed to disarm him rather than exhibit inter-personal skills of a more general nature.

On the other hand, in the above situation, it may not necessarily be the interviewee but the interviewer who, by use of cues, intrudes the candidate's sexual identity. Her responses may then be taken by the interviewer as an indication of her willingness to interact with him at other than a professional level. This is not to say that the manager necessarily wants a secretary willing to take dictation on his knee, but the temptation or desire to flirt at a relatively harmless level, and the prestige appeal of an attractive secretary may still remain. Another situation in which the intrusion of latent sexual identities is proverbial (though not necessarily true) is that of the attractive female taking a driving test. It is sometimes felt that the more the examiner sees of her legs, the less likely he is to notice her poor driving.

Latent sexual identities are fequently intruded in the context of industrial and commercial sales and marketing. The taking of certain vitamin pills and tonics for instance, is often linked not only with general well-being but also with youth and virility. Much the same could be said of techniques used to market certain brands of prestige cars, and cigarettes.

Certain identities may be either latent or manifest depending upon the value system of the wider society. Here, Gouldner gives the example of the role of 'elders' in a gerontocratic society. The deference and respect due to them by their juniors results in the elder constituting a manifest role. However, in modern Western industrialized society the role of 'elder' is a latent one because, in the context of the factory, it is not regarded as fully legitimate or clearly relevant.

Cosmopolitans vs. *Locals : 'Company Men'* vs. *'Itinerants'* Gouldner, in a study of a factory in the USA,[28] noted a type of company executive which he called the 'expert'. Experts, he claims, tend to be treated with some suspicion by other members of the organization, and top positions are usually withheld from them:

> Experts tend to be staff who never seem to win the complete confidence of the company's highest authorities and are kept removed from the highest reaches of power. Much like staff men in other companies, these experts can advise but not command. They are expected to 'sell' management on their plans, but cannot order them to be put into effect. It is widely recognized that these experts are not given the 'real promotions'. The expert is under pressure to forego the active pursuit of his speciality if he wishes to ascend in the company hierarchy. Among the reasons for the experts' subordination may be the fact that they are less frequently identified as 'company men' than others in the executive group.

Gouldner goes on to contrast this with the situation of company man:

> The 'company man' . . . is one who is regarded as having totally committed his career aspirations to his employing company, and as having indicated that he wishes to remain with it indefinitely. In effect, then, company personnel were using a criterion of 'loyalty to the company' in assigning social identities to members of their organization. A company man is one who is identified as 'loyal'.[29]

Experts, Gouldner claims, are less likely to be identified as company men because of their previous formal training which opens up opportunities for employment in a whole range of different organizations and gives them a feeling of commitment to their particular skill or discipline which may well transcend any commitment towards their current employer. In the extreme case, their current employer is regarded as a stepping stone in their career, to be rejected when possibilities for career advancement occur elsewhere. In a sense, they are 'in' but not 'of' the organization.[30]

This, it could be said, puts them in the position of itinerants, occupying a position intermediate between the line company man (whose main skill derives from his detailed knowledge of the practices of his own company, frequently to the exclusion of those of other companies), and an outside management consultant.

Around the positions of expert and company men, Gouldner has constructed the terms of 'Cosmopolitan' and 'Local' latent social identities respectively. These terms take their specific meaning from the situation whereby the expert (Cosmopolitan) relies for his continued standing as a competent professional on the esteem of peers elsewhere (i.e. others with the same skill and specialism in other organizations). On the other hand, the company man (Local) relies for his continued standing on the recognition of others within the same company.[31]

Cosmopolitans tend to exhibit:
1. a low degree of organizational loyalty
2. a high commitment to their own specialized skills
3. an identification with a peer-group situated outside the organization.

Locals, on the other hand, tend to exhibit:
1. a high degree of organizational loyalty
2. a low commitment to specialized skills
3. an identification with a peer-group situated inside the organization.

Gouldner says:

Cosmopolitans and locals are regarded as *latent* social identities because they involve criteria which are not fully institutionalized as bases for classifying people in the modern organization, though they are in fact, often used as such.[32]

This is not to say that all experts are Cosmopolitans—see the work of Cotgrove and Box (below).

Similarly, in trade unions, different identities may be assigned to people who orientate themselves to different reference groups. Some union officers and shop stewards may identify with an outside political reference group—the wider Labour Movement—whilst others are primarily orientated towards the more limited goals and objectives of their own particular union.

Gouldner, in his study of a college, succeeded in distinguishing groups of Cosmopolitans and Locals amongst teachers. Compared to the Locals, the Cosmopolitans were more likely to believe in light teaching and administrative workloads in order to allow time for research; they saw good research facilities as an important factor influencing job satisfaction; they were more likely to have, or be registered for, a Doctorate degree; they were less likely to define those around them as having similar professional interests, and were more likely to leave the college.[33]

The effects of these latent identities in practice were that cosmopolitans were less inclined to participate on college committees, they were therefore less influential in organizational decision-making, and they exhibited a higher propensity to question organizational rules.

It is perhaps surprising, in view of these findings, that the management of institutions of further and higher education is still often fraught with difficulties that need not arise if staff selection and staff development processes were more efficient. However, this is not to say that such problems always arise. In Britain, academic leadership normally rests with the universities. University departments are normally conscious, not only of the status of their university, but also of the status of their own particular department compared to similar departments in other universities. A good department, even in a generally low status university, can usually attract good staff, good students, outside funds, and even compete on strong terms for internal funds. A lecturer is unlikely to seek employment in such a department unless he is willing to undertake research and publish, and the department would not, in any case, look favourably upon his application.

In colleges of further education, on the other hand, heavy teaching loads frequently institutionalize mediocrity. That is not to say that they do not meet the demands of their market, but the heavy internal demands made on staff would be likely to spell professional suicide, job dissatisfaction, and conflict for a Cosmopolitan lecturer, unless he or she decided to drop any commitment to his or her specialism in favour of a long-term career in the institution. However, organizations do not always select the 'best' (most qualified) candidate for a vacancy but frequently opt for the candidate promising the 'best fit' with organizational objectives, i.e. mainly those of teaching.

Whilst the functions of the university (academic leadership) and the technical college (lower level teaching with high student throughput) appear fairly well understood, it could be argued that the function of Polytechnics is somewhere in between the other two and not well-defined. Teaching loads here are fairly high (though not normally as high as in technical colleges) and the temptation exists to compete with the universities in terms of reputation—post-graduate courses are offered and research is undertaken. Identity problems are likely to result here and probably nowhere more than in a department of management where teachers are recruited both from industry (usually Locals) because of their practical experience and also from more academic backgrounds (often Cosmopolitans). However, once recruited, all staff are expected to conform to a common pattern of behaviour—the master of all trades utility man—doing teaching, administration, some research and also, possibly, consultancy work. The first to suffer is usually research and this coincides frequently with an increase in the likelihood of the individual gaining promotion—the individual having resolved the role strain here by confirming a commitment to a Local identity.

Scientific identity and role strain

The increasing application of science and technology to the field of production has seen correspondingly larger numbers of scientists being employed in industrial organizations. However, this can create certain difficulties both for the scientist himself and also the employing organization. Scientific research has a certain ethos, values, and beliefs. Salient amongst these are: the need for autonomy to exercise scientific expertise, communication of findings across organizational boundaries through publication, and the pursuit of knowledge for its own sake over and above other goals such as profitability and personal gain.

Box and Cotgrove[34] have constructed a typology of scientists based on attachment to these values. Two of these scientific identities approximate closely to Gouldner's Cosmopolitan and Local identities but Box and Cotgrove have also interposed a third identity. Their three occupational scientific identities were as follows:

1. *Public*—identifies with the ethos of science, stresses autonomy and the need to publish in order to gain recognition.
2. *Private*—here satisfaction lies in the task itself and getting results. Little interest in publishing—does not regard the scientific community as his reference group.
3. *Organizational*—does not seek scientific recognition outside the organization. Interested in occupational advancement and will abandon his scientific skills if necessary to achieve this.

The authors' research indicated that both self-selection and organizational selection processes were likely to direct *public* scientists towards research positions in university or government laboratories or, at the least, more fundamental research in industry. At the other end of the spectrum, *organizationally* oriented scientists were more likely to opt for industry with the prospect of better pay, welfare benefits, and promotion opportunities. Most frequently they were found in routine research work most closely associated with production.

Role strain amongst scientists is most likely where there is a lack of congruence between the aspirations and interests of the individual and the demands of the organization. This would be at a maximum in the case of the public-minded scientist doing highly production-oriented work in industry. However, careful selection of both employees by organizations and employment situations by individuals reduces the chances of mis-match and high levels of role strain.

However, with industry a major employer of scientists, mis-matches can occur given the limited number of openings for *public* scientists in universities and the emphasis which universities place on quality of first degree as a pre-requisite for research work. Where role strain does result, however, it may diminish in intensity over time. There are various reasons for this. First, the individual may become socialized over time into accepting the value system of the organization employing him, just as social forces earlier influenced his adherence to a public-minded scientific identity. Second, over time, his knowledge in the areas in which he had previously desired to carry out more fundamental research would become dated, thus reducing even further the possibilities of his gaining an employment situation suited to his earlier identity. The increasing realization that his earlier identity is unlikely to be satisfied may lead him to accept his earlier aspirations as unrealistic, and to modify them over time. Finally, changes in life-cycle position, e.g. marriage, and parenthood, may lead to a re-definition of his priorities, with financial rewards becoming more prominent, thus precipitating a greater level of acceptance of his current role.

Role activation conflict

The case of the industrial inspection department   Pugh,[35] in a study of an inspection department in an engineering factory mass-producing electrical goods, has questioned whether the conflict between production and inspection departments is in fact a case of role conflict in the traditional sense and has developed the term 'role activation' conflict. When discussing role conflict earlier, we said this occurs when an individual is subjected to conflicting role expectations. This may happen when the actor occupies multiple roles (e.g. the working wife) or, more important here, when a person occupying a single position is subjected to conflicting role-set expectations. The classic example, discussed earlier, is the conflicting expectations that management and workers have of the foreman—'the man in the middle'.

Two functions of an inspection department are (1) *quality assurance* (comparing product to a given standard) and (2) *production auxiliary* (giving feedback to production on quality and causes of failure to help prevent re-occurrence). Role conflict, in the sense mentioned earlier, occurs here if the inspection department conceived their role essentially in terms of the quality assurance function whilst production departments expected inspection to function essentially as a production auxiliary. Pugh did find some evidence that this was the case, with inspection sometimes taking the view: 'Inspection is here to ensure that only good products go out of the factory gate' and production taking the view: 'Inspection is here to help us make a good product, not to sit in judgement on us.'

However, and of greater interest, was the fact that production did not feel that they ought to have control over inspection. They felt that it ought to remain independent. Further investigation indicated that each department saw each others expectations as being legitimate:

> . . . there is basic agreement upon the inspection functions of quality assurance and production auxiliary among *both* inspection and production. These two sets of expectations are accepted as legitimate, yet they are often incompatible, and role conflict certainly occurs.[36]

Thus, there was agreement by both sides on the legitimacy of *both* of the potentially conflicting functions of the inspection department. Pugh claimed that:

> The conflict arises because Production questions not the legitimacy of the quality assurance function, but only the relevance and priority of the particular judgement involved.[37]

Inspection departments do not normally operate straight forward standards, but make judgements. They have to assess not only the degree of error in a product but also whether or not the error is *critical*. Further, they remain flexible in the light of pressures put upon them. They react to *cost* pressures because any insistence that every part be made exactly to drawing measurements would result in sky-high costs. They also react to *schedule* pressures in order to give production a chance to produce to target. Finally, they react to *sales* pressures which often vary, depending whether there is an expanding market or a contracting market for the product. In an expanding market, demand for production comes to the fore, and salesmen are less likely to follow up customer complaints on quality.

Hence, Pugh claims:

> Standards of acceptability are thus the end result of a social process, and it is clear that inspection accepts the need to adjust these standards to the obligations of the situations, and that the production auxiliary expectations laid on them in this respect, are legitimate.[38]

Hence, conflict centres around which facet of the inspection function should be *activated* at a particular time—quality assurance or production auxiliary. Conflict is most marked when only *one* of these legitimised functions or expectations is activated to the exclusion of the other. This may occur when, say, the production department appeals to a higher authority in an attempt to get standards relaxed to meet high production schedules or, alternatively, when the inspection department appeal to attempt to uphold a high standard of quality assurance.

On the other hand, conflict is least likely when *both* facets of the inspection function are activated, for instance, when inspection grant a temporary concession on standards in order to assist production. Here they are insisting that the work represents a departure from standard (quality assurance function) while allowing a temporary concession (production auxiliary function). An intermediate situation may arise where both functions are activated but there is an inbalance. For instance, inspection may reject some product (activation of quality assurance function) but, at the same time, agree to sort the bad product from the good in a particular batch, and help to identify the causes of scrap (activation of production auxiliary function though to a lesser extent).

Thus, in conclusion, Pugh claims there are two types of role conflict which may result from occupancy of a single role. They are as follows:

ROLE ACTIVATION CONFLICT (e.g. the Industrial Quality Inspector)	ROLE LEGITIMATION CONFLICT (e.g. the Foreman, 'Man in the Middle')
All Expectations Perceived as Legitimate	Legitimacy of Incompatible Expectations Called into Question
Relevances and Priorities Challenged	Role Content Challenged
Conflict Resolved by Simultaneous Activation of Multiple Expectations	No Obvious Solution to Conflict

The usefulness of role theory

We said at the beginning of this chapter that role theory is not strictly a theory in the sense that the physical scientist uses the term, and it could be criticized inasmuch as it cannot make any claim to direct explanatory power. However, the usefulness of role theory concepts lies in their power to organize data for purposes of analysing and understanding various features of organizational behaviour. Thus it has a heuristic usefulness in that it can suggest alternative hypotheses to those which might be arrived at using different kinds of organizing principles; Pugh's discusssion of industrial inspectors is an example of this.

It would perhaps not be too adventurous to say that many attempts at decision-making and problem resolution in the workplace often fail through an incomplete understanding and analysis of the social relations concerned. A role theory approach can be of considerable use here both in aiding an understanding of problems and in offering pointers for improvements.

An additional strength of role theory is that it acts as a useful point of articulation between the individual and the wider social environment. Whilst role theory has usually been used to examine behaviour at the micro-scale, it could be argued that the social forces which arise here and influence behaviour patterns are those which are likely to arise also at a macro-level.[39]

REFERENCES

1 LINTON, R., 'Status and role', in COSER, L. A. and ROSENBERG, B. (Eds.), *Sociological Theory: A Book of Readings*, pp. 276–81, Collier-Macmillan, 4th Edn., 1976.

2 ABEGGLEN, J. C., *The Japanese Factory*, Free Press, 1958; ODAKA, K., 'Traditionalism, democracy in Japanese industry', *Industrial Relations*, pp. 95–103, Oct. 1963.

3 PAHL, J. M. and PAHL, R. E., *Managers and their Wives*, Pelican, 1972.

4 *ibid.*, p. 222.

5 *ibid.*, pp. 242–51.

6 MERTON, R. K., 'The role-set: problems in sociological theory', *British Journal of Sociology*, **8**, pp. 110–20, 1957. Also in WORSLEY, P. (Ed.), *Modern Sociology—Introductory Readings*, pp. 245–54, Penguin, 1970.

7 WILLIAMS, D., 'Uses of role theory in management and supervisory training', *Journal of Management Studies*, pp. 346–65, Oct. 1969.

8 JAQUES, E., *Equitable Payment*, Ch. 4, Heinemann, 1961.

9 For a discussion of role conflict and role ambiguity in an organizational context *see*: KAHN, R. L., WOLFE, D. M., QUINN, R. P. SNOEK, J. D., and ROSENTHAL, R. A., *Organizational Stress: Studies in Role Conflict and Ambiguity*, Wiley, 1964.

10 BURCHARD, W., 'Role conflicts of military chaplains', *American Sociological Review*, **19**, pp. 528–35, 1954.

11 DUNKERLEY, D., *The Foreman, Aspects of Task and Structure*, Routledge & Kegan Paul, 1975.

12 THURLEY, K. and WIRDENIUS, H., *Supervision: A Reappraisal*, p. 217, Heinnemann, 1973.

13 *ibid.*, p. 218.

14 MERTON, R. K., *op. cit. see also*: JOHNSON, HARRY M., *Sociology—A Systematic Introduction*, pp. 35–8, Routledge & Kegan Paul, 1960.

15 KAHN, R. L., *et al.*, *op. cit.*, p. 73.

16 HANDY, C. B., *Understanding Organizations*, p. 56, Penguin, 1976.

17 LINTON, R., *op. cit.—see* ref. (1) above. This view has not been confined to Linton alone. Talcott Parsons, like Linton, sees roles as *externally given* in accordance with the demands of normative order, and adopted unproblematically by the actor via processes of socialization. The view of Max Weber here is somewhat similar except that bureaucracy acts as the external force defining the role. *see*: LEVINSON, DANIEL, 'Role, personality and social structure in the organizational setting', *Journal of Abnormal and Social*

Psychology, **58**, pp. 170–81, 1959. Also in: SALAMAN, G., and THOMPSON, K., *People and Organizations*, espec. pp. 226–8, Longman (for The Open University Press), 1975.

18 TURNER, R., 'Role-taking: process versus conformity', in ROSE, A. M. (Ed.), *Human Behaviour and Social Processes—An Interactionist Approach*, p. 38, Routledge & Kegan Paul, 1962.

19 MEAD, G. H., *Mind, Self and Society*, University of Chicago Press, 1934.

20 PARK, R. E., *Principles of Human Behaviour*, The Zalaz Corporation, 1915.

21 ROSE, A. M., 'A systematic summary of symbolic interaction theory', in ROSE, A. M. (Ed.), *op. cit.*, p. 12.

22 *ibid.*, p. 12.

23 SALAMAN, G., 'Symbolic interaction', *Social Interaction, The Sociological Perspective Units 5–8*, p. 16, The Open University, 1972.

24 Reported in HARGREAVES, D., *Interpersonal Relations and Education*, Routledge & Kegan Paul, 1972.

25 HAMILTON, P. and WORTH, V., 'Social interaction', *Social Relations, Making Sense of Society Units 18–20*, p. 70, The Open University, 1975.

26 GOULDNER, A. W., 'Cosmopolitans and locals: toward an analysis of latent social roles', *Administrative Science Quarterly*, pp. 281–306, Dec. 1957, and pp. 444–80, March, 1958.

27 *ibid.*, p. 285.

28 GOULDNER, A. W., *Patterns of Industrial Bureaucracy*, Free Press, 1954.

29 GOULDNER, A. W., *op. cit.* (Administrative Science Quarterly), pp. 287–8.

30 *ibid.*, p. 449.

31 *ibid.*, pp. 281–306.

32 *ibid.*, p. 290.

33 *ibid.*, pp. 444–80.

34 COTGROVE, S. and BOX, S., *Science, Industry and Society*, Allen & Unwin, 1970.

35 PUGH, D., 'Role activation conflict: a study of industrial inspection', *American Sociological Review* **31**, pp. 835–42, 1966. Also re-printed in SALAMAN, G. and THOMPSON, K., *op. cit.*, pp. 238–49, Longman (for The Open University Press), 1975.

36 *ibid.*, p. 244.

37 *ibid.*, p. 244.

38 *ibid.*, p. 243.

39 SALAMAN, G., *op. cit.*, p. 25. Salaman claims that the interrelationship between the two levels of analysis (macro and micro) is well illustrated by Weber's analysis of bureaucratization which operates as a macro process and as a form of interpersonal action.

VII

THE ORGANIZATION OF WORK

Few managers are called upon to develop a new organization from the drawing board or to carry out major changes to a large scale undertaking. But viewed from a more realistic level most managers still have a considerable interest in the organization of work. Today most managers work for an employer with a large work force. This inevitably creates internal problems of work organization but, whatever the size, the behaviour of employees is going to be strongly influenced by both the formal structure of the organization and the informal relationships that exist within it. An understanding of such influences can contribute to more effective management. A similar point has already been made in our examination of leadership styles (Chapter V). Successful leadership is contingent upon critical factors in the situation such as power, the nature of the task, the type of organization, and group behaviour.

Furthermore, managers may or may not agree with the way in which their superiors choose to plan and co-ordinate. Either way a recognition of the theories on which they base their actions, however dated they may be, helps managers to act in an appropriate manner. Usually too, there is frequent daily interaction with other organizations, be they customers, suppliers, or public services. Some understanding of the way they organize their own work will be to our advantage. Finally, an opportunity may come to carry out a reorganization, perhaps not of a whole undertaking, but a department or section. That can be a daunting task without adequate guidelines.

The term 'organization' has a number of different meanings and so requires definition. By 'organizations' we mean 'formal organizations' that employ people, have a name or title, and are usually recognized in law as corporate bodies. Such organizations are social systems by virtue of bringing people together, who then act and react as individuals, groups, and departments in a recognizably social manner. Organizations are frequently economic systems as well, having to pay for goods and services and raise funds for this purpose. Sometimes their overt aim is to produce and sell goods and services for profit, sometimes to provide a public service, sometimes to serve the recreational or spiritual needs of members.

Management thinking has tended, in the past, to be dominated by a concern for private enterprise organizations, probably because competition provided a spur to the search for better ways of organizing private companies, but in recent years attention has moved to other areas, particularly the public service sector. Attention has also now to focus on the commitment of employees to the stated goals of the organization. This can vary according to whether they join of their own free will, are only in it 'for the money', or have a strong moral attachment. Prevailing cultural and social values also affect peoples' attitudes and therefore the way they behave in organizations. As we probably know from personal experiences the formal organization chart is only the starting point in gaining a real understanding of what takes place in a work organization. The problem of classifying organizations by type is considered again later in this chapter.

Our framework in looking at organizations is essentially historical, concentrating on developments during this century. Henry Ford may have said that history is 'bunk', but this is just not true when we are trying to understand human behaviour. Human behaviour is, to a large degree, the product of history and culture. The organizations we work for and deal with have been fashioned by their recent past. The actions of their leaders are heavily influenced by theories, whether consciously or sub-consciously, that were popular ten or twenty years ago. And the latest theories about the organization of work, as with all other scientific theories, need first to be put into understandable and practical shape, and then be tested and gain acceptance before being put into effect.

We begin with the early years of this century. Shortly before the first World war a book was published in the United States that was to have a profound effect upon management thinking about the organization of work. Its author was Frederick Winslow Taylor, probably best known as the pioneer of Work Study, and the book was titled, *The Principles of Scientific Management*.[1] Taylor was to become a leading figure in the so-called 'scientific management' movement, whose ideas remained influential until the middle of this century.

The scientific management movement

The advent of the Industrial Revolution and the growth in size of industrial corporations created a need for principles upon which to base the organization of people at work. In the past there had of course been large military, religious and civil organizations, but these provided little guidance to the leaders of industry. So rule of thumb methods prevailed, based mainly on the division of labour and a belief in hierarchical structures.

At the same time exciting developments in the physical and biological sciences were taking place, and it seemed logical enough to try to develop a science of management along similar lines. Taylor and his followers tried to do this and failed. What they came up with was a set of general statements about the way in which organizations 'ought' to be set up and run. These statements possessed the merit of being fairly systematic and appealed to what then prevailed as common sense (rather like the quest for the Holy Grail the search for a science of management has attracted many since those days and still continues to do so. Unfortunately such people are frequently confused as to what the term 'scientific' really means).

Major contributions were made to the Scientific Management movement by such prominent authorities as Gulick[2] in the United States, by Fayol[3] in France, and by Urwick[2] in England. In time a general synthesis took place, of which a representative set of statements is given below. Some of these still possess a familiar ring:

1. Employees should be formally grouped and organized in specialist functional departments.
2. These departments and the persons within them should occupy a hierarchical structure, with authority emanating down from the board of directors.
3. An organization chart should be produced to show this structure, with lines depicting the chain of command and the proper channels for official communications.
4. Each employee should report to only one superior.
5. The span of control of subordinates by superiors should be limited to permit effective supervision. This number was unlikely to exceed 8.
6. Jobs should be described, and the nature of the duties prescribed, preferably in writing.
7. The number of levels of authority in the organization should be kept to a minimum to ensure effective control and communication from director to manager to supervisor and to worker.
8. Authority should be commensurate with responsibility.
9. Departments could be categorized as either 'line' or 'staff'. Using a military analogy, line departments were depicted as those directly responsible for success in the market place, and therefore included production and sales. The function of staff departments was to give specialist advice and services to line departments, but they should never usurp the authority of line managers over their own functions. Typical staff departments might be Work Study or Personnel.

Implicit in the statements emanating from the Scientific Management movement were assumptions about human behaviour. These assumptions have been parodied as the 'rabble' hypothesis, as they assumed that work people behaved like a rabble of isolated individuals motivated chiefly by a desire to earn money. The authority of management to give orders, and the generally hierarchical nature of society, were also taken for granted.

We can see how a number of the 'principles' put forward by these writers appeal to common sense. It is difficult to argue with the idea that authority should be commensurate with responsibility, because it would be unfair to give one without the other. It is of course much harder to define either of these terms, let alone weigh them quantitatively in order to achieve a balance. Two of the 'principles' appear to conflict with one another. The more we limit the span of control, the more we widen the gap between workers and management by increasing the levels of authority.

In their time these 'principles' probably helped a large number of managers and contributed to increased efficiency. In other cases the reverse may have been true, for reasons we shall discuss in the rest of this chapter. By the nineteen twenties empirical evidence was already accumulating that questioned the basis of many of these principles. For example, successful organizations were revealed containing very wide spans of control. Advances in the Social Sciences led to criticism of the behavioural assumptions of these theories. Psychologists suggested that workers were influenced by many factors other than money. Sociologists began to question their assumptions about social order at the place of work.

One of these sociologists was a contemporary of Taylor, although their paths never crossed. He was the German sociologist Max Weber, whose work we have already met, but whose writings did not become widely known and influential until a quarter of a century later. Probably best known today for his writings on bureaucracy, and the Protestant ethic, his description of bureaucracy with its hierarchical and impersonal structures possesses similarities with the 'principles' of scientific management. And his description of the Protestant ethic, which extolls thrift, hard work, and a sense of duty, reminds us that large organizations run on traditional lines rely far more than is often recognized upon an inculcated set of values. Current thinking, as we shall see in our final section in this chapter, is very much concerned with these issues.

Human relations

Organizations are composed of people. This simple truth is frequently overlooked because questions of finance and production take pride of place. But it does mean that human relations at the place of work have long been the subject of speculation. During the nineteen thirties and forties a number of prominent writers and researchers were led to place great emphasis upon the significance of human relationships at the place of work and its impact upon productivity, laying particular stress upon group behaviour, joint consultation, and the 'informal' organization.

By the 1920's, psychologists had begun taking an active interest in what went on at the place of work. It was a team of psychological researchers from Harvard University who carried out the famous investigations into the Hawthorne plant of the Western Electric Company in Chicago, subsequently described by their leaders Roethlisberger, Dickson, and Elton Mayo.[4, 5]

Most interest in this particular piece of research has centred on two of the investigations. In the first, a small group of female operators whose task it was to assemble telephone relays, was transferred to a room by themselves along with their equipment, and asked to continue with their task. This they did whilst the researchers made changes to their working conditions in order to see whether these had any appreciable effect upon output. The workers continued to be paid by the company on an incentive scheme. In one set of experiments the quality of lighting was improved in stages, and in another, rest periods and refreshments were introduced. It was found that output increased significantly as compared to previously recorded levels as these improvements were made. But what was far more startling was that it remained at this high level even after a return to the original conditions. Furthermore, sickness and absenteeism decreased. The workers themselves had no clear explanation of why they worked so much faster, nor were they conscious of a speed-up and increased productivity.

In a second investigation by the researchers at Hawthorne, discreet observation was kept on male workers in the bank wiring room in the factory. Here again, the workers were on individual incentive schemes. However, instead of asserting maximum effort, they worked well below their real capacity. Individuals who showed signs of outpacing the rest were brought into line and made to conform.

Arising from this and other studies that took place in the thirties the general conclusion was drawn that the key to increased output lay not in individual incentive schemes and traditional authoritarian management, but in fostering better relations upon the shop floor. As higher output seemed to require the active co-operation of employees, supervisors had to be trained to show greater consideration and a more democratic style of leadership. Stress was laid upon better communications, interpreted as passing on more information as well as operating counselling programmes, and the creation of good morale in work groups. Put at its most simple, Human Relations advocated a human face to capitalism, with the promise of a pay-off to all concerned.

This emphasis upon the individual and the work group has been carried on during the 1950's and 60's under the impetus of the American behavioural scientists mentioned in earlier chapters, such as Maslow,[6] Likert,[7] McGregor,[8] Argyris,[9] and Herzberg.[10] In its modern sophisticated form this approach is more correctly referred to as neo-Human Relations. Emphasis is placed upon the factors we have already discussed of job satisfaction, group dynamics, participative leadership styles, and motivation. Whilst this important approach to behaviour at work (which in turn is very relevant to the organization of work) has been dealt with in appropriate detail elsewhere in this book, it is important to note that their general message with regard to organizations was and still is to the effect that the proper place for intervention when trying to modify the behaviour of workers and increase productivity is at the level of human relations on the shop floor or in the office.

From this group of American behavioural scientists we single out for special mention the work of Chris Argyris. Writing as a psychologist he shows concern for the well being of people working in organizations. In consequence he underlines the dangers inherent in situations where psychologically healthy individuals are constrained to work in formal organizations run on traditional lines. By definition, a psychologically healthy individual will be 'predisposed toward relative independence, activeness, use of their important abilities, control over their immediate work world'.[11] But this is 'not congruent with the requirements of formal organisation, which tends to require agents to work in situations where they are dependent, passive, use few and unimportant abilities, etc.'. Note how as a psychologist Argyris emphasizes the concept of an ideal type of psychologically healthy individual. This begs the question of who has the right to define just who is psychologically healthy and who is not. But more important in this context, it demonstrates the manner in which experts tend to judge human institutions from within their own frame of reference.

Properly conducted organizations can contribute to this psychological health suggests Argyris. Healthy organizations need healthy people, and healthy people need healthy organizations. Successful organizations can only remain successful for long periods of time if they are composed of psychologically healthy individuals, who can react appropriately to changing circumstances. Traditional formal organisations are liable to condition their members to such an extent over time that they become inflexible and unwilling to step out of line. In turn, individuals need to belong to 'healthy' organizations if they are to mature psychologically. Therefore organization structures must be modified and traditional hierarchies broken down in order to permit self-actualization by individuals at their place of work. This will have a pay-off in more responsible actions by employees, as well as being defensible in terms of their contribution to psychologically healthier individuals.

Such an approach leads naturally to an advocacy of organizational change programmes where an attempt is made to break down barriers between individuals and to encourage frankness and an open exchange of views. This has been tried, sometimes successfully, sometimes not so successfully, in management by objectives, T-Groups, and organization development programmes.[122] This will be discussed more fully in Chapter IX.

In fact a neo-Human Relations approach to the organization of work is probably the most popular one to be found amongst managers in industry and commerce today. It is an approach which can easily be understood, and again accords with much that is common sense. It tempts us with the promise of both higher productivity and a more contented and satisfied work force. The harsh fact of the matter is however, that working groups seem to be becoming more militant or appear less well satisfied with their working conditions in spite of several decades of human relations orientated company policies. Clearly we need a wider analysis of the problem of organizing people at work than that provided by the Human Relations School alone. So now we turn our attention to those social scientists who have concentrated on the context within which work takes place, particularly the factors of technology, structure, and social values.

Technology and work

Why is it that some industries seem to be the focus of industrial unrest, whilst others are rarely in the news? Should work be organized in exactly the same way in mass production firms, oil refineries, hospitals and the civil service? How much attention should we pay to the way technology dictates the nature of work? Can the contents of a job so alienate the worker that no amount of human relations technique will make him satisfied? Some see the key to this and related questions in an analysis of the technology of work.

A simple approach to the technology of work is to classify organizations on the basis of their production technology. This has been used to great effect by Robert Blauner[13] in the United States, and Joan Woodward[14] in England. Concentrating upon industrial production methods, we can follow Blauner in classifying work according to whether it is:

(a) a 'Craft' industry such as printing, or
(b) 'Machine minding' such as textiles with considerable standardization and mechanization, or

(c) 'Assembly line', such as the car industry where workers carry out repetitive unskilled work, or

(d) 'Process' industry, using continuous process methods, such as in chemicals and oil refining.

Of these four kinds of work situation the assembly line probably has the most notorious reputation. Blauner was much concerned with the problem of 'alienation' discussed already in Chapter II, which he defined in terms of workers' feelings of powerlessness, meaninglessness, isolation and self-estrangement. His conclusion, after investigating a large sample of workers in the United States, was that alienation increased as the degree of mechanization of work increased up to a peak when the assembly line is reached, and then improves considerably as continuous process methods take over in the technologically advanced industries.

If this is true then forms of organization structure which create harmony and high output in a craft industry might well prove a failure in a mass production situation. Evidence along these lines was produced by Joan Woodward as a result of a study of one hundred firms in south-east England. She used a similar method of classification categorizing the firms as to whether they used unit, mass, or process production methods. Like Blauner, she found evidence of greatest tension between workers and management in the mass production firms. But what is of greater significance is that she also analysed the organization structures of the firms concerned, using many of the headings put forward by the advocates of scientific management, such as span of control and number of levels of authority.

Her findings dealt a serious blow to the claim of the Scientific Management writers that the application of their principles would promote the success of the organization irrespective of type or place. What she did find of a positive nature was that the outstandingly successful firms had one feature in common. Many of their organizational characteristics approximated to the media of their production group. For example, in successful unit-production firms the span of control of the first line supervisor ranged from 22 to 28, whereas in successful mass production firms it ranged from 45 to 50. Also, mass production firms who conformed with the principles of scientific management appeared to do better than the mass production firms who did not, although this did not apply to firms in the other two production categories.

The lesson here appears to be that conformity and a 'follow my leader' approach to organization structures pays off, at least in an industrial context. But this is a very crude rule of thumb. Findings from other studies, in particular one conducted by Tom Burns and G. M. Stalker[15] into the organization of the electronics industry in Scotland in the 1950's, underlined the importance of the marketing and social environment in which a firm operates. A firm operating in a fairly bureaucratic (sometimes termed 'mechanistic') manner had a good chance of remaining stable and successful if its product market also remained stable, but a turbulent economic environment required a far more informal organization that could quickly produce the appropriate multi-disciplinary task orientated work groups to meet the challenge of change (sometimes referred to as an 'organic' structure). The principles of reporting to only one boss, hierarchical and rigidly separated functional departments, detailed job descriptions and little delegated authority appear to mitigate against rapid change.

Recent work dealing with the influence of the technology of work has tended to concentrate on the actual task which workers are expected to carry out. Factors such as the variety of work, skill required, and control over the place of work have been underlined.[16] This focus on the actual job has come about at the same time as many behavioural scientists have begun to advocate a process of job enrichment in order to increase motivation. Productivity bargaining between management and unions has also led to greater flexibility in work-manning arrangements.

A number of limitations are apparent if one concentrates too heavily upon technology and task, not least of which is the human dimension. In trying to organize the work of say an engineering workshop in an African state, one is likely to use a different approach to that in Britain, even if the technology is common. Furthermore, many organizations cannot be categorized simply by their production technology, because they may employ a variety of technologies, and furthermore possess a large administrative office. Whilst accepting that the technology of work is a major factor to be considered, we must now attempt to bring other major variables into the equation. One of these is the degree of bureaucratization.

Bureaucracy

For many people the term 'bureaucracy' is synonomous with 'organization'. Most of us grumble from time to time about bureaucracies, 'faceless' bureaucrats, and endless form-filling. Bureaucracies appear to be a general characteristic of modern industrial societies, whatever their political creeds or ethnic populations. Frequently the term 'bureaucrat' is used as a form of abuse.

It may therefore seem somewhat surprising to us that Max Weber depicted bureaucracies as an 'ideal' type. He did not mean 'ideal' in the sense of being functionally perfect, but 'ideal' in the sense of describing an extreme type of structure useful for comparative purposes, a kind of model or standard. As we have noted, bureaucracies are not very different from the form of organization advocated by the scientific management school. But do bureaucracies actually work efficiently? Is it right that so many work organizations today should be bureaucracies?

The criticism levelled by the Human Relations School at scientific management can also be levelled at extreme bureaucracies. Most of us know from personal experience that they can be impersonal and inflexible as well as neglecting the psychological needs of employees and clients alike. Insight into their actual efficiency is given by two case studies.

In the first example Alvin Gouldner[17] described the imposition of a bureaucratic structure upon a gypsum company, a small plant employing just over 200 employees in a semi-rural community in the United States. In this situation kinship meant a great deal, and family relationships were important both outside and inside the plant. Local people were united in their distrust of outsiders. A so-called 'indulgency pattern' of relationships operated in the plant, which meant that supervisors were not strict, management frequently turned a blind eye to petty misdemeanours, and tradition and custom were highly valued.

A sudden change was precipitated when head office appointed a new manager, with instructions to make the plant more efficient. This was interpreted as a requirement for more beaucratic procedures and stricter controls. The 'indulgency pattern' was attacked. Work study, production control, paperwork procedures and formalized promotion and selection methods were imposed. As can be imagined, there was immediate resentment, and an increase in tension. In order to counter this, supervision was made even tighter, which in turn generated further tension.

The outcome was a series of bitter disputes and a 'wild cat' or unofficial strike. Eventually an uneasy peace was established, but the immediate consequence of imposing bureaucratic procedures was a decline in efficiency. It is important however, to note the circumstances. The new manager had to act out a role imposed upon him by head office. The local workers were also acting out roles. In this particular case bureaucracy did not work because individual expectations were not taken into account.

By way of contrast, Peter Blau describes a situation where the workers were accustomed to bureaucratic procedures.[18] This was in a public employment agency in a city where the interviewers he described worked in two sections, A and B. Their duties were alike, and involved finding suitable jobs for job seekers. However, there was considerable competition between interviewers, particularly section A, to see who could achieve the largest number of satisfactory job placements. In a period of job shortages this competition took the form of trying to utilize job openings as they were notified before anyone else did. Instead of leading to greater efficiency, this led to subterfuge by interviewers in section A in order to boost their own individual success rate. For example, incoming notices about job vacancies were concealed, or deliberately amended in order to confuse other interviewers. Members of section B were more co-operative, and helped each other with placements. When a productivity index was created, it showed section B to be better than section A. Interpersonal competition had the effect of reducing the efficiency of part of that bureaucracy.

The effect of more recent studies, such as that by Burns and Stalker already referred to[15] have shifted the focus of interest away from the internal workings of bureaucracies to the question of their appropriateness to their economic and social environment. Because bureaucracies tend to be both inflexible and particularly adapted to a prevailing set of circumstances, they may well provide the most efficient (defining 'efficient' in a fairly narrow economic sense) form of organization at the time. But should circumstances begin to change, then trouble ensues, as Burns and Stalker highlighted in the study referred to. In fact the recent economic history of this country is littered with examples of large organizations which have failed to adapt to the rapid change in markets and technology, and therefore have gone to the wall.

In an attempt to throw light on this question of 'best fit' in the design of organizations in relation to changing environments, and the relationship between constituent internal parts, we now turn our attention to the Systems Approach.

The systems approach

Frequently changes are made in the organization of work for which there seems an obvious need. Unfortunately such changes sometimes lead to repercussions in other parts of the organization which cancel out the initial benefits. This situation may arise simply because the organization has not been viewed as a 'system' by those initiating the changes.

In the 1940's, social scientists from the Tavistock Institute observed some technical changes being carried out in the coal mining industry in Durham.[19] The object of these changes was to mechanize the system of extracting coal underground, thus enabling coal to be extracted on a 'longwall' method. This replaced the old single place working method where a small group of miners worked their own place in the coalseam. Each miner had formerly been an all-rounder, and belonged to a self-selecting group of miners with strong interpersonal ties. The new method replaced this with shift working, each shift specializing on a different task, namely preparing, cutting, or loading. The new system did not prove successful because of lack of co-operation within the shift, and between shifts, resulting from specialization. Technical change had taken place, but an appropriate social system had not been developed to match this change. What was needed in the opinion of the social scientists, was a 'socio-technical' systems approach. Applied to this particular problem area this approach led to the development of the 'composite longwall method', where a multi-skilled role was reintroduced, shifts carried out composite tasks, and social cohesion was restored.

The two diagrams shown in Figure 7.1 contain many of the basic

Figure 7.1   (a) Simple open system model
           (b) Essential processes in organization viewed as a system

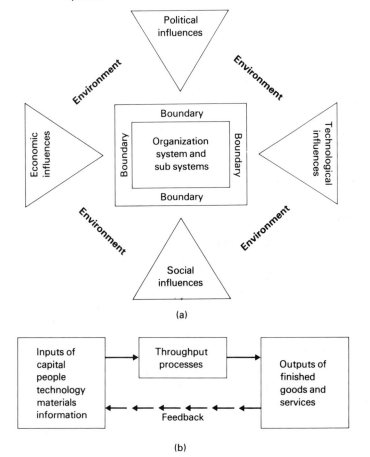

elements to be found in 'systems' models. Instead of emphasizing just the social and technical factors, as in the early socio-technical system used in the coal-mining study, an attempt is made in a more advanced general systems model to bring in all the relevant factors, of which economic ones are the most obvious addition to be made.

Recent systems theory has become highly sophisticated and complex. Leading exponents of systems theory as applied to organizational design in the United States are Paul Lawrence and Jay Lorsch.[20] This following quotation, taken from their book, *The Individual in the Organization: A Systems View*, gives a good insight into this type of approach:

> Any work organization is an open system consisting of the patterned activities of a number of individuals and engaging in transactions with the surrounding environment. The system has a boundary which separates it from its environment, and most organizations having several sub-units also have a number of internal boundaries. The organization takes in inputs from the environment and executes transformation processes which turn these inputs into outputs. Thus, a manufacturing company imports raw materials, converts them into products, and acquires a profit from selling the product. It also recruits employees, trains them, assigns them to jobs, and sooner or later exports them by resignation, retirement, or dismissal. It imports and consumes supplies and power. It also collects intelligence about its market and its competitors, analyses this information, makes decisions about the quality, quantity, and price of the product, and issues communications of different kinds as a result of the decision made.
>
> The environment of the system is important in a number of ways. In the first place it is the source of the inputs and the market for the outputs, Second, other organizations also exist in this environment which may well be competing with the organization under consideration. Furthermore, the environment in general may influence the organization directly or indirectly, and in a way not connected with the major operating task of the organization. For example, in the last few years concern with the rights of black citizens has put pressure on organizations to hire more blacks.
>
> In order to perform its task of converting inputs to outputs, an organization essentially engages in two types of processes: maintenance and task performing. The maintenance process is essentially those activities which the organization engages in to remain viable. It must build and maintain staff, plant, etc., in order to perform any task at all. The second set of processes, task performing, are the actual activities by which raw materials are transformed into finished products. Finally,

there are import and export processes across the organization
boundary, as organization members gather resources and distribute
products or services.

Lawrence and Lorsch go on to develop from this foundation a set of
guidelines to the design of organization structures that has direct practical
application. The label frequently given to this type of approach is
'contingency theory', because it reminds us of the need to have regard to
the contingencies in the situation. In particular, there exists the need to
adapt the specialization, and the co-ordination between specialist
departments, to the demands of the different parts of the organization's
environment. More formalized and centralized methods of integration are
seen to be appropriate in less turbulent and diversified environments. Put
very simply, this requires us to take account of the market for our goods
and services, the labour market, the political and social system impinging
upon our organization, and the technology of the work processes and in
response to develop internal departments and liaison procedures that can
cope with this environment, and also integrate with each other. The major
contribution of contingency theory has been this emphasis upon the
selection of a configuration that will best suit the prevailing situation.

A good practical example of the application of a systems approach to a
particular problem area, namely that of wages, is provided by Tom
Lupton.[21] Too often wages are seen as a necessary but unfortunate burden
upon the organization. Lupton's model (Figure 7.2), reminds us that

Figure 7.2   From 'Best fit in the design of organisations', T.Lupton[21]

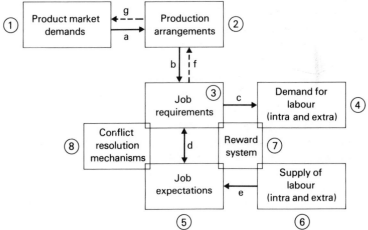

rewards should be seen as occupying a very positive role in maintaining an equilibrium between a number of pressures, both internal and external.

In this diagram, Lupton highlights the way in which wages and the fringe benefits which make up the reward system help to maintain a balance between the supply of labour, by attracting labour from the labour market and the demand for labour. Furthermore, workers bring certain expectations with them to the work situation concerning the demands which the job will impose upon them. The reward system plays a function in satisfying workers job expectations, and in getting them to accept the requirements of the job. The situation is of course a dynamic one, with continual re-adjustments being made within all the 'boxes' in order to keep the organization going.

Systems theory has come under attack from a group of sociologists, who see in its use a danger that the needs of the organization will be over-emphasized at the expense of the individual. This is a salutary reminder that organizations are in the last resort made up of individuals and exist to serve individuals and the community.

The emphasis upon the 'goals' of the organization by many systems theorists is also criticized. Individual human beings can have goals, so this argument runs, but an organization is just a collection of individuals and cannot be said to have a mind of its own. To go further means that one is 'reifying' the organization. In other words, treating the organization as real, rather than a collectivity of individuals. This criticism comes particularly from Social Action theorists.[22] In reply, Systems theorists argue that organizations are in fact real, because they are part of what we define as the reality that is the world around about us. The Civil Service or the Electricity Board are quite real enough. For the practising manager this debate probably seems rather too philosophical and abstract to have much to do with his tasks as a manager. But it is a timely reminder that organizations often do not achieve the goals to which they have been publicly committed. Indeed a major failing of many so-called 'management by objectives' schemes can be linked to the imposition of goals or objectives upon uncommitted subordinates.

Another criticism frequently levelled against the systems approach is that it is 'managerialist'. That is to say, it views the situation from a management point of view. This means that it cannot aspire to being a value free scientific approach, and is inevitably biased. As Systems theorists are sometimes consultants, there is also the criticism that 'he who pays the piper calls the tune'. Again, this is a useful reminder to the manager that consultants are frequently tempted to tell the manager what he would like to hear, rather than the truth. This links with the temptation the manager feels for a nice instant 'package' to remedy his situation. Of course, in the last resort, a manager has to make decisions and has to make prescriptions, whereas the academic theorist can sit out on the sidelines. Criticism of systems theory serves to highlight the difference in objectives between the manager and the social scientist. But the manager ignores the findings of the social scientist at his peril. Provided this is recognized, then the systems models can supply us with a useful approach to the improvement of work organization. In particular, contingency theory[23] reminds us that any person responsible for initiating major changes in the organization of work must spell out the pertinent economic, social and technological factors, both within the organization and at the boundary where it relates to the world outside. This seems so obvious that one wonders why it is so frequently overlooked. Perhaps the answer lies in the political nature of most organizations, the internal balance of power and the self-interest of participants who may not treat the material success of their organization as their over-riding priority (see next chapter).

Discussion of the Systems Approach has underlined the significant differences that exist between organizations, and the importance of the relationship between an organization and its environment. We turn our attention now to the problem of establishing an adequate system for classifying organizations that takes these factors into account.

Ways of classifying organizations

Scientific progress requires the development of adequate systems of classification. The physical, chemical and life sciences all rest on logical systems of classification. Early writers on organizations tended to use over simple methods of classification. But when we consider organizations as diverse as the Civil Service, a general hospital, a school, I.C.I., or the local youth club, we can see the need for a more sophisticated system. We have already touched on some of the simpler methods of classifying organizations, including the following:

—by ownership, e.g. public versus privately owned.
—by size, e.g. large versus small.
—by 'ideal' type, e.g. similarity to Weber's ideal type of bureaucracy.
—by membership, e.g. is membership voluntary or compulsory?
—by technology, e.g. unit production or mass production?

Clearly an adequate system of classification is going to have to take account of these and other significant facets of organizations. One of the best known modern attempts to classify organizations from a sociological perspective was that made by Etzioni.[24] He used compliance as the major source of differentiation. Put quite simply, an organization would cease to exist if it did not achieve a degree of compliance on the part of its members. Etzioni sees compliance, and the authority which exerts compliance, as resting upon the manner in which the individual member becomes and remains involved in the organization. This may come about because of coercion, desire for financial reward, or because of moral or normative feelings. If, suggests Etzioni, coercion is the basis of authority, then compliance will be alienative. If remuneration is the basis, then compliance will be utilitarian or calculative. And if moral feelings and norms are the basis, then the compliance itself will also be moral. Etzioni further suggests that there will be a tendency for alignment or 'congruence' between authority and compliance such that organizations will tend to be one of three types: coercive-alienative, remunerative-utilitarian, or normative-moral. Also, congruent types would be more 'effective' than non-congruent types. Examples of these three types would be prisons, work organizations, and voluntary associations, respectively.

This typology is valuable in that it reminds us of the dependence of organizations upon compliance, a fact which is often skated over, particularly by management. However, it still leaves a number of questions unanswered. These include the significance of technology, the way in which organizations might become 'incongruent', and certainly as to the meaning of 'effectiveness'. Practical difficulties have also been found in applying this system of classification to a wide range of actual organizations.[25] Some organizations show a diversity of involvement on the part of their members. Individuals join and work in organizations for a variety of reasons. Etzioni's system of classification then does not fit the bill, although it reminds us that the manner of involvement of its membership is crucial to the classification of an organization.

A highly systematic approach to the classification of organizations has been put forward by Pugh and Hickson.[26] In it, they have attempted to blend ideas highlighted by such diverse authorities as Max Weber, Wilfred Brown (a British industrialist) Henri Fayol (a French industrialist), and Bakke (an American writer on organizations). Five dimensions of organization structure, or 'primary variables' are elucidated. These are:

Specialization	Centralization
Standardization	Configuration
Formalization	

Most of these variables reflect terminology, used everyday within organizations. Thus we speak of the degree of specialization within a job, the standardization of procedures and methods, the formalization or official rules on communication channels and procedures, the degree of centralization of decision-making at head office, and finally, the shape or configuration of the organization chart, including spans of control and distance between the chief executive and the shop floor worker. Scales are put forward for measuring these variables. Other variables are also introduced into their scheme in an attempt to do justice to the complexity of the problem. For example, the context in which an organization operates are given special treatment, including factors such as size, technology, ownership, and location.

This 'dimensional' approach was tried out on work organizations in the West Midlands using a sample of fifty-two medium and large-sized firms employing a variety of technologies. It was shown that structural profiles could be drawn up, using the primary variables described. This suggests that we have the basis here for a rather more satisfactory system of classification than has been available hitherto. At the present time it still remains a basis rather than a fully developed scheme, although it has been used in some empirical studies.[27] Part of the problem in developing a fully worked out and comprehensive system of classification is of course the considerable time, resources and co-operation of management required. Because the Pugh and Hickson approach combines so many of the significant variables we are concerned with in studying organizations, their scheme which forms the basis for further research is shown in Figure 7.3.

Figure 7.3

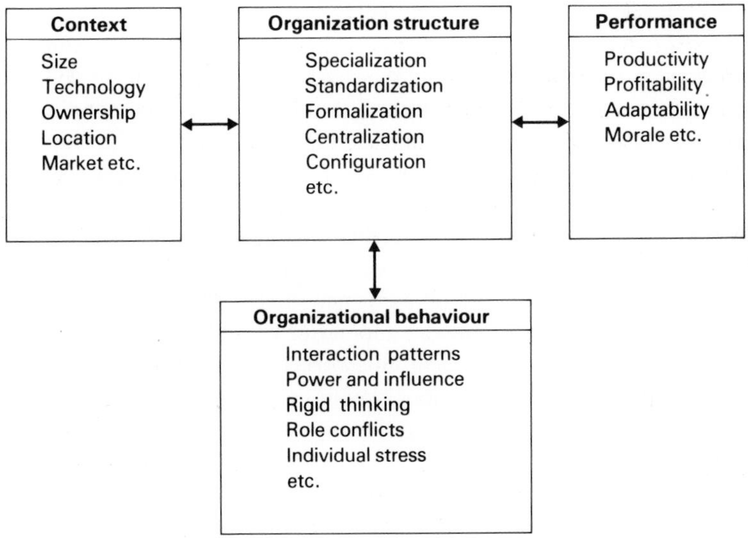

Context	Organization structure	Performance
Size Technology Ownership Location Market etc.	Specialization Standardization Formalization Centralization Configuration etc.	Productivity Profitability Adaptability Morale etc.

Organizational behaviour
Interaction patterns Power and influence Rigid thinking Role conflicts Individual stress etc.

A social action view of organizations

In contrast to the Systems Approach, with its emphasis upon the organization, a Social Action view is essentially humanistic. It tries to view the organization from the point of view of the individual participant. In part, it can be taken as a philosophical point of view, a reaction against big business, big Trade Unions, and a bureaucratized state. In part too, it is hard-headed and practical, because it reminds us that the decision to comply or to deviate is taken by private individuals in accordance with their perception of the situation. An organization is, at the same time a social system, and a plurality of social systems. Different groups have different objectives and different values. A conflict of interests has to be lived with.

In our discussion of Social Action theory in chapter two, we noted that as an approach it is more concerned with the way in which individuals construct their own realities than with looking at the way in which impersonal systems or structures influence behaviour and attitudes. Systems and structures are viewed sceptically because they accord with a particular and probably biased definition of the situation, rather than the actual definitions of the situation held by the participants themselves. This being so, the social action approach can help the manager at one level, namely that of understanding the behaviour of people in organizations, and is really rather similar to modern theories of motivation which emphasize the significance of people's expectations in influencing their perception of situations and consequent behaviour. However, it does not lend itself readily to the task of designing and improving organizations.

One practical example of where such an approach can usefully be applied is in Industrial Relations. We saw in Chapter II that the concepts of anomie and alienation are constantly recurring in the study of attitudes to work. Their significance to Industrial Relations was brought out in a well-known essay by Fox and Flanders.[28] The key issue, they stated, was 'whether the whole normative framework governing the production and distribution of wealth becomes further fragmented and splintered in a manner which threatens further disorder, or whether we are still capable of reconstructing larger areas of agreement upon which larger units of regulation can rest'. It is therefore anomie, or breakdown in agreed norms of conduct between management and workers, that is seen as the crucial issue. Another related key issue is simply one of trust. If managers don't trust workers, and workers no longer trust managers, then social institutions fall apart.

Now this may seem somewhat pessimistic and over-dramatic. It does of course go to the root of social order; but if we recognize that an organization is a form of social institution, operating within society, and we also recognize that employees, particularly when organized in strong unions, have usurped much of the authority which management used to claim as of right, then we are led to consider ways of maintaining and improving the social order within our own organizations. This must be on the basis of greater consensus between the parties concerned, and the attempt to attain mutual reconciliation as to the norms and standards of work-place behaviour. The alternative is increased conflict, with few winners and many losers. Current emphasis upon participation can in fact be seen as an attempt to apply a form of social action perspective to the problem of the organization of work (see also Chapter IX).

We started this chapter by saying that as managers we are interested in the study of work organizations from three different points of view. First we are active participants, within organizations, and need to understand our situation. Secondly, we deal with a variety of organizations both in business and leisure, and therefore can benefit from an insight into their structure and working. Finally, as managers, we wish to make decisions that bring about the right consequences.

But what we consider to be the right consequences will depend on our definition of the situation. Building an empire may be good for me, but may be bad for my organization. The head of a state enterprise may reorganize the enterprise after seeking the advice of the most fashionable consultants, but still fail to secure the support of the workforce because he is too distant from their definition of the situation. Then again, a giant firm like General Motors may reorganize successfully, but we may still conclude that what is good for General Motors is not always good for the United States.

At manager level, the Social Action perspective reminds us that the best laid plans often go astray because men are complex creatures with minds of their own; this, in turn, increases the homework which managers need to do. Making a realistic start on the organization of work is going to be better in the long run than the easy acceptance of a consultant's package, particularly now that traditional organizations are undergoing immense strain and need to adapt. Organizations are created by the actions of men, and there are a variety of options open to us.[29]

REFERENCES

1 TAYLOR, F. W., *The Principles of Scientific Management*, Harper & Brothers, New York, 1911.

2 GULICK, L. and URWICK, L. (Eds.), *Papers on the Science of Administration*, Institute of Public Administration, New York, 1937.

3 FAYOL, H., *General and Industrial Administration*, Sir Isaac Pitman & Sons Ltd., London, 1949.

4 ROETHLISBERGER, F. J. and DICKSON, W. J., *Management and the Worker*, Harvard University Press, 1939.

5 MAYO, E., *The Human Problems of an Industrial Civilisation*, The Macmillan Company, New York, 1933.

6 MASLOW, A. H., *Motivation and Personality*, Harper & Row, 1954.

7 LIKERT, R., *New Patterns of Management*, McGraw-Hill Book Company, 1961.

8 McGREGOR, D., *The Human Side of Enterprise*, McGraw-Hill Book Company, 1960.

9 ARGYRIS, C., *Integrating the Individual and the Organization*, John Wiley & Sons Inc., 1964.

10 HERZBERG, F., MAUSNER, B. and SNYDERMAN, B. B., *The Motivation to Work*, John Wiley & Sons Inc., 1959.

11 ARGYRIS, C., *Understanding Organisational Behaviour*, Tavistock, 1960.

12 BENNIS, F., *Changing Organisations*, McGraw-Hill, 1966.

13 BLAUNER, R., *Alienation and Freedom*, University of Chicago Press, 1964.

14 WOODWARD, J., *Industrial Organisation Theory and Practice*, Oxford University Press, 1965.

15 BURNS, T. and STALKER, G. M., *The Management of Innovation*, Tavistock, 1961.

16 WEDDERBURN, D. and CROMPTON, R., *Workers Attitudes and Technology*, Cambridge, 1972.

17 GOULDNER, A., *Wildcat Strike*, Harper, New York, 1965.

18 BLAU, P. M. and SCOTT, W. R., *Formal Organisations*, Routledge & Kegan Paul, 1963.

19 TRIST, E. A. and BAMFORTH, K. W., 'Some special and psychological consequences of the longwall method of coal-getting', *Human Relations* 4, No. 1, pp. 6–24 and 37–8, 1951.

20 LAWRENCE, P. R. and LORSCH, J. W., *Developing Organisations: Diagnosis and Action*, Addison Wesley, 1969.

21 LUPTON, T., article on 'Best fit in the design of organisations', *Personnel Review* 4, No. 1, Gower Press, Teakfield Ltd.

22 SILVERMAN, D., *The Theory of Organisations*, Heinemann, 1970.

23 LUPTON, T., *Management and the Social Sciences*, Chapter 4, Penguin, 1971.

24 ETZIONI, A., *A Comparative Analysis of Complex Organisations*, Free Press of Glencoe, 1961.

25 HALL, R. H., HAAS, J. E. and JOHNSON, H. J., 'An examination of the Blau-Scott and Etzioni typologies', *Administrative Science Quarterly*, **12**, No. 1, June 1967.

26 PUGH, D. S. and HICKSON, D. J., 'The comparative study of organisations', in *Industrial Society*, PYM, D. (Ed.), Penguin Books, 1968.

27 WARNER, M. and DONALDSON, L., *Dimensions of Organisation in Occupational Interest Groups: some preliminary findings*, Working paper, London Graduate School of Business Studies, 1971.

28 FOX, A. and FLANDERS, A., The reform of collective bargaining: from Donovan to Durkheim, in *British Journal of Industrial Relations*, **VII**, 1969.

29 CHILD, J., 'Organisation; a choice for man', in *Man and Organisation*, Ed. J. Child, George Allen and Unwin, 1973.

VIII

SOCIAL CHANGE AND THE MANAGER—QUESTIONS OF POWER, AUTHORITY AND CONFLICT

'Under any social order from now to Utopia a management is indispensable and all enduring', wrote Sidney Webb the Socialist historian half a century ago, 'the question is not: "Will there be a management elite?" but "what sort of elite will it be?"' The same question continues to be posed today, but with added force, prompted by changes in the power and authority which managers are able to wield and an increase in conflict within our industrial relations system. Earlier chapters have outlined a variety of ways in which the findings of behavioural scientists could be of use to managers, but many of these are dependent upon managers being allowed to exercise some degree of authority and to take fresh initiatives. Managers in all sectors of the economy, both public and private, are contained today by legislation, the power of the trade unions, and the aspirations of working people in a manner rarely experienced by their predecessors.

There exists a temptation to shy away from uncomfortable facts. Behavioural scientists have been as guilty as others in seeking to avoid the awkward problems posed by considerations of power and conflict. Further work still remains to be done. But enough research has been carried out to provide a useful insight into the challenge currently facing managers, and these are outlined in this chapter. Methods and philosophies that assist in adapting to and coping with such problems are outlined in the subsequent chapter, featuring aspects of participation and organizational change.

Much of the relevant research has been carried out at one of two different levels. On the one hand, some studies have considered the work and behaviour of managers in particular situations and have featured specific aspects of power and authority. On the other hand, general questions have been asked and pursued concerning the nature and function of management, the meaning and measurement of power and authority, and the endemic nature of conflict in our society. Aspects of both these approaches have already been encountered. For example, in Chapter Five the discussion of leadership inevitably touched on the authority of a manager in a group situation, and in Chapter VII the discussion of contingency theory reminded us that the success of an organization in relation to its structure is contingent upon a number of factors, including those of power and authority.

The focus in this chapter will rest initially upon the nature and function of management in our society, and then move to an examination of relevant findings concerning power, authority and conflict.

The manager in society

Definitions of management are numerous and varied and much time can be wasted in fruitless discussion of who does and who does not qualify for the title. Most of the attention has been paid to so called 'top management' in our society, the supposed decision takers within both public and private sectors of our economy, but in recent years account has had to be taken of the swelling ranks of 'middle' and 'junior' management who control day to day operations, and who can bring considerable collective pressure to bear when major decisions are taken. In this section attention is given to the three principal perspectives used by behavioural scientists when considering the nature of management in the context of the issues of power, authority and conflict. These constitute, in turn, an examination of the control managers are in a position to exert over the means of production in our society, the function of managers within work organizations, and the typical day to day behaviour of managers within different positions of responsibility.

The debate on the influence which managers are in a position to exert in society and on the means of production conducted by economic historians and political writers as well as social scientists stems from changes which have taken place in our economy over the last hundred years. In the course of our industrial revolution the legal ownership of most business organizations has passed from private hands to shareowners by means of the stock market. Because the share owning public, made up of a large number of individuals and institutions, is rather diffuse and not concerned with the control of the business in the same manner as the founding fathers, it has been suggested that a divorce has taken place between ownership and control, and control has effectively passed into the hands of managers. These managers are likely to be more interested in feathering their own nests and building up their power than in serving the interests of shareholders. This has given rise to that much quoted phrase 'the managerial revolution', used as the title to James Burnham's well-known book.[1] In recent years the debate has been taken a stage further by writers such as J. K. Galbraith[2] who have warned of the influence of giant organizations on our daily life, and suggested the need for some 'countervailing power'. The general situation in Britain today with regard to control of the means of production is somewhat confused, by virtue of it being a 'mixed economy'; large sections of the economy are under direct public control, and the remaining parts are heavily influenced by government directives.

This brief excursion into economic and social history may at first seem surprising in the context of a discussion of power, authority and the manager. However its direct relevance swiftly comes across to any manager who has had his authority to make decisions questioned by articulate shop stewards, particularly if they have challenged the legitimacy of his position. We will return to this point again shortly.

A systematic examination of the relative influence shareholders and managers are in a position to exert in publicly quoted industrial concerns has been provided by Sargant Florence[3] in a study of 268 large English companies over the period 1936–51. He analysed the composition of shareholding groups and concluded that about two-thirds of these companies were not owner-controlled by the end of the period, and the trend was towards greater divorce of ownership from control. Evidence of a widely distributed shareholding can of course mean that considerable scope exists for control to be exerted by a minority interest. In recent years the influence of institutional shareholders, such as pension funds and insurance companies (and indeed government economic agencies) has grown, but it is interesting to note that a firm like ICI could report in 1976 that no person held an interest in stock comprising more than ten per cent of the ordinary share capital of the company.

Evidence on how decisions are made by boards of directors and senior management committees is very limited and understandably hard to come by. Some sociologists have suggested that evidence showing that both managers and shareholders come from the same social class is sufficient to establish that this section of society both owns and controls the means of production, although the objectivity of some sociologists on questions of this sort is open to serious question. Theo Nichols[4] in a study of senior managers and shareholders in a northern English city claimed to find a considerable overlap in the financial interests of business owners and managers, suggesting that both ownership and control remained in the hands of a traditional elite. Richard Whitley[5] examined the network connecting directors of financial institutions in the 'City' with directors of forty large industrial companies and found evidence of a common educational background based on wealth, common membership of expensive clubs, and overlapping directorships. 'This suggests,' concluded Whitley, 'that the financial institutions play the central role in co-ordinating companies' policies, and that seemingly disparate industries may be united through the financial elite.' By way of contrast he also noted that 11 out of 18 directors of Marks and Spencer, GUS, Thorn Electric, Sears, and Tesco for whom educational data was available did not go to public school, and were relatively unconnected with the 'City'.

Anxious questions have been asked recently about the calibre of British managers in the light of our economic performance, and attention is being given to the contribution made by institutes of higher education. A large proportion of graduates choose not to enter management careers, and colleges are not generally geared to the needs of the world of work. A survey carried out by *European Business* in 1971 indicated that chief executives in European countries were more likely to possess a university degree than their counterparts in this country. About half of the chief executives investigated in Britain were graduates, compared with 83 per cent in France, 81 per cent in Germany, 85 per cent in Belgium and 77 per cent in Sweden. A study published by David Granick[6] analysed the proportion of top management who had attended the best known institutes of higher education within their own countries. The figures when standardized by the numbers that attended these institutions show that in France 15 per cent of top management attended the Grandes Ecoles, between 3 and 5 per cent of the top U.S. managers attended the Ivy League Universities, but only 1 per cent of Britain's top managers went to either Oxford or Cambridge.

When their authority to make decisions and give orders is challenged many managers are liable to fall back upon two arguments. The first is that authority has been properly delegated by superiors, who are in turn answerable to the legitimate owners of the business. This argument holds force, as will be illustrated in the next section of this chapter, provided the legitimacy of the ownership is accepted. The second argument is based upon competence. A manager may claim the right to make decisions and give orders because he is an expert or possesses special skills. However, the special expertise of a manager, acting as a manager, is also open to question, and further support may be required.

Some would claim that management itself is a 'profession', with attendant rights and responsibilities. A number of managers are of course 'professionals' in the sense that they have qualified for membership of one of the well established professions, such as accountancy or engineering. But whether management itself is a profession is doubtful. Consider for example the following list of criteria provided in abbreviated form from the report of the Monopolies Commission in this country:

1. A specialized skill and service
2. A well ordered intellectual and practical training of a high order
3. A high degree of professional autonomy and responsibility
4. A fiduciary (i.e. fee paying) relationship with clients
5. A sense of collective responsibility
6. An embargo on certain methods of conducting business (i.e. advertising)
7. Regulation of competence, standards, and discipline.

This may seem an unduly restrictive list, but even if items 4 and 6 are excluded it is hard to make out a case for including management *per se*. Efforts by business schools and institutions such as the British Institute of Management have led to considerable advances in skill, training and standards but managers would do well to support their authority by additional arguments, examples of which are put forward in the next section.

The function of management within the work organization has received considerable attention in management literature. Writers in the scientific management tradition have been considerably influenced by the writings of Henri Fayol,[7] a former French industrialist turned writer. He defined the function of management (or 'administration') as to plan, organize, command, co-ordinate, and control. A modern version of this approach is rendered by the well-known American writers Koontz and O'Donnell[78] as planning, organizing, staffing, directing, and controlling. By way of contrast the former Chairman of the Glacier Metal Company in England, Wilfred Brown,[9] defined a manager as 'a member who has subordinate to him authorized roles into which he can appoint members and determine their work; he is accountable for his subordinates' work in those roles'. He further observed that two criteria distinguished a manager—'the right to choose and the right to dismiss subordinates'. This definition would of course rule out the majority of individuals accorded the title of manager in contemporary work organizations, but this serves to remind us of the diminished authority of the manager in respect of control over his subordinates.

Peter Drucker[10] has attempted what he describes as a reinterpretation of the role of the contemporary manager in the light of economic and social change. He puts forward six new assumptions 'that correspond to the realities of our time'. In abbreviated form, these are:

1. Management is generic and the central social function in our society, rather than the isolated peculiarity of the business enterprise
2. Because our society is rapidly becoming a society of organizations, all

institutions, including business, will have to hold themselves responsible
for the 'quality of life'

3. Managers in these new large scale organizations will have to learn to
'innovate' in order to replace the vacuum left by the demise of the small
scale entrepreneur

4. 'Knowledge workers', well educated and trained, will increasingly
replace manual workers as the back-bone of industry

5. Management is the means through which a given society makes
productive its own values and beliefs

6. There are no 'underdeveloped' countries, only 'undermanaged' ones. It
is the manager who creates economic and social development.

It will be seen from this list that Drucker is not concerned by any decline in
the power and authority of the manager; rather like Webb in the quotation
that opened this chapter, Drucker sees management as a pervasive activity
in contemporary society. However, he is concerned about 'conflict'.
'Managers' he says 'have to accept that Industrial Relations will become
increasingly bitter' (*ibid.*) principally because the replacement of manual
workers by 'knowledge workers' will lead to opposition and redundancy.

The development of a scientific approach requires detailed observation
and the careful reporting and interpretation of facts, as well as general
theories. The task of observing and classifying the work done by managers
is a forbidding one, considering the number of managers in employment.
Rosemary Stewart[11] has recently supervised a major research project in
Britain which has included just such a detailed observation of a large and
representative sample of managers. These have been found to spend on
average two-thirds of their working time in conversations of one sort or
another, underlining the significance of communication in a manager's job.
As might be expected, different types of management position make
different behavioural demands on job holders, in addition to the specialist
knowledge and skill required in the position. This is demonstrated in the
chart in Figure 8.1, from an article she wrote for the journal *New
Behaviour*[12] featuring the behavioural demands made by a manager's
relationships, work pattern, exposure, uncertainty and private life.

Most of us would agree with her conclusion that, 'For good selection
and training we need to identify the pattern of demands in each job.'
However, her approach does more than this, including a reminder that
management is not a neat and tidy unitary concept, but is rather a general
term in need of continual redefinition according to time and circumstance.

Figure 8.1 The jobs illustrated are specific jobs. The works manager was in charge of a small subsidiary process plant with 50 employees. The production superintendent was in charge of a section with 62 employees in a large process plant. The bank manager worked for one of the big clearing banks, and was in charge of a branch with 15 staff. The training manager was the regional training manager for a large company with eight training managers reporting to him. The group accountant, although he had 40 staff, worked mainly with the general manager. The management accountant had a staff of two. (Courtesy of Rosemary Stewart, *Contrasts in Management*, McGraw-Hill Book Co. UK, 1976.)

Contrasts in job demands on managerial behaviour

	Works manager	Production superintendent	Branch bank manager	Training manager	Group accountant	Management accountant
Relationships						
Contact time	⊠	■	⊠	⊠	☐	⊠
Supervision	⊠	■	☐	⊠	☐	☐
Cooperation without authority	☐	⊠	☐	■	☐	■
Role conflict	☐	⊠	☐	■	☐	■
Short-term contacts	☐	☐	⊠	■	☐	☐
Work pattern						
Responding	⊠	⊠	⊠	☐	⊠	⊠
Fragmented	⊠	⊠	☐	☐	☐	⊠
Time deadlines	☐	⊠	⊠	⊠	☐	⊠
Exposure						
People to consult	☐	☐	☐	☐	☐	☐
Mistakes identifiable	⊠	⊠	■	☐	☐	■
Uncertainty	☐	⊠	⊠	⊠	☐	⊠
Private life	☐	☐	⊠	■	☐	☐

Key: ☐ = Low demand; ⊠ = Moderate demand; ■ = High demand.

Power and authority at work

Power may 'grow out of the barrel of a gun', but writers from Machiavelli to the present time have reminded us that there is more to it than the use of money or fear. The contemporary organization has been likened by Antony Jay[13] to Machiavelli's political state, and the prince to the senior manager, in a book which contains much insight into power and authority in the contemporary work organization. 'One can make this generalization about men', wrote Machiavelli, 'they are ungrateful, fickle, liars and deceivers, they shun danger and are greedy for profit; while you treat them well, they are yours. They would shed their blood for you, risk their property, their lives, their children, so long, as I said above, as danger is remote; but when you are in danger they turn against you. Any prince who has come to depend entirely on promises and has taken no other precaution ensures his own ruin.' Managers should take note!

A good starting point is provided by Robert Dahl's definition of power:[14] 'A has power over B to the extent that he can get B to do something B would not otherwise do'. The exercise of power at the place of work is not the sole prerogative of managers; it can also be seen in the work of shop stewards, technical experts, and natural leaders. Sources of power which can be observed in everyday life include the following:

—financial rewards, e.g. pay increases and fringe benefits
—non-financial rewards, e.g. time off, praise, transfer to more interesting work
—punishment, e.g. dismissal, fine, transfer to unpleasant work, withdrawal of a trade-union card, 'sending to Coventry'
—physical coercion, e.g. aggressive strike picketing, or calling in the police
—respect for authority, e.g. referring to a trade-union official or director's 'authority'
—interpersonal skills, e.g. persuasive language, force of personality, or manipulation of group dynamics
—technical expertise, e.g. demonstrating special knowledge which is in demand
—resources, e.g. control of needed physical financial and human resources.

A number of these sources of power have been touched upon in the earlier chapters featuring motivation and leadership; the ability to motivate or lead, for example, is a manifestation of the power to change another's behaviour in a desired direction. In practice a manager may be able to draw on a number of sources of power simultaneously; a subordinate might obey an order for a combination of the reasons listed above. Arising from social change these sources of power are also changing. Legislation and bureaucratization have noticeably constrained the first four power sources listed above. New knowledge has enhanced power sources six and seven. But it is probably in the area of authority that the greatest changes have taken place in recent years.

The concept of authority has frequently been associated with that of power, because it has been thought that authority permits the exercise of power without the necessity for coercion. In this classic treatment of the subject Weber interpreted the term in much the same way.[15] To him, compliance with authority was a voluntary act that rested on a common value system, and he analysed the term under the three headings of traditional, charismatic and legal authority. Legal authority rests on a belief in the right of those in high office to give orders and to be obeyed. Charismatic authority rests on the personal influence of the individual, giving him power over devoted followers. Traditional authority is based on a belief in the traditional order of things, including respect for those in authority.

A number of attempts have been made to improve on Weber's typology of power. A generally satisfactory example is provided by French and Raven,[16] based on the determinants of interpersonal power as they influence the relationships between power holders and power recipients. Their typology covers five perceived determinants of power: 'reward', 'coercive', 'legitimate', 'referent' and 'expert' power. Reward power is based on the ability to offer a reward, attractive to the recipient, coercive power on the ability, perceived or real, to punish, legitimate power on an acknowledgement by the recipient of the authority of the power holder, referent power on the admiration the recipient has for the power holder, and expert power on special knowledge and expertise. This typology of power has been adapted in turn by Etzioni[17] in order to develop the typology of organizations referred to in the previous chapter. The three forms of power Etzioni observed to be particularly relevant to modern organizations were coercion, remuneration, and normative, to which he added three forms of involvement by members of organizations termed calculative, moral, and alienative. The principal virtue of this approach probably rests in its reminder that the power of a reward to induce a change in behaviour is dependent on the involvement of the employee in his job, career, and organization. The power to facilitate promotion only carries weight with the ambitious subordinate.

Two relevant examples of the influence of power and authority are provided by Pelz and Milgram. The first concerns leadership. As noted in Chapter V, successful leadership is contingent upon a number of factors, including power. As reported by Pelz[18] the power which supervisors were perceived to hold by their subordinates influenced their success. Holding constant such variables as size of the work group, kind of work, and length of time on the job. Pelz found that relations between supervisors and subordinates differ from the expected pattern. For example, 'giving honest and sincere recognition for a job well done' depressed morale in groups of white collar workers. Further analysis showed that these perplexing findings were due to the amount of power which the leader was perceived by his subordinates to possess. When supervisors perceived to have 'influence upstairs' followed supervisory practices generally considered to represent effective leadership behaviour, workers tended to respond favourably, but when supervisors lacked such influence then they secured far less favourable results.

The second example concerns authority and obedience. Milgram[19] conducted an experiment which tested whether individuals would carry out acts dangerous to fellow human beings in obedience to the orders of someone perceived as being a technical expert. Subjects were invited to participate in an experiment concerning learning under the stimulus of electric shocks. The subject was in the one room along with the expert, whilst the learner was supposedly seated in a chair next door wired to electrical terminals. The learner was asked questions, and when he got the answer wrong the subject was instructed to administer an electric shock. With each mistake the voltage was increased in a manner visible to the subject, and clearly marked at the different stages of slight moderate and dangerously severe levels of shock up to 450 volts. When the subject pulled the generator switch following each mistake the generator lighted up and buzzed, but unknown to him, no shock was actually transmitted to the learner.

It was observed that subjects were willing to carry on administering shocks to the unseen learner even after the danger level had supposedly been reached. At these levels the learner could be heard screaming and pounding on the walls, and thereafter lapsed into an ominous silence. At this stage most subjects turned anxiously to the instructor, who advised them to treat no response as an incorrect response and to proceed with the administration of the shocks. Out of forty subjects, all proceeded past the very strong shock readings and some even proceeded beyond 450 volts, although most were visibly disturbed and under stress. When the experiment was repeated with forty new subjects, it was found that the absence of the experimental instructor from the room, using a telephone to communicate his orders, led to a dramatic fall in obedience, although some serious shocks were still administered.

Power and authority can of course be wielded by departments or groups as well as individuals. The power of groups over individuals was examined in Chapter V. The power of a department within a work organization is likely to be influenced by the general perception of whether it fulfils a function critical to the success of the organization. In a typical industrial organization this might be the sales, production or finance departments. In the public sector it might lie with a powerful committee. Perrow[20] investigated twelve industrial firms in the United States asking the question, 'Which group has the most power?' He found that the sales departments were invariably perceived as having the most power, as illustrated by the graph, Figure 8.2.

Figure 8.2   Overall power of departments in industrial firms (courtesy of Charles Perrow 'Departmental power and perspective in industrial firms', in Zald, Mayer N. (Ed.), *Power in Organizations*, Nashville, Tenn., Vanderbilt University Press, 1970)

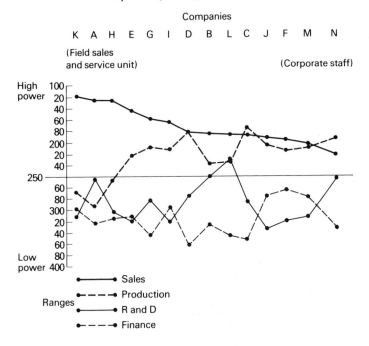

Perrow argued that this came about because sales possessed the most critical function in such industrial concerns. 'As the link between customer and producer, it absorbs most of the uncertainty about the diffuse and changing environment of customers.'

The influence of attempts to adapt to a changing environment on organization structures, and hence on matters of power, authority and locus for decision-making were discussed in the previous chapter. Studies of particular relevance in this context include those by Burns and Stalker[21] and Lawrence and Lorsch.[22] As was noted, Burns and Stalker put forward the concepts of 'mechanistic' and 'organic' organization structures, the former being appropriate to a stable environment and the latter to an unstable one. In the former, power and authority were likely to be retained at the top of the management hierarchy, whereas in the latter they were delegated to the appropriate task groups. Lawrence and Lorsch pay considerable attention to the extent of differentiation between departments and functions within a firm, in relation to the needs of the system to adapt to environmental demands. They found that in their most differentiated industry, plastics, the perceived amount of influence was spread evenly amongst the six highest levels of management. But in the container industry, operating within a more stable environment, influence was concentrated at the top. Where a diverse environment existed, such as in plastics and food, the research and sales divisions were perceived to possess greater power than production. In a stable environment, power might be vested in production.

To the extent that the authority of the manager resides within the hierarchical structure of the organization, managers are dependent on a general acceptance of the legtimacy of such a situation. Where acceptance does not hold, and positional authority is challenged, managers need to resort to their other potential sources of power, such as threat of punishment, the ability to reward, or manipulative skills. The situation then becomes an interesting and potentially disturbing one, when a body such as a trade union challenges this authority, and union members are protected by legislation or other means from coercion. On the whole the legitimacy of management has been recognized by official trade-union leaders, usually in return for a reciprocal recognition that they have the right to negotiate on behalf of the work force. But the conflict of interests is frequently apparent, and is being further exacerbated by pressure groups challenging the rights of managers to 'manage'. Within management itself, conflict also frequently prevails, with departments and departmental heads vying for power. A consideration of authority leads inevitably to a consideration of conflict.

Conflict

The ever present reality of conflict and internal politics for managers is well illustrated by the following example provided by Charles Handy.[23] When a group of middle managers were asked to comment on conflict and the major problems facing them in their work,

(a) 87 per cent felt that conflict was rarely coped with, and attempts to solve conflict were inadequate;

(b) 65 per cent thought that the most important unsolved problem of the organization was that top management appeared unable to help them overcome inter-group rivalries, lack of co-operation, and poor communications;

(c) 53 per cent said that if they could alter one aspect of their superior's behaviour it would be to help him to see the dog-eat-dog communication problems that existed in middle management.

The quest for power, rewards, and security inevitably lead to clashes of interest, and considerable time and energy is taken up in most organizations over matters to do with 'internal politics'. Earlier studies by behavioural scientists found considerable evidence of conflict between so called 'line' and 'staff' managers.* Line managers were usually held directly accountable for results, and tended to be long-service employees 'who had come up the hard way'. They frequently showed resentment at the form and manner of the advice they received from the better educated younger staff experts. In one of the best known studies of line-staff relationships, Melville Dalton[24] found that staff managers also tended to be more concerned with correct dress and manners, and to show greater concern for theory. However, line managers held greater power in controlling promotion procedures, whilst hiding their anxiety that the staff managers might come up with bright ideas that would embarrass them. Turnover was rather higher amongst staff managers, who showed impatience at not making faster progress.

As the standard of education and training of line managers has improved in recent years, this cause of tension has decreased. Interest has shifted to the related problem of professional-organizational relationships. As was noted earlier in this chapter, a proportion of managers consider themselves to be 'professional' by virtue of belonging to the accepted professions such as accounting or engineering. Studies by Kornhauser[25] Box and Cotgrove[26] and Hall[27] have shown most such 'professional' managers to be strongly committed to their work, without necessarily being committed to their own organizations. In place of this they identify with the persons regarded as their professional peers and take a pride in membership of their professional institute. This can result in conflict between what is perceived as good professional practice, in combination with an internalized need for a measure of autonomy, and the discipline of complying with the procedures that characterize the bureaucracy for which they work. At the same time the professional is anxious about his career prospects, because senior positions tend to go to the good 'all rounders' and competent administrators.

Three psychological bases of conflict within the organization have been

* Terminology explained in Chapter VII.

identified by Katz.[28] The first is 'functional conflict induced by various subsystems within the organizations'. Certain departments within a typical work organization are concerned with internal procedures; they '. . . face inward in the organization and are concerned with maintaining the status quo'. Other departments face outwards on the world and so develop different norms and priorities. Hence the seeds of conflict between cost accountants and sales personnel. The second source of conflict arises from similarity of function, leading to competition for power and status. The final form of organizationally based conflict arises from interest group struggles for status, prestige and money. Subgroups join forces to increase their power base, which can lead to workers versus managers ('us and them') or inter-departmental factions.

Sociology reminds us of the influence which structure has upon behaviour within organizations. So the technology of work may frequently lead to conflict. Joan Woodward reported after her South East Essex study that the level of conflict and the 'tone of industrial relations' appeared to be related to technology[29] and commented that, 'In firms at the extremes of the scale (of technology) relationships were on the whole better than in the middle ranges. Pressure on people at all levels of the industrial hierarchy seemed to build up as technology advanced, became heaviest in assembly line production and then relaxed, so reducing personal conflicts' (ibid. p. 18). The technology of the assembly line has frequently been blamed for the high incidence of industrial disputes in the car industry. In the United States Kuhn[30] investigated the relationship between technology and 'fractional bargaining' (the unauthorized pursuit of demands backed by unofficial sanctions) and concluded that 'the incidence of fractional bargaining is greatly influenced by the technology of production'. In the investigation into human relations in the Durham coalfield by Trist[31] and his colleagues, already referred to in earlier chapters, the general conclusion was that changes in the technology of work had had major social implications for work groups (i.e. a 'socio-technical' situation) which in turn led to considerable conflict between the different shifts.

Wedderburn and Crompton[32] reported after research into the attitudes of workers employed on a large chemical manufacturing complex in the north-east of England that the different technologies used in the three works located in close proximity to each other (labelled works A, B and C), particularly as they affected the control workers had over their tasks, influenced attitudes and hence the level of conflict. Works C provided least satisfaction to the workers in this respect. Wedderburn and Crompton's comment: 'In the case of Works C, we would argue that the constraints imposed by the technology were predisposing factors making for discontent which expressed itself around the bonus and pay levels.'

Industrial conflict cannot be understood without reference to the meaning which workers attach to their work, and therefore the points made in Chapter II are highly relevant to an understanding of what goes on when disputes and disagreements arise. Goldthorpe, Lockwood and their colleagues[33] investigated workers attitudes to management, employment and trade unions in their Luton research study and concluded that, 'the manner thus in which they define their work situation can be regarded as mediating between feature of the work situation objectively considered and the nature of the workers' response'.

As anyone knows who has been involved in an industrial dispute, it is very difficult to provide or obtain an objective account of events, and to provide an adequate explanation of the real reasons that have led to trouble. Individuals and parties to the dispute will put forward different and frequently conflicting explanations, depending on their orientation. This also applies to observers, for as McCarthy[34] put it, 'one assigns causes to strikes according to one's personal bias or predictions. A Marxist will draw up one list, and an industrial psychologist another.'

Industrial conflict inevitably features large in the study of Industrial Relations. Our understanding of what is happening in the sphere of industrial relations can be helped by viewing it as a system, in much the same way as organizations were viewed as systems in the previous chapter. This provides a more balanced approach than analysis entirely dependent on psychological or social-action frames of reference. A general model has been provided by Stanley Parker[35] which attempts to isolate the significant variables and demonstrate their interrelationship. This is reproduced in Figure 8.3.

This model has been confined to five clusters of variables, and the sub-headings illustrate the major part the behavioural sciences have to play in our understanding of industrial relations. The further relevance of this model to the subject of conflict is made clear by reference to the cluster headed 'quality of industrial relations', which features 'level of conflict'. The level of conflict can then be seen as influencing, and being influenced by all the other clusters in the diagram. Parker adds the caution that 'This (does) not imply any necessary casual connection between the absence of conflict and good industrial relations. The absence of conflict may be a sign, not of positive agreement between management and workers about ends to be achieved or means to achieve them, but disengagement or alienation of one or both sides from the problems of the other or of the whole enterprise' (*ibid.*, p. 29).

Such a model provides a useful tool for the manager anxious to get to grips with an industrial relation situation, with a view to effecting an improvement. Much contemporary interest in Industrial Relations is

Figure 8.3   General model of scope of workplace industrial relations (courtesy of Parker, Stanley, *The Sociology of the Workplace*, Warner, M. (Ed.), Allen & Unwin)

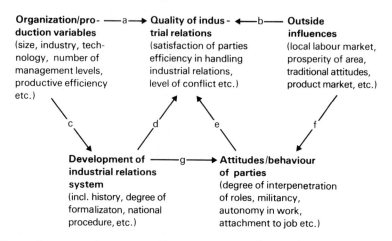

focused upon work groups, as these are seen as a key to the understanding of what happens at plant or office level. The first chapter of Hugh Clegg's major exposition of the industrial relations system in this country commences with a chapter headed 'Work Groups and Shop Stewards'.[36] Conflict also needs to be considered in terms of group behaviour; aspects of inter-group rivalry and hostility were discussed in Chapter IV. Group behaviour was also examined in Chapter VII whilst discussing the human relations approach to organizations. It will be remembered that the research team investigating the Hawthorne Electrical Works drew attention to the importance of work groups on conduct at work, and how in the bank wiring room group norms effectively restricted output. Leonard Sayles[37] subsequently noted in a major study in the United States of the behaviour of 300 industrial work groups employed over a wide range of manufacturing industry, referred to in Chapter V, that the behaviour of work groups was influenced by a wide variety of influences, including technology, status and the nature of the text. Lupton[38] came to similar conclusions in this country following his study of work groups in an electrical-engineering workshop and in a garment producing workshop.

The behavioural sciences serve to remind us of the endemic nature of conflict, and therefore of the inevitability of industrial disputes. The manager influenced by the human relations tradition who aims to achieve 'one happy family' at the place of work is liable to disappointment, and more importantly, to act in an inappropriate manner in the handling of industrial relations. This approach was described by Fox in a research paper to the Donovan Commission as based on a 'Unitary frame of reference'.[39] He went on to urge that the industrial enterprise be treated as a 'pluralistic system', arguing that 'The full acceptance of the notion that an industrial organization is made up of sectional groups with divergent interests involves also a full acceptance of the fact that the degree of common purpose which can exist in industry is only of a very limited nature.' One example of a constructive response to conflict within a pluralistic frame of reference is provided by recent attempts to improve collective bargaining machinery by both management and trade unions. This view comes through in the comment by Kessler and Weekes[40] that 'Once it is accepted that collective bargaining consists of a rule-making process by independent organizations of work people and management, then this has to be recognized as a permanent state of affairs. It is unrealistic to expect a conflict-free situation,' and 'If management negotiates, it is far better that unions are effective.'

This approach to conflict by use of 'joint regulation' rests on a fair measurement of agreement between the parties concerned (bearing in mind that a 'pluralistic system' may frequently include different trade unions with conflicting interests, such as those representing manual, craft and managerial groups which blurs the distinction contained in the slogan 'them and us') to play according to the rules of the game. This in turn rests on a shared value system, i.e. as to what is legitimate and reasonable. The essence of this situation is contained in the following passage from Alan Fox's 'A Sociology of Work in Industry'.[41]

'In establishing this procedural system, the two parties are jointly creating another social organization with its own division of labour, status relationships, and communications pattern. Insofar as this social organization is congruent with the aspirations of both sides, they will share certain values and norms relevant to it. The desirability of peaceful settlement; the importance of observing the other party's expectations in respect of procedure; the restraints and conventions of social interaction which maintain an environment favourable to compromise; these are at once the pre-conditions and the consequences of successful conflict-regulation. Insofar as there is normative agreement about these behaviours, it embodies a recognition by both sides that any immediate tactical advantage resulting from violation of shared expectations would be outweighed by damage to the system within which they had hitherto accomplished satisfactory results.

'Failure on the part of either side, or of any collectivity level on either side, to achieve what they regard as speedy and just results may thereby create a strain upon the system, and possibly lead to withdrawal of support. The independent power enjoyed by many work-group collectivities in post-war Britain enables them not infrequently to challenge the social organization of conflict-regulation, more especially in certain industries. Impelled by rising aspirations; faced with the anomalies and inequalities of pay systems distorted by managerial weakness and inflationary conditions; impatient with the cumbersome inefficiencies of the conflict procedures to which higher collectives have committed them; work groups have increasingly violated institutional values and norms by using coercive action in defiance of procedure. This may create for some managements a downward spiral into disaster. Fearful of escalating the conflict with reprisals, they appease with concessions, hoping to draw the rebellious group back into the paths of institutional settlement. But this rewarding of coercion may simply add another motive for violating procedure.'

Should agreement break down on this shared value system or 'normative agreement' then the nature of the conflict changes radically, and the rules of the game no longer apply. It is worth noting that more than one party to the system can decide to withdraw their acceptance of the rules and norms. This may come about through the influence of a new political philosophy, or a general breakdown in law and order, or both. This is the situation Fox and Flanders[42] warned against when they wrote in their much quoted article in the *British Journal of Industrial Relations*, 'The loss of integration and predictability is also expressed in such things as chaotic pay differentials and uncontrolled movements of earnings and labour costs. And the political consequences are decidedly no less important. Growing disorder may threaten the government's ability to govern and starts to generate strong popular demands for authoritarian State intervention to restore order.'

In the next chapter we shall consider some possible methods for coping with conflict within the work organization for managers caught up in social economic and technological change. In the meantime we can add one further task to the job of the manager, namely 'coping with conflict'!

REFERENCES

1 BURNHAM, J., *The Managerial Revolution*, John Day, New York, 1941.
2 GALBRAITH, J. K., *The Affluent Society*, Hamish Hamilton, London, 1958.
3 FLORENCE, P. S., *Ownership, Control and Success of Large Companies*, Sweet & Maxwell, London, 1961.
4 NICHOLS, T., *Ownership Control and Ideology*, Allen & Unwin, 1969.
5 WHITLEY, R, in STANWORTH and GIDDENS (Eds.), *Elites in Britain*, Cambridge University Press, 1974.
6 GRANICK, D., *Managerial Comparisons of Four Developed Countries: France, Britain, USA, Russia*, M.I.T. Press, 1972.

7 FAYOL, H., *General and Industrial Management*, Pitman Publishing Corporation, New York, 1949.

8 KOONTZ, H. and O'DONNELL, C., *Principles of Management*, 4th ed., McGraw-Hill, 1968.

9 BROWN, W., *Exploration in Management*, Penguin, 1965.

10 DRUCKER, P., *Technology Management and Society*, Heinemann, 1970.

11 STEWART, R., *Managers and their Jobs*, Pan Books, 1967.

12 STEWART, R., 'The manager in his job: a behavioural viewpoint,' in *New Behaviour*, April 24th 1975.

13 JAY, A., *Management and Machiavelli*, Pelican Books, 1970.

14 DAHL, R., 'The concept of power', *Behavioural Science*, **2**, July 1957.

15 WEBER, M., *Theory of Social and Economic Organisation*, The Free Press, New York, 1947.

16 FRENCH, J. R. P. and RAVEN, B., 'The bases of social power', in CARTWRIGHT, D. and ZANDER, A. (Eds.), *Group Dynamics*, 3rd ed., Harper & Row, New York, 1968.

17 ETZIONI, A., *A Comparative Analysis of Complex Organisations*, The Free Press, New York, 1961.

18 PELZ, D., 'Influence: a key to effective leadership in the first line supervisor', *Personnel*, 1953.

19 MILGRAM, S., 'Behavioural study of obedience', *Abnormal Psychology Journal*, 1963.

20 PERROW, C., 'Departmental power and perspective in industrial firms', in ZALD, MAYER, N. (Ed.), *Power in Organisations*, Vanderbilt University Press, 1970.

21 BURNS, T. and STALKER, G. M., *The Management of Innovation*, Tavistock, 1961.

22 LAWRENCE, P. R. and LORSCH, J. W., *Organisation and Environment*, Harvard University Press, 1967.

23 HANDY, C. B., *Understanding Organisations*, Penguin, 1976.

24 DALTON, M., *Men who Manage*, Wiley, New York, 1959.

25 KORNHAUSER, W., *Scientists in Industry*, University of California Press, 1965.

26 BOX, S. and COTGROVE, S., 'Scientific identity, occupational selection, and role strain', *British Journal of Sociology*, March 1966.

27 HALL, R. H., 'Professionalisation and bureaucratisation', *American Sociological Review*, **33**, 1968.

28 KATZ, D., 'Approaches to managing conflict', in KAHN and BOULDING (Eds.), *Power and Conflict in Organisations*, Basic Books, New York, 1964.

29 WOODWARD, J., *Industrial Organisation, Theory and Practice*, Oxford University Press, 1965.

30 KUHN, J. W., *Bargaining in Grievance Settlement*, Columbia University, 1961.

31 TRIST, E. L. and BAMFORTH, K. W., 'Social and psychological consequences of the longwall method of coal-getting', *Human Relations*, **4**, No. 1, 1951.

32 WEDDERBURN, D. and CROMPTON, R., *Workers Attitudes and Technology*, Cambridge University Press, 1972.

33 GOLDTHORPE, J. H., LOCKWOOD, D. et al., *The Affluent Worker, Industrial Attitudes and Behaviour*, Cambridge University Press, 1968.

34 McCARTHY, W. E. J., 'The reasons given for striking', in *Bulletin of the Oxford University Institute of Statistics*, **21** (esp. page 17), 1959.

35 PARKER, S. R., 'Workplace industrial relations', in WARNER, N. (Ed.), *The Sociology of the Workplace*, Allen & Unwin, 1973.

36 CLEGG, H. A., *The System of Industrial Relations in Great Britain*, Basil Blackwell, 1972.

37 SAYLES, L. R., *Behaviour of Industrial Work Groups*, Chapman & Hall, 1958.

38 LUPTON, T., *On the Shop Floor*, Pergamon, 1963.

39 FOX, A., 'Research Paper Number 3', *Royal Commission on Trade Unions and Employers' Associations*, HMSO, 1966.

40 KESSLER, S. and WEEKES, B. (Ed.), *Conflict at Work* (esp. pages 10, 11), British Broadcasting Corporation, 1971.

41 FOX, A., *A Sociology of Work in Industry* (esp. page 149), Macmillan, 1971.

42 FOX, A. and FLANDERS, A., *British Journal of Industrial Relations VII* (esp. page 163), 1969.

IX

THE CHALLENGE OF CHANGE

We are all influenced by 'the winds of change', and for many of us the pace of change appears to be quickening. Change has been vividly described by Alvin Toffler as 'a roaring current' that '. . . overturns institutions, shifts our values and shrivels our lives'.[1] The challenge of change to the manager is represented by the daunting task of creating and maintaining an efficient and adaptive organization that can cope with the forces of change. This means that managers have in turn to make changes within their own organizations in order to achieve the appropriate levels of efficiency and adaptability. As the primary vehicle for the creation of change is people, behavioural scientists have been much concerned with internal change processes. Change has been mentioned frequently in earlier chapters; in this chapter the special contribution which the behavioural sciences can make to planned organizational change is examined. One consequence of major change in our social values is examined in the latter part of this chapter, that is, the question of participation at work.

The forces of change external to the organization that necessitate internal change derive from changes in the economy, technology, legislation and social values. Rosemary Stewart[2] listed the sources of major change affecting management as:

1. Innovations which lead to new products and new methods of manufacture.
2. Shifts in market patterns as a result of innovations, of changes in consumer wants and of new methods of selling.
3. Greater competition, especially as a result of lower tariffs.
4. Changes in government regulations and taxation.
5. New tools of management such as the computer.
6. Changes in the background, training and occupation of those employed.

In order to complete this list we need to add further:

7. Changes in social values and in attitudes to work.

As we noted in Chapter VII, economic and technical change can lead to social change, and *vice versa*, hence the usefulness of a 'socio-technical' approach to change by managers. An example of the former is provided by the major political economic and technical changes which have taken place in the international trade in oil in the last twenty years. As a consequence enormous new seagoing oil tankers have been developed which, because of developments in technology and automation, require a far smaller crew. At times these super tankers have had to be at sea for extended periods, with the consequence that small groups of people have been cooped up together, causing dangers of tension and internal dissension. Fortunately the findings by behavioural scientists outlined in Chapter V, on group behaviour, have provided assistance in the selection and training of crew members to cope with this problem. An example of external social change leading to internal economic and technical change is provided by recent developments in the Swedish car industry. Because indigenous Swedish workers were no longer willing to put up with the tedium and frustration created by assembly-line production methods, an enlightened management has changed the production technology to group assembly, along lines suggested at the conclusion to Chapter V.

Resistance to change

Change is frequently resisted. Most of us look upon change with suspicion. Change may require personal readjustment, and this can sometimes prove to be painful. Change may be resisted by collective action, and economic and social history bears witness to numerous occasions when groups of work people have refused to adapt or co-operate. In contemporary society newspapers frequently carry stories which feature refusals to operate new machinery or adopt new procedures. Managers also earn their share of criticism for their reluctance to change, or for implementing change in an inconsiderate manner. Sometimes it is easy to see and understand why particular changes are being resisted, as when jobs and career prospects are being threatened. Furthermore the word 'progress' is sometimes misused as a pretext for inflicting change of dubious value. But sometimes resistance to change appears to be irrational and damaging to the long term interests of those concerned. Managers need to always take into account the likelihood of an element of irrational behaviour in even the best planned programme of change.

Resistance to change occurs at individual group and organizational levels. Goodwin Watson[3] listed the principal reasons for individual resistance to change under the following headings:

1. Homeostasis, or the pressure to maintain equilibrium.
2. Habits, which are not easily changed.

3. Primacy, or the lessons learnt in successfully coping with past situations.
4. Selective perception and retention.
5. Dependence, or incorporation of the values, attitudes and beliefs of those we were once dependent on.
6. Super-ego, a Freudian term for conscience and self-imposed moral standards which may inhibit innovation.
7. Self-distrust, which inhibits the desire to change.

All of these have to be taken into account by managers. Chapter III provides further useful insight into the reasons why the individual may resist change, and reminds us that the individual needs to be positively motivated to change. The key to achieving this lies in satisfying individual expectations, and many of the critical factors were well represented in the model presented on page 47. Faced with change, an individual will normally consider the likelihood of a favourable outcome in terms of financial or intrinsic rewards if he co-operates. This may seem so obvious that it is necessary to remind ourselves that all too frequently little account is taken of individual expectations when changes are promulgated. Individuals may, of course, make an incorrect assessment of the likely benefits of change, and this can arise for a number of reasons. For example, communications may be poor, individuals may be stupid or prejudiced, or group pressures may distort the individual's understanding. Individual perceptions of the situation may be distorted in the manner described on pages 69 and 70, Chapter IV.

Age is frequently associated with resistance to change, although we all know exceptions to this rule. In part this may come about because of a deterioration in physical and mental attributes, and in part because of lessons learnt from experience. Whilst we all 'age' at different rates, 35 is a figure that frequently features as a turning point. Eli Chinoy[4] found 35 to be the crucial age at which concern for security began to dominate, superseding economic incentives, amongst American car workers. The extensive survey into training methods for older industrial workers by the Industrial Training Research Unit located at Cambridge also decided to draw the line at the age of 35 years.[5] Michael Crozier[6] found, however, that seniority, rather than age or occupation, made the significant differences in determining attitudes towards mechanization in a large manufacturing concern. 'Workers', he concluded, 'become hostile little by little through a sort of learning process corresponding to their acculturation in the workers' group. The important factors seem to be the norms of the group and not the peculiarities of the situation.' On the other hand, a study of technical change in the steel industry in Britain by a team led by W. A. Scott, [7] found that occupation did make a significant difference. Crew-men and unskilled workers were least favourably inclined towards change, as against management and skilled workers. This was hardly surprising in the circumstances seeing that they were the groups most affected by the changes in production methods. The results are represented in the Figure 9.1.

Figure 9.1   Responses of personnel in a steel mill to the statement 'The firm should put in the new machinery' (adapted from Scott *et al. op. cit.*, Table 29, page 177)

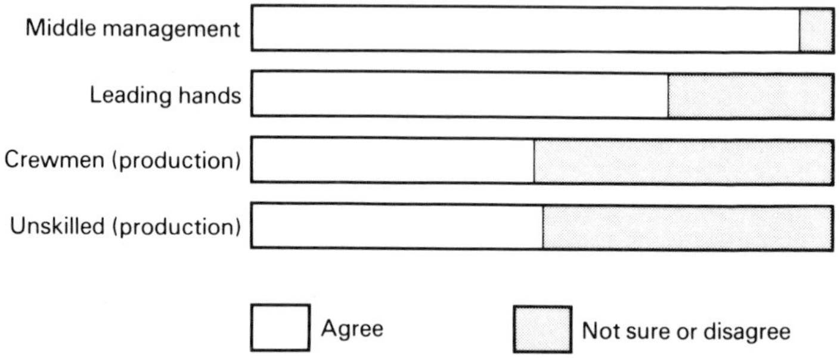

Individual perceptions of the likely effects of change are strongly influenced by group pressures. Some possible reasons for resistance to change within groups were detailed in Chapter V. Once group norms have been established, particularly within a cohesive group, they are difficult to change. If such norms do not favour the proposed change, then problems lie ahead. Note has been made in earlier chapters of Sayles' 'conservative' work groups[8] which consisted of skilled workers capable of a highly tactical approach in securing their own best interests. In Britain skilled printing workers combine to provide examples of such groups, successfully delaying technical change and innovation in what they assume to be their own (short term) interests.

Resistance to change may be a characteristic of the nature of the organization. Bureaucratic structures are notorious for their inability to adapt to change. Burns and Stalker's study[9] of the Scottish electronics industry, discussed in Chapter VII, showed the difficulty which 'mechanistic' structures presented when attempts were made to introduce innovative technology that would have ensured commercial success. The Fulton Report in Britain made a number of suggestions for modernizing the Civil Service, but few persons inside or outside the Civil Service would concede that much has really changed. Interdepartmental and vested interests conflict, and frequently lead to jealousy and internal politics, rather than attention to the world outside. Crozier[6] goes so far as to define the bureaucratic organization as, 'an organization that cannot correct its behaviour by learning from its errors'. This is further accentuated by centralization of decision making and a tendency to universalistic solutions for specific problems.

The social environment external to the organization may inhibit or encourage change. Again, economic history is witness to the manner in which certain countries appear to be capable of economic 'take off', whereas others, frequently possessing superior natural resources, have stagnated. In a perceptive article (in the *Sunday Times*) on the contemporary Scottish economy, James Poole commented on the continuation of class divisions in Scotalnd and noted that, 'The worker gets his lower status rubbed in here more than anywhere else I have seen. The whole country seems littered with little notices saying 'manual grades through tunnel' and 'this door staff only'.'[10] Such class divisions manifestly inhibit change and progress. But management is not solely responsible for the social and status divisions that impede change. Britain's antiquated trade union structure leads to the presence of several different and frequently competing trade unions within many firms and industries and puts the country at a grave disadvantage compared to overseas competitors. This can hardly be in the best long term interests of working people.

Changing individual attitudes

We have seen that resistance to change on the part of the individual is frequently associated with his or her attitudes, and attitudes in turn influence such critical factors as perception, habits and self confidence. Successful change programmes sometimes involve changing individual attitudes; this can present a difficult task. In this context it is useful to make a distinction between the terms *value, attitude* and *opinion*. Values derive from our fundamental beliefs and upbringing which serve as an ultimate justification for the manner of our living; they are rarely changed in adult life. Attitudes are less fundamental, but are still related to personality and therefore not easily changed. Opinions refer to relatively superficial ideas on topics of general interest and are therefore more easily changed. Thus a television commercial might aim to change our opinions, whereas a political or religious leader may be concerned with attitudes or values. Such distinctions are somewhat arbitrary, because values, attitudes and opinions are part of a continuum which may be likened to an iceberg; only the tips show, represented by opinions, but the main part lies concealed in the individual's personality. Change may be directed at the visible part, but the invisible remainder must also be considered.

Attitude has been variously defined as 'a frame of reference that influences the individual's views or opinions on various topics, and that influences his behaviour' (Tiffin and McCormick)[11] and 'a predisposition to respond in a favourable or unfavourable way to objects, persons, concepts or whatever' (Scott and Mitchell).[12] It will be clear that attitudes based on firmly held value systems which are derived from childhood upbringing and socialization are not easily changed. This point, along with the equally significant point that attitudes are more easily changed by group pressures than by individual pressures, is well illustrated by the example of the United Nations prisoners of war captured by the Communist forces in the Korean War in the 1950's. Considerable consternation was created in the United States by the large number of American soldiers taken prisoner of war who made statements, subsequent to capture, expressing sympathy with the Communist cause. The findings of a team of enquiry set up by the United States government, reported by Edgar Schein,[13] showed that their captors first took away from the prisoners the officers and men who demonstrated leadership qualities, and then proceeded to use political discussion groups, led by trained propagandists, to inculate new attitudes into the confused and leaderless groups of captured soldiers. Whilst a number of American and British soldiers were influenced in this way into expressions of pro-Communist support, not one of the captured Gurkha soldiers succumbed. The religious and cultural values of the Gurkha soldiers were proof against this technique.

Probably the best known theory concerning attitude formation and change, which has demonstrated its practical application, is Leon Festinger's theory of Cognitive Dissonance. Festinger and Aronson[14] state that '. . . the simultaneous existence of cognitions which in one way or another do not fit together (dissonance) leads to effort on the part of the person to somehow make them fit better (dissonance reduction)'. In other words, when we are forced to make a decision which entails choosing between a number of different alternatives, we are rarely faced with a clear cut situation. Choosing one course of action involves the rejection of alternative courses of action which possess their own attractions. In order to justify this course of action we overcome our mental reservations by a shift in our attitudes which in effect paints our chosen course of action in relatively glowing colours. According to Festinger, the greater the inconsistency, the greater is the shift in attitude to reduce the initial dissonance. This is illustrated by the classic experiment by Festinger and J.

M. Carlsmith (see reference 14, page 132), in which they asked students to spend an hour by themselves performing a very boring task, and then asked them to tell the next student waiting to perform the task that it was both enjoyable and interesting. Some were paid one dollar, some twenty dollars for making this false statemnt. As predicted, those who were paid the smaller amount changed their original attitude about the task, having convinced themselves that they were not lying to their fellow students. However, those paid the relatively large sum of twenty dollars did not change their opinion on the task after lying to their fellow student; they were able to rationalize their action and lessen their dissonance by reference to the heavy bribe they had accepted.

Planned intervention in the culture of a work organization, with the objective of changing attitudes and creating an improvement in the degree of co-operation between managers and departments, has in recent years gone under the title of 'organizational change'; to this we now turn our attention.

Organizational change and organizational development

In recent years behavioural scientists have, on a number of occasions, been invited by top management to join in a planned programme of intervention into the social processes of the organization, so as to create changes in attitudes and behaviour that will lead to greater effectiveness. Where these organizational change programmes are associated with an examination of the effectiveness of the total organization, they are frequently referred to as 'Organization Development', or 'O.D.' for short. According to French[15] the objectives of organizational development programmes are:

1. To increase the level of trust and support among organizational members.
2. To increase the incidence of confrontation of organizational problems, both within groups and among groups, in contrast to 'sweeping problems under the rug'.
3. To create an environment in which authority of assigned role is augmented by authority based on knowledge and skill.
4. To increase the openness of communications laterally, vertically and diagonally.
5. To increase the level of personal enthusiasm and satisfaction in the organization.
6. To find synergistic solutions to problems with greater frequency (synergistic solutions are creative solutions in which 2 + 2 equals more

than 4, and through which all parties gain more through co-operation than through conflict).

7. To increase the level of self and group responsibility in planning and implementation.

This systematic and systemic approach to organizational change can be represented by the diagram in Figure 9.2.

Figure 9.2   Organizational Change: A systematic approach

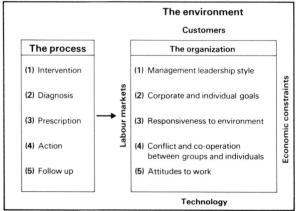

The process can be set in motion either by external change agents, or by managers within the organization possessing the necessary expertise. Expertise is essential, because it will be appreciated that mistakes can be costly. Organizational change programmes arouse people's expectations, and a failure to deliver the goods can lead to a state worse than before the innovation. Three stages are frequently used in change programmes, deriving from the pioneer work into Group Dynamics by Kurt Lewin. These three stages are represented by Edgar Schein[16] as:

1. Unfreezing: creating a motivation to change.
2. Changing: developing new responses based on new information.
3. Refreezing: stabilizing and integrating the changes.

Before individuals are prepared to listen attentively to new viewpoints they must be induced into a receptive state; the method used will depend on the results of stages 2 and 3 in the process, shown in Figure 9.2. Obviously, captured prisoners of war are dealt with differently from groups of managers or shop stewards! Once receptiveness and motivation have been created, new ideas can be introduced and discussed. If a measure of agreement is reached, then the new ideas must be consolidated in a manner that ensures that they are firmly retained by participants and subsequently put into practice.

Organization Development, as propounded by the main body of interested behavioural scientists in both the United States and in Britain, possesses a number of distinctive features, which mark it off from other approaches to organizational change. These features include the following (based on an authoritative study by French and Bell[17]):

1. Programmes aim to be 'normative-re-educative' and 'rational-empirical', based on the assumption that norms form the basis for behaviour and change comes through a re-education process in which old norms are discarded and supplanted by new ones, and that men will change if and when they come to realize that change is advantageous to them. Thus the use of power and coercion are ruled out as vehicles for change.
2. A 'systems' approach should be adopted which appreciates the interrelatedness of organizational phenomena; one must aim to change systems, not just component parts.
3. Strong emphasis is placed on the value of data concerning human and social processes within the organization and members of the organization must learn how to collect and utilize such data for solving problems.
4. People learn best how to do things by doing them, and therefore participants are encouraged to learn about organizational dynamics by reflecting on their own experiences, aided by an expert 'change-agent'.
5. Both organizations and individuals need to manage their affairs against goals which are explicit, measurable, and attainable.
6. Membership of normal organizational working-groups should, as far as possible, be maintained within any learning programme, as this helps to ensure that effective team building takes place within the organization.

This approach can be seen to differ considerably from the more traditional approaches to development and change based on management training programmes or the use of management consultants. In management training the emphasis tends to be on individuals rather than teams, and many managers experience difficulty in applying what they have learnt upon returning to their own departments after a period of absence. Management consultants may deal with departments and work groups but all too frequently they take their skills away with them upon completing an assignment.

A number of techniques have been developed as vehicles for organizational change, some of which have become widely known. Whilst each technique requires many pages of exposition for a complete understanding, a brief introduction will give an indication of their aims and methods.

Sensitivity training

The aim of sensitivity training is to lead group members to a point where they become more perceptive of other people's feelings, and hence more adept at inter-personal relations. This is usually achieved by participation in so called 'T Groups' (Training Groups), where a group of individuals spend a period of time together, and are led to express frank comments ('feedback') about each other's behaviour. This form of training is sometimes referrred to as 'laboratory training', with the implication that such groups are carrying out experiments into their own behaviour.

When used for the purposes of organizational change, membership of the T Group frequently consists of selected members of management and the work force plus a leader. Clearly this type of group requires very careful preselection and handling by an expert leader, in order to prevent possible damage to individuals unable to stand up to criticism and feedback. Anxiety on this issue should be mitigated by follow up studies reported by Cooper[18] which show that in only about 2% of cases can any adverse effects be measured subsequent to participation.

In the early days of organizational change programmes, sensitivity training was the most commonly used method of implementing behavioural change, but other methods have since found greater favour. The results were mixed, with some managers claiming to have achieved greater awareness of their impact on others; but all too frequently little significant change in organizational processes could be observed subsequently. As Derek Pugh expressed it: 'The T Group, by affecting only the individual, attempts to affect the whole social system on too narrow a front. It is not the individual, but his network of social relationships which is basic, and attempts to alter it through the individual must remain only marginally effective.'[19]

Leadership style

Organizational change that leads to organization development can sometimes be achieved by a programme aimed at the leadership styles of selected managers. One of the best known programmes is provided by the Managerial Grid developed by Blake and Mouton[20] and discussed in Chapter V.

A more sophisticated version of this is provided by Reddin's 3-D (three dimensional) approach.[21] The three dimensions of leadership style referred to, and which are translated into a three-dimensional 'grid', are 'Relationships', 'Task' and 'Effectiveness'. Different positions on this grid indicate different styles of management, including the following stereotypes:

'The Deserter', who rates very low on all three dimensions.
'The Missionary', who rates high on relationships, but low on the other two dimensions.
'The Autocrat', who rates high on task, but low on the other two.
'The Compromiser', who rates high on task and relationships, but is ineffective.
'The Bureaucrat', who rates high on effectiveness, but low on the other two.
'The Benevolent Autocrat', who rates high on tasks and effectiveness, but low on relationships.
'The Developer', who rates high on effectiveness and relationships, but low on task.
'The Executive', who rates high on all three dimensions.

As with the managerial grid approach, managers participate in exercises and questionnaires which provide them with feedback as to their perceived style of leadership. A major strength of recent versions of the 3-D approach is this emphasis upon situational analysis. Instead of attempting to pressurize managers into adopting a particular stereotype, such as 'Executive', emphasis is placed on a developing or consolidating a style appropriate to the situation. As Reddin says: 'If you want to help a manager to change, talk to him about his situation, not about himself.' This approach can readily be developed into a full scale organizational development programme aimed at changing and improving interpersonal processes within the organization.

Whilst further research is required on the results of the 3-D approach, it does appear to have satisfied a number of large organizations, and has the merit of incorporating situational analysis.

Confrontation goal-setting

Here the aim is to bring out into the open the conflict that frequently exists between departments and managers within an organization. A change expert will meet separately with members of conflicting departments or groups of employees, and ask them to prepare a statement of how they perceive the other department or group with whom they are in conflict, and also ask them how they think the others in turn perceive them.

The two groups are then brought together in order to discuss all four statements and to thrash out their differences.[22]

Team building

Organizational Development programmes in Britain tend to avoid publicity, for understandable reasons. Their greatest impact has probably been in changing the style and philosophy of training departments in large organizations in the direction of a 'systems' approach that recognizes group processes and inter-personal relationships.[23]. Where training departments have invited in O.D. specialists to assist in programmes, this has frequently taken the shape of 'team building' exercises that adopt a pragmatic approach.

In a typical programme (see for example, Knibbs[24]), the usual stages of diagnosis, analysis and action planning are gone through. Work teams then spend a period of two or three days together away from the job, possibly in a training centre or hotel. Reassurance sometimes needs to be given that no attempt at sensitivity training will be attempted. Led by the change agent, the team members then participate in discussions centring on topics such as leadership, authority, roles and relationships, and the climate of trust within the team. The aim is to develop a work team that is more effective because it has faced up to problems blocking co-operation and teamwork.

Such innovations do not always succeed. Attempts to 'unfreeze' British managers encounter a number of problems. These have been summarized by Fritz Steele[25] as stemming from the widely held fear of 'rocking the boat', emphasis upon tradition, a desire for stability and security, fatalism, 'a stiff upper lip', and a general mistrust of all outside experts, including behavioural scientists. This is a salutary reminder that the management of change is not to be undertaken lightly, although the urgency for change is only too apparent in the poor economic performance of many organizations that can frequently be traced back to lack of co-operative effort.

Management by objectives

In this well-known technique, the emphasis is upon mutual agreement between managers and subordinates on the targets to be achieved on the job, and the time and manner of the review of performance. The sequence of events is generally as follows:

1. Top management agree on corporate objectives.

2. Departmental managers meet with subordinate managers to discuss departmental contributions to corporate objectives.
3. Subordinate managers discuss and agree the targets they aim to achieve so as to make a proper contribution to corporate objectives. These targets are usually set in what are termed 'Key Result Areas', aiming at a few quantifiable results in critical areas of the work.
4. Departmental managers agree to provide the support and training necessary to the achievement of targets.
5. The progress towards achieving the agreed targets is discussed subsequently on dates agreed to in advance by both manager and subordinate.
6. The whole process is conducted in a systematic company-wide fashion, with emphasis upon the motivation of participants through a sense of achievement and involvement.

Management by objectives can be seen as an attempt to make explicit what many people might regard as simply 'good management'. However, it can act as a powerful change-agent if introduced and conducted skilfully. Unfortunately, a too mechanistic approach has sometimes been adopted, with too much emphasis upon paperwork and procedures. It has also sometimes foundered due to conservatism and a suspicion of any change that involves greater participation. Like many change programmes, it suffers from the 'chicken and egg' dilemma. It aims to develop a more open and flexible style of management, yet it can only successfully be introduced if managers are ready for such a change. Therefore its successful introduction requires awareness by management of those aspects of individual, group and societal behaviour, emphasized in the preceding chapters of this book.

Productivity bargaining

The change techniques described above are mainly concerned with the behaviour of managers. Frequently an organization may wish to induce changes that encompass the entire working force, and this will normally involve consultation and negotiation with trade unions. Productivity bargaining is not normally listed as a change technique, yet in Britain it has probably had more effect on major companies than any of the other methods listed. Its mention also serves to remind us that trade unions need to be taken into account when change programmes are introduced. The three stage approach to change recommended by Schein, mentioned earlier, applies equally here. Attitudes have to be 'unfrozen' to permit a constructive discussion of the proposed changes that will lead to greater productivity and improved working conditions.

A 'classic' study of productivity bargaining is provided by the Fawley Productivity Agreement.[26] A more recent example of productivity bargaining, associated with a widespread attempt to change attitudes and inculcate new ideas into management thinking and practice, is provided by ICI's weekly staff Agreement, that followed on from their Manpower Utilization Programme. The end result aimed for was weekly staff status for manual workers, and improved pay and conditions of service, in return for greater flexibility in manning. In addition, training courses and literature were provided for management in an endeavour to achieve more participative management styles. In a number of plants the scheme met tough opposition from trade unions and managers. Its successful introduction into one of their plants is described in a most interesting study by Cotgrove, Dunham and Vanplew entitled *The Nylon Spinners*.[27] At the time of its introduction to one of their plants, Eric Wigham commented in an article in *The Times*.[28]

'Of course the cost in time and effort is great. At ICI headquarters they estimate that the introduction of WSA takes about 10 per cent of management time and that this will continue after it is in operation. But at Rocksavage they said that at the peak period they had eight out of forty managers and senior engineers working full-time on the project and other managers spending 10 or 20 per cent of their time on it. Shop stewards and workers were frequently away from their jobs at meetings or undergoing training for their new functions. There were fifty meetings with groups of men lasting on average three hours. "It was only by co-operative effort that we kept production going", I was told.'

Organizational change programmes, then, are not to be lightly undertaken! However they do provide a unique opportunity for management to take the initiative in breaking out of chains imposed by tradition, hostility and bureaucracy. In order to underline the need to bring the behavioural sciences and industrial relations together, if many of industries' problems are to be solved, this section concludes with a quotation from the deputy chairman of the Rod Division of Delta Metal following a period of innovation and change in their industrial relations procedures, quoted from Daniel and McIntosh:[29]

'We need to change the defensive attitudes that have so often dominated us in the past, replacing them where we can with a constructive relationship. Our industrial relations should not be dominated by a narrow exchange of views on money, which promotes defensiveness on both sides, but expanded into a wider discussion on which money will be only one of the matters which is under debate. We need to start bargaining about conduct and conduct is not money.'

Participation

Participation at the place of work is seen by some managers as an opportunity but by others as a threat. Unfortunately, participation is too frequently portrayed as either the answer to all industrial problems, or as a dangerous innovation advocated by left-wing radicals. Yet there will be few readers of this book who do not wish to have some say in the way in which they work, and to be consulted by their superiors on decisions affecting them; whether readers are also equally willing to concede such rights to their subordinates may be a different matter. In one interesting study of leadership styles and behaviour,[30] it was found that members of a particular level of management expressed the wish to be consulted more often by their superiors. It was also found that their subordinates in a lower level of the management hierarchy were also anxious for a more consultative leadership style by their managers. We do not all practise what we preach!

Aspects of participation have already been touched on in earlier chapters. Thus Chapter V on Working in Groups considered participative styles of leadership, and Chapter III on Motivation considered participation by employees in matters of job design. In The Times Management Lecture for 1970, Professor Kenneth Walker distinguished four broad categories of participation. These were in ownership, government, management of the firm, and in setting the terms and conditions of employment. In this section we turn our attention to management, whilst recognizing that the other three categories all have a bearing on each other and on the changing task of the manager.

In attempting to evaluate the benefits of increased participation, behavioural scientists are faced with a problem concerning criteria. Should the effects of changes in the degree of participation at the place of work be measured in terms of productivity, job satisfaction or labour wastage? Or is increased participation an inevitable response to social and trade union pressures? Kevin Hawkins[31] commented that: 'If one believes that some form of participation, whether "on" or "off" the job, is essential to higher morale and higher productivity in the workplace, then one is automatically making a series of assumptions about the motivation of the workers concerned. In other words, one is implicitly assuming that workers want to participate and that they want to acquire more responsibility and a wider range of functional roles. It is then relatively easy to set up a field experiment and to obtain results which will validate the original assumption' (see reference 31, pages 1 and 2). Whilst he underestimates the problems in setting up field surveys, his comment serves to remind us of the difficulties associated with the provision of 'scientific' generalizations in the social sciences on issues of this nature.

An early 'classic' study concerning the influence of participation on facilitating change in the work organization was reported by the social psychologists Coch and French.[32] The Harwood Manufacturing Corporation in the United States was a medium-sized factory producing pyjamas, which because of changes in style had to change its work methods from time to time. As the workers were paid by piece-rate methods, their earnings were liable to suffer whilst they learnt to cope with changed methods, and this in turn led to a degree of resistance to such innovations. In the experiment carried out in this plant, four groups of sewing machine operators were formed, matching each other in background and experience. One group formed the control group, and were changed to new jobs by the normal factory procedures, which involved an explanation of why the changes were necessary, what the new job would be like, and what the new piece rates would be. A second group formed the first of the experimental groups. This group was given more information about changes than the control group, and were permitted to choose representative to participate in the design of the new jobs, the setting of piece rates, and in training procedures. The two remaining groups formed experimental groups 2 and 3. All members of these two groups participated directly on designing the job, and in setting piece rates. The results for the control group and experimental groups 2 and 3 are shown in Figure 9.3.

After the change, the control group dropped to an output of about 50 units per hour, a normal reaction in the circumstances. A number of workers in this group left the firm's employment. Experimental group 1 also dropped to about the same level, but soon began to improve, and ultimately reached about 65 units of output an hour. Groups 2 and 3, however, where all members participated in the new procedures, dropped hardly at all after the change, and thereafter showed a steady improvement which took them eventually to 70 units of output an hour. Additionally, the labour turnover was very low. Coch and French concluded that 'It is possible for management to modify greatly or to remove completely group resistance to changes in methods of work and the ensuing piece rates. This change can be accomplished by the use of group meetings in which management effectively communicates the need for change and stimulates group participation in planning the changes.'*

That participative methods do not necessarily lead to higher productivity, but can lead to other desirable results, was demonstrated by an experiment conducted by the Institute for Social Research of the University of Michigan.[33] Four divisions employing 500 clerical workers and carrying out similar duties were involved. The supervisors and

* Reference 31, page 532.

Figure 9.3   Output in a garment manufacturing company under three systems of management (from data collected by Marrow, Coch and French)[32]

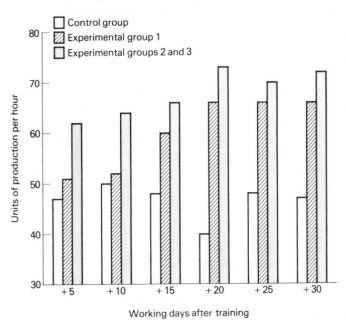

Working days after training

managers in two of the divisions were given a six months' training programme which established a participative climate of leadership, while in the other two divisions a training programme reinforced a hierarchical style of management involving close supervision and decision making confined to senior personnel. In addition method study was used in these last two departments to establish standard output times.

At the end of one year, productivity had increased by 20 per cent in the two participative divisions, and by 25 per cent in the two hierarchically controlled divisions. But in the hierarchically controlled divisions labour wastage had increased sharply, loyalty had declined, and work ceased when supervisors were absent from the department. In the participatively led divisions labour wastage was lower, workers continued to work in the absence of their supervisors, and there was a far more favourable attitude to management.

An interesting contemporary case study of participative methods applied throughout a workforce was provided in an article in *The Times* newspaper by Nancy Foy,[34] featuring Bristol Channel Ship Repairers (BCSR). Through the initiative of the Chairman, a structure of committees and quarterly conferences was created followed at a later date by small group discussions in which the company's finances were regularly discussed with all 1,500 employees. The need for more financial information and small group discussions became clear through the quarterly conferences, when the shop floor representatives began demanding clearer explanations. Subsequently all employees were given shares in the company, which created still further interest in the company's fortunes. The local shop steward of the Society of Boilermakers and Shipwrights is quoted as saying: 'Seven years ago if we had a problem at eight, it would have been a major dispute by nine; in 1975 a problem at eight is usually solved by nine.' There were of course some practical difficulties. For example, middle management felt threatened by the new system, and needed help in adjusting. Despite these, the AUEW (engineering workers) shop steward commented, 'I'd advise anybody to start the way we have. It's ordinary and mundane, but we are proud of our progress so far,' and, 'We explain why we gained or lost a contract. And people really give management a view of their real problems.' The Chairman was able to point to a productivity per man that was three times that of any other ship-repairing company in the country.

What is particularly notable about this last example is that it was not imposed by a unilateral management decision, but involved consultation and bargaining with the trade unions. Participation is sometimes seen as a clever manipulative device whereby management achieves its objects by devious means. Again, participation has been criticized because it involves no real shift in power from management to the work force. The workers are encouraged to put up suggestions, but management exercises the same degree of control as in the more traditional approaches. It is an obvious truth, sometimes overlooked by managers, that workers and their representatives are not easily fooled by a superficial approach to participation which does not involve a willingness to share decision making and genuine concessions. Participation has also to escape from the shackles of the Human Relations movement (discussed in Chapter VII), in which human relations techniques are applied as a device to secure greater compliance from the work force without any movement on the part of top management in the direction of power sharing.

Exercises in participation and plant bargaining of the type described at the Bristol Channel Ship Repairers require a large measure of respect for each other on the part of management and the workers' representatives. This respect is associated with a recognition of the legitimacy of each others' position, and of the rules that govern society. Unfortunately industrial history bears witness to many incidents where such recognition has not been given, and management have frequently been to blame. It would be foolish to overlook the fact that a powerful challenge has now arisen from those who seek to radically change society, and therefore do not recognize the legitimacy of management and 'the rules of the game'. This point was made in the previous chapter in the discussion of power and conflict. At a philosophical level it finds expression in the writings of Alan Fox, whose perceptive but barbed comments attract widespread attention in the industrial relations field. Writing from what he terms a 'radical' point of view he states in his book, *Beyond Contract: Power and Trust Relations*:[35]

'Those acting in accordance with the radical analysis will of course have very different perceptions. They see what pluralists define as "free and equal joint regulation" as no more than "bargaining under duress". If they aspire to demands which represent a repudiation of all or some of the conventionally received notions and principles which are the condition of their negotiating activities being tolerated by the major power holders, but are conscious of being contained within the conventional bargaining limits by those power-holders, they are likely to see such negotiating as they are permitted as being under duress', and he goes on to say that 'only a sense of equal participation can be expected to induce an observance based on moral obligation as aginst calculative expediency'.

This frame of reference would see the shop stewards at Bristol Channel Ship Repairers as having acquiesced to a system which upholds the present order of society, deemed to be dominated by the owners of capital. The essential point to be made here is that the types of successful participation and organizational change programmes described in this and other texts require a large measure of confidence in each other by all the parties concerned. The basis for this confidence is constantly under attack from political extremists on both the left and the right. Managements can only maintain the legitimacy of their position in the long run, at a time of social change, by encouraging genuine participation and powersharing. In the meantime more attention is needed by behavioural scientists, managers and politicians to the attitudes and expectations of ordinary workers. Speaking as General Secretary of the British Airline Pilots Association and a former ETU official, Mark Young[36] commented: 'The problem really is how to get workers to identify with the company in which they work, and to get them participating there. It is not a matter of structures. While the debate is going on at a high level, no one is asking actual workers what they want.'

REFERENCES

1 TOFFLER, A., *Future Shock*, Pan Books Ltd., 1971.
2 STEWART, R., *The Reality of Management*, William Heinemann Ltd., 1963.
3 WATSON, G. W., 'Resistance to change', in *The Planning of Change*, BENNIS *et al.* (Eds.), Holt, Rhinehart & Winston, 1966.
4 CHINOY, E., *Automobile Workers and the American Dream*, Doubleday, 1955.
5 BELBIN, R. M., *Training the Adult Worker*, HMSO, 1964.
6 CROZIER, M., *The Bureaucratic Phenomenon*, Tavistock, 1964.
7 SCOTT, W. H. *et. al., Technical Change and Industrial Relations*, Liverpool University Press, 1956.
8 SAYLES, L. R., *The Behaviour of Industrial Work Groups*, Wiley, 1958.
9 BURNS, T. and STALKER, G. M., *The Management of Innovation*, Tavistock, Social Science Paperbacks, 1961.
10 POOLE, J., 'Can Scotland pay the piper', article in *Sunday Times*, January 30th 1977.
11 TIFFIN, J. and McCORMICK, E. J., *Industrial Psychology*, 6th ed., Allen & Unwin, 1975.
12 SCOTT, W. G. and MITCHELL, T. R., *Organisation Theory*, Richard D. Irwin Inc. and the Dorsey Press, 1972.
13 SCHEIN, E. H., 'The Chinese indoctrination program for prisoners of war', in *Psychiatry*, **19**, pp. 149–72, 1956.
14 FESTINGER, L. and ARONSON, E., 'Arousal and reduction of dissonance in social contexts', in CARTWRIGHT, D. and ZANDER, A. (Eds.), *Group Dynamics*, 3rd ed., Tavistock Publications, 1968.
15 FRENCH, W., 'Organisation Development', *California Management Review*, **12**, Winter 1969.
16 SCHEIN, E. H., 'The mechanisms of change', in BENNIS, SCHEIN, STEELE and BARLOW (Eds.), *Interpersonal Dynamics*, Dorsey Press, 1964.
17 FRENCH, W. and BELL, C., *Organisation Development*, Prentice Hall, 1973.
18 COOPER, C., 'Taking the terror out of T Groups', *Personnel Management*, **9**, No. 1, 1977.
19 PUGH, D., *T Group Training*, WHITTAKER, F.P.G. (Ed.), Blackwell, 1965.
20 BLAKE, R. R. and MOUTON, J. S., *The Managerial Grid*, Gulf, 1964.
21 REDDIN, W. J., *Managerial Effectiveness*, McGraw-Hill, 1970.
22 BECKHARD, R., 'The confrontation meeting', *Harvard Business Review XLV*, 1967.
23 LIPPITT, G. L., 'The trainer's role as an internal consultant', *Journal of European Training*, **4**, No. 5, 1975.
24 KNIBBS, J., 'Realities of the organisation development workshop', *Industrial and Commercial Training*, **8**, No. 11, 1976.
25 STEELE, F., 'Obstacles to O.D. in the United Kingdom', *Journal of European Training*, **5**, No. 3, 1976.
26 FLANDERS, A., *The Fawley Productivity Agreements*, Faber & Faber, 1964.
27 COTGROVE, S., DUNHAM, J. and VAN PLEW, C., *The Nylon Spinners*, Allen & Unwin, 1971.

28 WIGHAM, E., 'Some spanners in the works', article in *The Times*, September 9th, 1970.
29 DANIEL, W. W. and McINTOSH, N., 'The Right to Manage', *P.E.P. Report*, MacDonald, 1972.
30 PETER, H., 'Survey of leadership styles in a large oil company', I.P.M., *Annual Conference Report*, 1968.
31 HAWKINS, K., *Conflict and Change*, Holt, Rhinehart & Winston, 1972.
32 COCH, L. and FRENCH, J. R. P., 'Overcoming resistance to change', *Human Relations*, **I**, 1948.
33 LIKERT, R., *New Patterns of Management*, pp. 62–9, McGraw-Hill Book Company, 1961.
34 FOY, N., 'Where participation by the workers solves problems instead of creating them', article in *The Times*, June 2nd, 1975.
35 FOX, A., *Beyond Contract: Work, Power and Trust Relations*, Faber & Faber Ltd., 1974.
36 YOUNG, M., 'What participation means', article in *Industrial Society*, September/October 1976.

X

THE SMALL FIRM—A NEGLECTED AREA OF MANAGEMENT

The overwhelming mass of literature in the field of management is directed essentially at the larger firm. This is not surprising since the bulk of managers and employees alike work for large firms. However, small firms do still exist in our economy and perform a vital and indispensable role and, as such, warrant more attention in a book of this kind than they normally receive.

Some of the material presented in earlier chapters, for example that on leadership, power, groups and interpersonal communications, does have relevance to the problems of the smaller firm but it has, almost without exception, been developed with the larger firm in mind. This being so, it is worthwhile re-examining these issues with the small firm specifically in mind.

The reasons for the previous neglect of the small firm are not difficult to pinpoint. The post-war boom and the spate of take-overs and mergers during the 1950's and 1960's led to the small firm being regarded as a hangover from the industrial revolution doomed to rapid extinction in an economy dominated by large-scale public and private enterprise. It was widely considered that the age of specialization and mass production, with its associated economies of scale, meant certain death for the smaller business.

Another reason for the neglect of the small firm stems from difficulties of access to such firms experienced by both researchers and management consultants. Because the small businessman often tends to talk a different language to academics and consultants and sometimes feels that his business methods may attract criticism and even ridicule if exposed to critical examination, he has tended to keep his distance from them. In addition, pressure of work has kept the level of participation of managers from small firms on outside formal management training courses at a low level and so, once again, the two worlds of large and small have not met.

The importance of the small firm in the economy

The 1972 Census of Production[1] reported that there are around 69,000 small enterprises (those employing less than 200) in manufacturing industry alone, employing nearly 1·5 million personnel and producing around £8,900m worth of goods. Small firms constitute approximately 95 per cent of all firms in manufacturing industry, though the average size of firm is very much smaller than 200 employees. In fact 66,119, or over 90 per cent, employ less than 25 personnel.

These figures indicate the importance of small firms in the manufacturing sector, and a similar pattern emerges from an examination of other areas of the economy. In fact, the figures themselves understate the importance of the small firm given the reliance of large firms on their small firm counterparts for goods and services. As the CBI has put it: if our small firms closed down tomorrow, 'most of the large firms would grind quickly and painfully to a halt'.[2]

The small firm *has* declined in importance in our economy during this century but, in absolute terms, it remains highly significant and, what is more, the rate of decline appears to have been slowing down. Wood,[3] analysing Census of Production data for manufacturing industry from 1935 to 1968, concludes '. . . it appears that the rate of decline is slowing down'. Between 1963 and 1968 there was a continued decline in the overall number of small firms (− 5 per cent), but the decline in the number of large firms during this period was even greater (− 13 per cent). Hence, the representation of small firms increased in percentage terms. It may well be that the current economic recession will take a high toll on small firms as against large, but it would be highly speculative to extrapolate any long-term trend from this.

United States experience in recent years again underlines the importance of the small firm, The Bolton Report[4] on small firms pointed out that the share of economic activity held by small firms in the U.S. is much larger than in the U.K. Over 98 per cent of firms in the U.S. employ less than 100 people and between them account for about 40 per cent of total employment.[5] Further, the decline of the small firm, in what is often considered the most advanced of industrial societies, appears to have been halted and may even have been reversed.[6]

As a final word on the importance of the small firm in Britain, the Bolton Committee, in its conclusion, made the following claim:

Our researches have shown that the small firm sector remains one of substantial importance in the United Kingdom economy: its output is equivalent to about one-fifth of the GNP and it employs more people than the entire public sector. If the range of our report were expanded to cover all owner-managed businesses, of which there are many larger than the size limits we have accepted, the contribution of the small firm sector would be seen to be much larger still.[7]

A definition of the small firm

Defining the small firm is no easy task. However, the Bolton Committee saw the small firm as a socio-economic unit with the following characteristics:

   (i) Economically, a small firm is one that has a relatively small share of its market.
  (ii) Managerially, the small firm is administered by its owners or part-owners in a personalised way, rather than through the medium of a formalised management structure.
 (iii) Finally, it is independent in the sense that it does not form part of a larger enterprise and owner-managers are free from outside control in taking their principal decisions.[8]

This definition can be criticized on several grounds. Some small firms, for instance, have quite large shares of their often specialized markets. However, a practical drawback here is the lack of available data on ownership, management structures and market shares of firms, which rules out the application of this definition. Instead, for manufacturing industry, the Committee was forced to adopt the less satisfactory statistical definition of '200 employees or less'.

No one simple definition of size fits all instances. Even using a definition of size in terms of numbers employed does not leave us without problems. For instance, a car firm employing a thousand personnel would be considered 'small' in the context of its industry. On the other hand, in the printing industry (the national newspaper sector apart) a firm employing 200 personnel would be considered by many to be medium-sized or even large. However, in any examination of the social character and social dynamics of the small firm, a definition of size in terms of numbers employed is usually the most appropriate. The Bolton Committee's definition of '200 employees or less' may be erring on the large side given that research suggests that many of the small firm's social characteristics are likely to have disappeared or become markedly modified by the time workforce size approaches 200. However, it is acceptable as a broad basis for discussion.

Outside manufacturing industry, the Bolton Committee used alternative definitions of a small firm. Sometimes these were still expressed in terms of numbers employed (e.g. 25 employees or less for the construction industry) but in other instances alternative bases were used for purposes of definition (e.g. sales turnover for the retail and wholesale trades, and numbers of vehicles in the case of the road transport industry).

A social profile of the small firm

The small firm owner-manager is often thought of as being in some way 'odd' or non-conformist in the way he manages his business. His methods often appear to fly in the face of popular management theory, and intrinsic satisfactions frequently appear high on his list of goals, often at the expense of rationality and profitability.

Golby and Johns, in their Bolton Committee Research Report,[9] supported the above view in their suggestion that owner-managers are, in general, different in temperament and character from other businessmen. They described the underlying motivation of many small firm owner-manager in terms of a need to 'attain and preserve independence':

This need for 'independence' sums up a wide range of highly personal gratifications provided by working for oneself and not for anybody else. It embraces many important satisfactions which running a small business provides—the personal supervision and control of staff, direct contact with customers, the opportunity to develop one's own ideas, a strong feeling of personal challenge and an almost egotistical sense of personal achievement and pride—psychological satisfactions which appeared to be much more powerful motivators than money or the possibility of large financial gains.[10]

Further, Golby and Johns claim that this desire for independence acts as a strong influence in determining the guiding strategies and policies of small firm managements:

The powerful underlying need to maintain and preserve independence and the strong feelings of personal satisfaction derived from one's own achievement go a long way to explaining the attitudes to outside help and assistance. Government assistance was seen as leading to Government intervention; using more sophisticated financial assistance than that provided by the local bank manager would lead to a loss of independence because the organisation giving the assistance would want some measure of control over the firm. Having rejected 'the boss', respondents didn't want to suffer the paternalism of Government or anyone else for that matter. Because the sense of satisfaction derived from personal achievement was so important, many of these respondents appeared almost to turn a deaf ear to any outside source of advice or help. They neither knew nor wished to know about it.[11]

Growth in the small firm

Given the strong influence of the owner-manager on the small firm's organizational style, it is clearly necessary to examine this key role in some detail. Before doing so, however, it is important to look at the aspect of small firm social dynamics that has received most attention from social scientists in recent years—its growth and development. Other features of the firm—its managerial style, leadership and decision-making procedures, attitudes towards outside sources of finance, trade unions and industrial relations, training, employers organizations and Government departments—are often linked to various stages in the models of growth developed by these writers.

A survey of the literature on management in the small firm reveals a number of contributions to an understanding of small firm growth and there are certain similarities between the various efforts.[12] Without commenting on each of these in great detail, and at the risk of some over-simplification, it can be argued that they reveal two different basic themes.

The dominant theme is that of a 'stage' model where the firm is seen as passing through a sequence of stages of growth. The number of stages varies from writer to writer but typically there are three or four, though sometimes as many as ten.[13] Stage models, regardless of the number of stages offered, display certain similarities. The initial stage, as might be expected, stresses the individual entrepreneur(s) with an idea for a product or service setting up an economic unit to produce the item in question. The next stage (or sometimes the next but one), is usually concerned with the division of managerial tasks.[14] As the entrepreneur or founding partners of the firm can no longer exercise total managerial control over the enterprise, non-owner managers are recruited, usually because they possess skills not possessed by the founder(s). The remaining stages tend to concentrate on organizational maturity and stability. The small firm becomes more bureaucratic and rationalized in its organization and takes on the general character of the large company; it evolves a board of directors who are essentially managers rather than entrepreneurs; it exploits a wide range of management, production and marketing techniques; and there is an acceptance that it must develop systematic working relations with other organizations in society such as outside pressure groups, government departments, trade unions and the media.

The other theme present in theorizing on growth in the small firm is the so-called 's-curve hypothesis'[15] which can, in effect, be seen as a special case of the stage theory. This suggests that the small firm will have a short formative period of existence which will be followed by a period of rapid growth perhaps reaching an exponential rate, before tailing off. The thinking behind this is that after the entrepreneur(s) have developed an idea for a product or service, there is an initial establishing period for the firm which ends with the clear demonstration of a market advantage. This leads to a high rate of profit re-investment to further exploit the advantage plus an injection of outside capital attracted by the firm's performance in the establishing period. This investment fuels the high rate of growth in the next period of the firm's history.

This exceptional rate of growth, however, tails off as competition is offered by other firms who become aware of the market opportunities. This is reinforced by a lowering of investment levels in the firm due to profit-taking by the owner-managers, and a decline in the firm's attraction as an investment due to increased competition as well as other possible changes such as market saturation. In order to survive and stabilize as an economic entity the firm, now relatively large, begins to behave in ways typical of other firms in its sector of the economy. Investment is restricted to conventional levels and tied to a product mix which appears to offer an approximation to the average rate of return in the relevant area of the economy.

The three broad phases delineated in this theory, formation followed by a high rate of growth and then a stabilizing phase, explain how the 's-curve hypothesis' derives its name. It will also be apparent from the aspects most discussed that this model is one primarily developed by economists rather than organizational theorists. Nevertheless, it would not be difficult to fit this model into most of the more explicit stage models discussed above.

A re-examination of growth

It cannot be denied that these various approaches to growth contain a considerable element of truth but this is often superficial. For instance, for stage models to define a first stage in terms of an individual or small group deciding that they can, by setting up for themselves in business, exploit a market for a product or service, is to say very little beyond defining the coming into existence of a new independent economic entity.

Another curious aspect of both the stage and 's-curve' models of growth is an implied ignorance of the size distribution of firms in our economy discussed earlier. Census of Production data reveal that this size distribution is highly skewed with over 95 per cent of manufacturing firms employing less than 200 people and the typical firm, in a statistical sense, employing less than 30. The remaining 5 per cent or so of firms employ about two-thirds of the labour force in manufacturing industry. To put it more simply, there are a great number of very small firms and a mere handful of large ones. This characterization of the manufacturing sector (which is broadly repeated in most other areas of the economy), has two important consequences for most stage models of growth in the small firm.

First, most firms will *not* grow to any considerable size in terms of the number of persons employed (which we may assume is broadly correlated with several other dimensions of growth) and that, in practice, growth of any significant proportion is a rather *exceptional* process. This point is reinforced by data which shows that the failure rate among small firms, especially in the years immediately following formation is very high, perhaps of the order of half of the new enterprises founded in any five-year period.[16] In other words, existing theories of small firm growth fail to discuss, let alone account for, the rarity of the process they purport to explain.

Second, an inspection of the implied characteristics of the organizational and managerial structure of the firm, contained within the later stages in most of the models, indicates that the authors are discussing a firm which has long since entered the 6 per cent of large firms in our economy. Since these writers are frequently vague on the size of the firm in these later stages, it is not possible to be absolutely certain on this point. But, discussion of problems of 'going public',[17] of the need for a rationalization of a multi-role management structure,[18] and the bureaucratic organization of the functions of industrial relations, production control, marketing and customer relations,[19] all hint at a mental picture of a firm of some size, employing a substantial number of people and making an extensive product-range. In short, most of these theories are weakened by attempting to explain too much. Instead of concentrating on growth in the *small* firm, a good deal of the theoretical effort is devoted to the growth processes of firms which are, by reference to the actual size distribution of firms, among the largest in our economy.

Coming down to a more individual level, and remembering earlier references to Golby and Johns, it would appear questionable that most owner-managers even desire to develop their firms to any substantial size. Thus, any analysis attempting to look at growth in the small firm and its associated human problems needs to achieve a much closer understanding of the owner-manager himself and what growth, or its absence, means to him. In doing this, it is necessary to move from a Systems approach (upon which the stage and 's-curve' models of growth are based) to a Social Action approach (see earlier chapters for a discussion of the Social Action school of thought). Using this approach, which allows us to place a greater emphasis on the owner-manager himself, it is important to look first at the owner-manager's basic reasons for even wanting to become self-employed in the first place. An understanding of this helps us to make sense of events later.

The decision to 'go it alone'

Given the very strong influence of the owner-manager on the small firm's organizational style then, it is important to examine this key role in some detail. Of particular importance here are the owner-manager's reasons for 'going it alone'. Individuals do not develop goals and aspirations in a vacuum but are influenced by values emanating from the wider society. In our society there is a strong cultural bias favouring individualism. This finds expression in various ways. Economic individualism, it may be argued, in the form of founding and operating a business of one's own, is one of the most legitimate of all culturally prescribed forms of individualism. Indeed, as Max Weber argued,[20] economic individualism, in this form, was given divine sanction in our culture and in fact was closely associated with the genesis of modern industrial society itself.

A writer on the small firm in America has claimed that starting one's own business has:

... always been considered an integral element of the American way of life. Our traditional concept of opportunity has carried and still carries, a heavy emphasis on 'freedom', on 'being on one's own', 'being one's own boss' and 'working for oneself'.[21]

While this cultural bias is not quite so highly emphasized in Britain's culture, survey data[22] shows that the ideal of self-employment, in order to increase autonomy and personal self-esteem, is nonetheless widespread.

However, going into business for oneself is a difficult role transition if only because Britain's educational system and vocational guidance processes operate to minimize practical consideration of this alternative.[23] Nevertheless, some people, albeit a minority, do take on the owner-manager role. It is important to know something about the backgrounds of these people, especially first generation entrepreneurs, if we are to achieve an adequate understanding of the small firm. It is also quite clear from the available data on entrepreneurship in Britain and the United States, that new entrepreneurs are far from randomly drawn from the population, but are in some measure self-selecting.

As a social grouping, entrepreneurs tend to share certain characteristics. For instance, they are not, on the whole, well educated. The Bolton Report stated that nearly three-quarters of a sample of small manufacturing firms' chief executives had received no higher education, and that only 1 per cent had a management qualification.[24] Other data supports this claim for both Britain[25] and the United States[26], though there have been exceptions reported for the latter.[27] The general conclusion, derived from the study of the backgrounds of new entrepreneurs, is that they tend to be people who consider themselves misplaced by the conventional role allocation processes of their society.

The main point here of the special social character of those who embrace the entrepreneurial role is well supported in this quotation from the largest American survey on entrepreneurship:

> . . . Entrepreneurs are men who have failed in the traditional and highly structured roles available to them in the society. In this, as we have seen, entrepreneurs are not unique. What is unique about them is that they found an outlet for their creativity by making out of an undifferentiated mass of circumstance a creation uniquely their own: a business firm.[28]

This claim accords well with a claim made by the Bolton Committee that:

> The small firm provides a productive outlet for the energies of that large group of enterprising and independent people who set great store by economic independence and many of whom are antipathetic or less suited to employment in a large organisation but who have much to contribute to the vitality of the economy.[29]

In previous publications[30] the notion of 'social marginality' has been used to focus attention on the special social characteristics of first generation entrepreneurs. This term is used to refer to a situation in which there is a perceived incongruity between the individual's personal attributes— intellectual make-up, social behaviour patterns, values, physical characteristics, etc.—and the role(s) he holds in society.[31] It could be argued that social marginality is not an uncommon phenomenon due to the very nature of the processes of role allocation—the latter are far from perfect in allocating individuals to social roles—and also because individuals strive to maintain a sense of personal autonomy in all social roles in opposition to social pressures pushing towards conformity. These common forms of social marginality are, however, unlikely to lead to dramatic social responses.

However, for some individuals and some areas of society, circumstances combine to produce experiences of high levels of social marginality. The historical example, *par excellence*, of a group displaying high social marginality has been the Jews. Being a Jew has, regretfully, tended to make a person an 'outsider' in non-Jewish society regardless of his personal and intellectual characteristics. To some extent Jewish communities have developed patterns of social integration to counter these deprivations, imposed from the wider society, but feelings of social marginality are still likely to be present to an extent rare in most other parts of society. And for a Jew with only a weak commitment to his religion and community, any feelings of marginality are likely to be much more pronounced.

Just as those who enter business for themselves are not randomly drawn from the population so also there are constraints and pressures which influence the choice of entrepreneurship as a solution to marginality rather than any alternative solution. For example, to return to the example of the Jews, as a socially marginal group for a long period of European history, many high status social roles were socially and even sometimes legally denied to those of Jewish origin. Entrepreneurship was one of the few remaining alternatives, and it is not therefore surprising to find a high level of Jewish representation in this kind of role.

The social bases of marginality and the solutions adopted by those involved are, of course, highly varied. Common examples of socially marginal people are the intellectually gifted manual worker and the fully acculturated second-generation coloured Briton. Solutions to intense feelings of social marginality are varied. In some cases it leads to adherence to 'extreme' political or religious ideologies which promise to re-construct social reality and thus 'solve' the individual's experiences of social marginality.[32] But for some people, a solution is setting up their own firm.

Published examples of social marginality being solved by entry into entrepreneurship have involved individuals with not uncommon histories. Social marginality has sometimes resulted from promising academic careers being shattered by domestic tragedy, or through the effects of war sharply diminishing career prospects in conventional industrial/ commercial life. Or again, social marginality can occur in middle age when, for example, a successful career in the armed services cannot be matched by attainment of a similarly responsible position in civilian life. Other cases have included instances of demonstrated talent being overlooked by large employers due to the individuals' unorthodox attitudes and personal idiosyncrasies.

It has been argued then that for many first generation entrepreneurs feelings of social marginality, of being 'shut-out' from other positions in society for which they feel their talents qualify them, explain the motivation to become self-employed. As will be shown later, it tends to be these first-generation owner-managers who later display the attitudes and approach to business described earlier by Golby and Johns.

Of course not all those who become owner-managers are socially marginal. Second and subsequent generation owner-managers, who inherit

an already established business, are often very different in their
motivational patterns and approaches to business. They are more likely to
have a conventional middle-class background and education and
subsequently adopt a more conventional view of management and running
a firm. Many of these would never have possessed the motivation to set up
firms of their own volition but are nevertheless content to follow in a
founders' shoes.

Further, there have been examples of even first generation entrepreneurs
who display no symptoms of social marginality. For example, in America
in the 1960's, very favourable opportunities existed for self-employment in
the defence and space industries and often highly qualified professionals
successfully set up their own firms with a view to rapid growth and high
profitability. But the available research strongly suggests that social
marginality often goes with the adoption of the entrepreneurial role and
this is important if we are to understand management in the small firm.

Small firm management profiles

The classical economists offered a picture of the entrepreneur as a
rational profit maximizer and this remains the popular stereotype despite
little support from research. An American study for example has reported
that, of a sample of 81 newly founded businesses, only six approximated to
the classical economists' model of the entrepreneur.[33] The stage and 's-
curve' models of the small firm, presented earlier, bear similarities to the
classical economists' view in that they postulate a single ideal pattern of
functioning and development for the firm and are largely at a loss to
explain departures from this.

The social characteristics of the small firm outlined by Golby and Johns,
with a strong emphasis on independence, while based on research comes
close to this kind of stereotyping also.

To develop a fuller understanding of the small firm which will integrate
these various approaches and explain departues from them, we must use a
Social Action approach, building on Chapter VII and view the small firm
through the eyes of its chief executive owner-manager. Use of this
approach can explain changes in the owner-managers' perceptions of his
role through time, and hence changes in attitudes and managerial style, for
recent research into the small firm indicates that there is no one single,
stereotyped entrepreneurial role.[34]

Following on from the concepts introduced earlier in Chapter VI on
roles, we can now use a role definition and role building approach (as
opposed to the Structural or Holistic approach employed by the Systems
School) in an analysis of the entrepreneurial role. Here, it is helpful again to

use Alvin Gouldner's concepts of manifest and latent social roles.[35] To refresh the reader's memory, the *manifest* role here is that largely based on cultural prescriptions stemming from the expectations of the business community, customers, employees, unions, banks, etc., and conforms largely to the text-book definition of what an efficient manager's role ought to be. However, the entrepreneur, so long as he meets with these expectations at a level basically acceptable to others, e.g. pays his staff and suppliers, files financial returns, maintains reasonable deliveries to customers, doesn't overdraw at the bank, etc., can also introduce his own more personalized goals into his role. For instance, he may pursue the goal of independence to the extent that a lower level of profit results than would otherwise be possible. However, short of threatening the firm's survival, he is often free to do this. These more personalized elements which he integrates into his entrepreneurial role may be termed the *latent* role components or latent social identities.

Research suggests that three main latent identities occur with some frequency in relation to the role of the owner-manager:

(i) *The 'Artisan' identity*

Here the entrepreneurial role centres around intrinsic satisfactions of which the most important are personal autonomy at work, being able to pick the people you work with, status within the workplace and satisfaction at producing a quality product backed by personal service.

These are not the only goals attached to the role, but they are the ones which predominate. Thus, whilst income is important, as it must be for anybody who works and has no other source of income, it remains secondary to intrinsic satisfactions.

(ii) *The 'Classical Entrepreneur' identity*

This identity most closely resembles the classical economists' view of the entrepreneurial role. Earnings and profit become key goals and hence influence the way the entrepreneur acts out his role. Again maximization of financial returns (consistent with the survival and possible expansion of the firm), is by no means the sole goal of the entrepreneur, but it is given great importance compared to the intrinsic satisfactions associated with the 'Artisan' identity.

(iii) *The 'Manager' identity*

Here the entrepreneurial identity centres on goals concerned with the recognition of managerial excellence. The entrepreneur structures his role performance to achieve this recognition from fellow members of the firm, and, more especially, from outsiders such as other businessmen. Other goals and values stressed here are security and a concern to ensure that the entrepreneur's off-spring eventually receive the benefits of his enterprise.

Strategies and policies for the attainment of entrepreneurial goals

These entrepreneurial identities are connected to other aspects of the firm's operations. The 'Artisan' identity for example, is most frequently found amongst owner-managers who have only recently adopted the entrepreneurial role. The owner-manager who defines his role in this way tends to be greatly motivated towards intrinsic satisfactions. His desire to demonstrate his personal abilities often results in high product quality (sometimes higher than the customer is willing to pay for) and his desire for independence often leads to a reluctance to use outside sources of aid and advice, management education services, employers' organizations, consultants, sources of finance other than their bank, hire-purchase facilities, etc. In short, his acceptance of current business ideology and practice is low.

When recruiting staff, he tends to put a high emphasis on the personal qualities and attitudes of potential employees, being very concerned about the 'atmosphere' in his firm. Frequently he employs ex-colleagues from his former days in employment. In so doing, he gets quality workers, few problems of personal incompatibility, and a constant and welcome reminder of his new status—as the owner of his own business.

The entrepreneur's desire for independence frequently leads to an organizational climate founded on an autocratic leadership style, combined with a strong element of paternalism, which minimizes dependence on others, and increases his own self-esteem. He is likely to perceive the firm as a 'contented team', under-utilize the skills of subordinates as a result of being autocratic, and be blind to certain kinds of industrial relations problems. Awareness on the part of the entrepreneur of these results of a particular managerial style can help reduce unwanted side effects, and outside advisors wishing to help the small firm should evaluate the likely success of their proposed strategies against their knowledge of social relations patterns within the firm resulting from the entrepreneur's self-identity.

The entrepreneurial goals associated with the 'Artisan' identity are not highly favourable to the firm's growth. Many owner-managers feel that growth would threaten the achievement of intrinsic goals such as independence. It is perhaps therefore not surprising that growth in the small firm is often more apparent than real. Growth, despite its important place in the social values of our society, is likely to be less frequent than many expect. The small entrepreneur may well make an assessment of the likely results of certain courses of action, and decide that, on balance the 'costs' (in social and psychological terms) of some of these are too high.

Adopting a conscious no-growth stance in our society is not easy. We live in a society with a strong growth ideology. Growth is 'progress' and businessmen are often judged by this criterion. It is not therefore surprising that small firm entrepreneurs are rather circumspect, even to the extent of self-deception, in not striving too hard for growth. Golby and Johns summed up the attitudes among their sample as being:

> ... roughly divided on this question (the amount of growth thought desirable). Rather more agreed that expansion was desirable than backed the maintenance of the status quo. But it was noticeable that they often tended to express their views in a somewhat generalized way, as if they were paying lip service to an abstract ideal of growth.[36]

The reasons given for not growing were often difficult to accept at face value. Relatively minor administrative chores such as collecting insurance contributions and PAYE were offered as 'barriers' to growth. It is likely that reluctance to grow has, in fact, much more to do with the consequences, in social terms, of growth than these vocalized reasons.

A Social Action view (see Chapters II and VII) of the small firm here, concentrating on the goals of the owner-manager himself, offers reasons as to why growth is usually much less common than the prevalent growth ideology would lead us to expect, given the data on the low level of rewards[37] (in material terms) of small businessmen, the popularity of self-employment remains. Further, this viewpoint explains why the attractions of working for a large firm, with all that this implies in terms of security and material rewards, are rejected by certain people in our society. Also, it explains in part the highly skewed size distribution of firms in advanced industrial societies; it is not simply economic but social and psychological factors which also influence this distribution.

A small firm which survives the formative period and enters a period of sustained profitability constitutes a situation conducive to the development of the 'Classical Entrepreneur' identity. The goals associated with the 'Artisan' identity will now have been at least partially realised and the new social and economic situation of the firm is favourable to the possible emergence of a new entrepreneurial identity for the entrepreneur.

Probably the most problematic situation occurs where the owner-manager exchanges an 'Artisan' for a 'Classical Entrepreneur' view of his role. The problematic character results from growth which is a strategy normally associated with this transition. The anticipated consequences of this are, in practice, often instrumental in the transition not being made. Even where it is made, the full consequences are sometimes not fully realized, and this results in problems and conflicts—both identity conflicts for the entrepreneur and structural conflicts within the firm.

The administrative necessity to use a more consultative leadership style, to delegate and 'negotiate' with professionally trained managers brought in from outside, is not easily reconciled with the owner-manager's desire for independence. To this extent, he is a captive of the new situation he has himself brought about to meet his new goals. Problems of a similar kind are likely to arise out of the increasing likelihood of unionization. Entrepreneurs appear mostly aware of the positive correlation between organizational size and degree of unionization. However, unionization is not always seen as an extension of the new order of things in a larger firm, presenting management with benefits as well as problems. Sometimes, a 'communications breakdown' or the actions of 'militants' among new workers are held responsible for the onset of unionization.

The emergence of these 'growth effects' depends on a variety of factors, and may not occur until the firm has grown a considerable size. But whether any dramatic take-off into sustained growth takes place at all, even when the external logic—the economic and market situation of the firm and social relations with outsiders—is highly favourable, is a matter for scepticism. The owner-manager may retain a belief that 'small is beautiful'.

If the firm does grow and forces emerge, both internally and externally, that push it towards a more rational and bureaucratic structure, management functions have to be delegated as they become too complex and time consuming for a single person to handle. The need for certain skills, almost certainly not possessed by the entrepreneur, becomes crucial and specialists must be recruited. Social relationships can no longer be conducted on a highly personal basis but must be more systematically and bureaucratically ordered. From the entrepreneur's point of view, therefore, the firm comes increasingly to resemble previous social situations in previous employment which the firm was established to get away from, and many of his earlier goals may become threatened. Entrepreneurs who take on the 'Classical Entrepreneur' identity often claim that despite financial success they begin to feel like employees in their own firm.

Some small firm entrepreneurs have little hesitation in deciding that growth is desirable or even necessary for survival and take on a 'Classical Entrepreneur' view of their role. Once having established that they can maintain a high profit growth company, they may come to re-define their entrepreneurial role yet again in terms of the 'Manager' identity. In addition to the elements listed above, other behaviour patterns indicative of this identity are an increased interest in management training and development, employers' organizations, using management consultants, and attempts at taking over other firms and merging with larger companies or attempting to 'go public'.

The processes of rationalization and functional specialization, already begun at a time when the owner-manager held a Classical Entrepreneur view of his role, continue. This tends to manifest itself in the following ways:

1. *Hierarchical relations.* There is an increasing emphasis on vertical authority in the firm shown, for example, by the creation and circulation of elaborate authority charts.
2. *Division of labour.* Roles in the firm become clearly defined in terms of the tasks attached to them and the standards of performance required.
3. *Qualifications.* Increasingly role holders are selected on the basis of formal qualifications. Experience is still taken into account but often becomes secondary to paper qualifications.
4. *Impersonality.* Relations among role holders becomes more formal and confined to work problems. Interaction which cuts across authority lines becomes less and less frequent.
5. *Written records.* Activities are increasingly made the subject of written records which are stored for future reference.
6. *Code of discipline.* Rules of conduct are generated around role tasks, publicised and impersonally applied.
7. *Career patterns.* Career-development paths are set up along which members of the firm may expect to progress with accompanying changes in salary and responsibility.

However, it should be pointed out that some researchers have indicated that bureaucratization need not be an automatic outcome of growth.[38] Burns and Stalker,[39] in particular, have attempted to demonstrate its unsuitability to conditions of rapid changes in markets and technology. Here, they claim, a loose and flexible organization structure is more efficient than a rigid bureaucratic structure. Given that a period of growth represents similar instability, strenuous efforts to avoid excessive bureaucratization may be a prescription for successful growth. However, the transition to the 'Manager' identity on the part of the owner-manager can lead to an uncritical acceptance of ideas about management currently fashionable in management literature. This increases the danger of moving in a bureaucratic direction. The over enthusiastic adoption, for example, of a 'Systems Theory' approach to planning a firm's organization structure may merely result in a rigid bureaucratic structure.

Accompanying this process of bureaucratization is an increasing tendency towards unionization. This is largely the outcome of two interrelated processes both linked with increasing size:

1. The development of group consciousness on the part of workers who share very similar work situations. As the firm grows, it produces groups of workers who do similar jobs and who come to see advantages in acting collectively.
2. The standardization of conditions of employment by management as a strategy to ensure orderly management-worker relations and avoid charges of favouritism and victimization, etc.

Often the process of unionization is resisted by management but this sometimes only serves to harden relationships and cause more problems later on. There are, in fact, good reasons why management may wish to actually encourage unionization.

Unionization may be seen as the bureaucratic development of worker-management relations. It occurs when the individual worker feels he cannot go to the owner-manager personally to iron out a problem. The increased size of the firm creates barriers made up of additional levels of authority between shop-floor and the top level of the firm. From managements' point of view, workers cease to be individuals in a 'name' sense and a tendency to treat them as identical to each other emerges. This also has the advantage of avoiding individual charges of injustice and victimization.

The union provides a means for workers to have their own representatives who have access to top management. Management may now come to prefer to deal with a union because it is more convenient to deal with one worker representative than a large and increasing number of individuals. To some extent the union becomes a management tool in that it can help in disciplining workers who fail to reach agreed work standards, help in gaining acceptance for wage differentials and help in the smooth introduction of new techniques. While it is true that unions can promote worker-management conflict, the positive aspects of unionization should not be forgotten. In other words, unionization is a means of providing a channel of communication between shopfloor and top management in a firm once it has grown beyond the point where these relations can still be conducted in an individual face-to-face manner.[40]

Whilst most first generation owner-managers are unlikely to adopt the Manager identity during the early period of their firm's history, if ever, second and subsequent generation entrepreneurs, or even first generation entrepreneurs from conventional business backgrounds, may adopt either the 'Classical Entrepreneur' or even the 'Manager' identity from the outset.

However, the mere fact that these three different entrepreneurial identities occur with some frequency means that there can be no simple set of prescriptions for the efficient management of the small firm, and that techniques developed for the large firm may have little applicability for the small firm. It is on the basis of the now more widely appreciated importance of the small firm that a considerable amount of effort is now being made both in trying to help the small firm and in understanding the owner-manager,[41] The role of the owner-manager is the key to an understanding of human relationships and behaviour in the small firm. Unless we learn to see the entrepreneur's role as he himself perceives it, any discussion of the small firm by 'outsiders' is doomed to the status of a monologue punctuated by criticism and preaching, unlikely to be listened to by the small businessman himself.

The most common conclusion of such an approach is that the owner-manager is frequently 'failing' to meet the needs of the firm in a manner which appears to be the most efficient to an outsider well versed in modern management and personal techniques. But this is to neglect the key factor—the personal goals and values of the owner-manager himself. To put it another way, we must abandon the moralizing of the 'objective-outsider' approach and attempt to see the small firm through the eyes of its chief participant—the owner-manager. If we look at the small firm as it is, rather than in terms of an idealization, we shall obtain a surer understanding of it.

The future of the small business

If small businesses are to remain an important part of our economy, it is vital that there should be a continuing supply of individuals wishing to take up the owner-manager role. Following on from the evidence presented earlier that a major source of budding entrepreneurs is that group of people who consider themselves misplaced by conventional systems of occupational placement, there appear to be just grounds for optimism.

Numerous studies in recent years have warned against the danger of exaggerating the degree to which improved living standards and changes in the educational system have produced greater equality of opportunity.[42] Further, the level of knowledge that school leavers have of available occupational opportunities is often very incomplete.[43] These factors combined with imperfections in the personnel selection and promotion procedures employed by large firms continue to leave room for significant mis-matches between personal ability and positions held in employment.

If the future supply of entrepreneurs seems assured, what of the fate of the small firm itself? Here again we can be optimistic. There are many examples of recent technological developments and changes in patterns of consumption working in favour of the small firm.[44] Further, and of particular relevance to the theme of this book—people and work—there is increasing resistance to 'bigness' in our society. This is not only because many of the economies of scale normally thought to be associated with 'bigness' have been brought into question but, more specifically, because of the loss of individual identity often involved.

Ralph Turner, has argued:

Today, for the first time in history, it is common to see violent indignation expressed over the fact that people lack a sense of personal worth—that they lack an inner peace of mind which comes from a sense of personal dignity. . . . The urgent demand that the institutions of our society be reformed, not primarily to grant man freedom of speech and thought and not primarily to ensure him essential comforts, but to guarantee him a sense of personal worth is the new and recurrent theme in contemporary society.[45]

If Turner has pinpointed the central idea of contemporary social protest it bodes ill for the present large-scale economic enterprise. Such a unit is hardly suited to meet the challenge of providing participants with a feeling of individual self-importance. Though management may attempt to counteract the seemingly inherent impersonality of the modern large organization, so far no one has suggested a convincing means for doing this.

The small establishment, on the other hand, can claim an ability to recognize every participant as a significant contributor. It does not follow, of course, that this heralds the return of a small business economy, but it could produce a social climate more favourable to this kind of enterprise than has existed for most of this century.

REFERENCES

1 *Report on The Census of Production 1972*, Summary Tables, Table 8, HMSO, 1977.
2 'Britain's small firms: their vital role in the economy', Confederation of British Industry, p. 3, November, 1970.
3 WOOD, G., 'Where have all the small firms gone?', *The Financial Times*, p. 11, August 14th 1974.
4 *Small Firms—Report of the Committee of Inquiry on Small Firms*, HMSO (Cmnd. 4811), November 1971.
5 DEEKS, J., 'The small firm—asset or liability?', *Journal of Management Studies*, pp. 25–47, February 1973.

6 The Bolton Report, *op. cit.*, Ch. 6, and DEEKS, J. *op. cit.*, pp. 26–8. For a more recent, and less optimistic view, see BANNOCK, G., *The Smaller Business in Britain and Germany*, Wilton House Publications, 1976 and BANNOCK, G., 'The small man's burden', *The Guardian*, p. 14, November 22nd 1976.

7 The Bolton Report, *op. cit.*, p. 342.

8 The Bolton Report, *op. cit.*, pp. 1–2.

9 GOLBY, C. W. and JOHNS, G., 'Attitude and motivation', *Committee of Inquiry on Small Firms, Research Report No. 7*, HMSO, 1971.

10 *ibid.* p. 5.

11 *ibid.* p. 5.

12 Among the best known are: SCHUMPETER, J. A., *The Theory of Economic Development*, Harvard University Press, 1934; URWICK, L., 'Problems of growth in industrial undertakings', *Winter Proceedings*, 1948–9, No. 2, British Institute of Management; PENROSE, E., *The Theory of the Growth of the Firm*, Basil Blackwell, 1957; COLLINS, O. F., MOORE, D. G. with UNWALLA, D. B., *The Enterprising Man*, Michigan State University, 1964; THOMASON, G. F. and MILLS, A. J., 'Management decision-taking in small firms', *European Business*, pp. 29–41, October 1967; LUPTON, T., 'Small new firms and their significance', *New Society*, pp. 890–2, December 21st 1967; MATTHEWS, T. and MAYERS, C., *Developing a Small Firm*, BBC Publications, 1968; STEINMETZ, L. L., 'Critical stages of small business growth', *Business Horizons*, pp. 29–34, February 1969.

13 As in, e.g. URWICK, L., *op. cit.*

14 URWICK, *op. cit.*, and THOMASON and MILLS, *op. cit.*, provide examples of the division of managerial roles occurring in stage two while LUPTON, *op. cit.*, and MATTHEWS and MAYERS, *op. cit.*, offer examples of this occurring in stage three.

15 A review of the literature on this view of growth in the small firm is provided in MUELLER, D. C., 'A life cycle theory of the firm', *Journal of Industrial Economics*, pp. 199–219, July 1972. *see also* STEINMETZ, *op. cit.*, for one version.

16 Exact data on the death rates of small firms is very difficult to come by but see the discussions in DEEKS, *op. cit.*, and the Bolton Report.

17 MATTHEWS and MAYERS, *op. cit.*, pp. 142–4.

18 THOMASON and MILLS, *op. cit.*, p. 34.

19 LUPTON, *op. cit.*, p. 891.

20 WEBER, MAX, *The Protestant Ethic and the Spirit of Capitalism*, Unwin University Books, 1965.

21 MAYER, KURT B., 'Business enterprise: traditional symbol of opportunity', *British Journal of Sociology*, p. 160, June 1953.

22 *see*, e.g. GOLDTHORPE, J. H., LOCKWOOD, D., BECHHOFER, F. and PLATT, J., *The Affluent Worker: Industrial Attitudes and Behaviour*, pp. 131–6, Cambridge: Cambridge University Press, 1968 and BATSTONE, E., 'Deference and the ethos of small town capitalism', in BULMER, M. (Ed.), *Working Class Images of Society*, pp. 116–30, Routledge and Kegan Paul, 1975.

23 For instance, a recent survey of material on this topic, WILLIAMS, W. M. (Ed.),

Occupational Choice—A selection of papers from the Sociological Review, George Allen & Unwin, 1974, contains no discussion of this occupational alternative.

24 The Bolton Report, *op. cit.*, pp. 8–9.

25 DEEKS, J., 'Educational and occupational histories of owner-managers', *The Journal of Management Studies*, pp. 127–49, May 1972.

26 COLLINS, O. F., MOORE, D. G. with UNWALLA, D. B., *op. cit.*, Ch. V.

27 ROBERTS, E. B., and WARNER, H. A., 'New enterprises on Route 128', *Science Journal*, pp. 78–83, December 1968; COOPER, A. C., 'Entrepreneurial environment', *Industrial Research*, pp. 74–6; September 1970; LILES, P. R., 'Who are the entrepreneurs', *MSU Business Topics*, pp. 5–14, Winter 1974. These sources seem, however, to refer to a special variety of entrepreneurship which emerged under conditions of a kind not frequently encountered in private enterprise societies. *see* the discussion below.

28 COLLINS, O. F., MOORE, D. G. with UNWALLA, D. B., *op. cit.*, pp. 243–4.

29 The Bolton Report, p. 343.

30 CURRAN, J. and STANWORTH, M. J. K., 'The way of the small businessman', *New Society*, August 19th 1971; STANWORTH, M. J. K. and CURRAN, J., *Management Motivation in the Smaller Business*, Gower Press, 1973 and STANWORTH, M. J. K. and CURRAN, J., 'Growth and the small firm—an alternative view', *Journal of Management Studies*, pp. 95–110, May 1976.

31 For a comprehensive history of the concept of 'social marginality' *see* DICKIE-CLARK, H. P., *The Marginal Situation*, Routledge & Kegan Paul, 1966.

32 Examples of these are given in: MEWTON, K., *The Sociology of British Communism*, Allen Lane, The Penguin Press, 1969 and YINGER, M. J., 'Religion and social change: functions and dysfunctions of sects and cults among the disprivileged', reprinted in his *Sociology Looks at Religion*, pp. 39–64, Collier-Macmillan, 1969.

33 MAYER, K. B. and GOLDSTEIN, S., *The First Two Years: Problems of Small Firm Growth and Survival*, Small Business Research Series, No. 2, Washington, D.C., Small Business Association, 1961, reported in DEEKS, J., 'The small firm—asset or liability?', *Journal of Management Studies*, pp. 25–47, February 1973.

34 See especially STANWORTH, M. J. K., and CURRAN, J., *op. cit.*

35 GOULDNER, A. W., 'Cosmopolitans and locals: an analysis of latent social roles', *Administrative Science Quarterly*, pp. 282–92, December 1957 and pp. 444–80, March 1958.

36 GOLBY, C. W. and JOHNS, G., *op. cit.*, p. 17, HMSO, 1971.

37 *see* MERRETT CYRIAX ASSOCIATES, 'Dynamics of Small Firms', *Committee of Inquiry on Small Firms, Research report No. 12*, p. 35, HMSO, 1971, for data for the United Kingdom. COLLINS, O. F., MOORE, D. G., with UNWALLA, D. B., *op. cit.*, suggest that a similar relatively low level of material rewards are received by small firm executives in the United States.

38 HALL, R. H., 'Bureaucracy and small organizations', *Sociology and Social Research*, pp. 38–46, October 1963.

39 BURNS, T. and STALKER, G. M., *The Management of Innovation*, Tavistock Publications, 1961.
40 EVANS, E. O., 'Cheap at twice the price? Shop stewards and workshop relations in engineering', in WARNER, M. (Ed.), *The Socioloy of the Workplace*, pp. 82–115, George Allen & Unwin, 1973.
41 For example, see the series of articles in *Personnel Management*, November 1974–June 1975.
42 *see* BANKS, O., *The Sociology of Education*, Batsford, 1971 and WESTERGAARD, J. and RESLER, H., *Class in a Capitalist Society, A Study of Contemporary Britain*, Penguin, 1976.
43 *see* FEGELMAN, K., *Leaving the Sixth Form* (National Foundation for Educational Research), reported in the *Guardian*, August 4th 1972. Also, VENESS, T., *School Leavers*, Methuen, 1962; CARTER, M., *Into Work*, Penguin Books, 1966 and WILLMOTT, P., *Adolescent Boys of East London*, Routledge & Kegan Paul, 1966 and WILLIAMS, W. M., *op. cit.*
44 On technological developments in particular *see* The Bolton Report, *op. cit.*, pp. 76–7.
45 TURNER, R. H., 'The theme of contemporary social movements, *British Journal of Sociology*, pp. 390–405, December 1969.

XI

THE BEHAVIOURAL SCIENTIST AT WORK

In the preceding chapters we have looked at the nature of our knowledge and understanding of work, work behaviour and work organization as represented in the theory and research of the behavioural sciences. This range of knowledge is now fairly extensive, although in some areas it remains a question of being clearer about what it is we do not know. One particular limitation is that of deciding how existing knowledge becomes applied. The use of the term 'applied' can itself be misleading. Most of what has been written in this book so far is applied in the sense that it is *about* people in organizations. Much of it, however, is still not applied in the sense of the ideas actually being *used* in organizations. The last chapter did examine some of the approaches to facilitating change that have their origin in the behavioural sciences. Despite this, however, as recently as June 1976 it was possible for a group of researchers to state:

> Empirical studies of the utilization of applied social research in organizational decisions are practically non existent. . . . Apart from a restricted number of case studies based upon participant observation . . . few systematic studies exist about the transformation of applied science information into organizational action[1]

Clearly, if the behavioural sciences are going to be used as well as being merely useful in organizations, greater attention needs to be paid to the application process; this implies a need for greater understanding of the behavioural scientist at work. In this chapter we briefly examine how some of the concepts already elaborated in this book might be used to increase understanding of some of the problems and potential barriers to effective utilization.

It would be misleading to suggest that behavioural scientists working in this particular applied field represent a unified body; there are certainly some major differences in their orientations to their work. for some, the prime interest in the area is essentially academic; their main aim is to expand the body of knowledge about people in organizations by testing theories or at least throwing light on theoretical problems. The impetus for their research is external to the organization itself and the results are intended to feed back into the store of knowledge. This does not mean that these results will not have any relevance for the solving of organizational problems; but this is not the prime objective and so results will often be presented in a form which is not readily usable by a practising manager.

At the opposite extreme there are those whose prime concern is the solving of organizational problems. The impetus for their activity is internal; they bring the knowledge, concepts and methods of the behavioural sciences to bear on a particular problem with the aim of finding some operational solution. The findings of their research are fed back into their own action in the organization, and into recommendations for action by other organizational members, in a form which is usable in and specific to the particular organization. This does not mean that such research cannot make a contribution to the general body of knowledge but that is not its prime intention. So the feedback is likely to be in the form of published case studies which, as we mentioned in Chapter I, can be useful for generating hypotheses, but are limited in their application to other settings.

Obviously these two approaches represent extremes and there are approaches which fall somewhere between them. Cherns,[2] for example, labels the first 'pure basic research' and the second 'action research'. In between he suggests there is 'basic objective research' and 'operational research' (which should not be confused with the widely used quantitative aid to managerial decision making). The former he regards as having greater generality than the latter. Despite this, however, there is growing concern that the gap between the extremes may be widening.[3]

This widening gap may be understood in terms of the motivations and reward systems associated with the two approaches. Wadell and Naslund[4] point out that:

> The main factor which influences promotion in the academic hierarchy is 'scientific' research. Teaching skill is sometimes considered to a small degree, but rarely is skill in design and implementation of organizational change rewarded.

This means that the behavioural scientist interested in advancement in an academic career is frequently more concerned with getting articles published in 'academically respectable' journals than in his research findings being used. Such an orientation is accentuated by the problems associated with gaining financial support for carrying out the research in the first place as Smith[5] emphasizes.

It is acknowledged by many who seek public funds for research that panels to whom the research design is submitted are more likely to pay scrupulous attention to methodological elegance than to the potential applications of the research findings. Academic criteria take higher preference over the criteria of any potential client.'

The consultancy orientated behavioural scientist, on the other hand, is more likely to be interested in enhancing his reputation with his clients than with his academic peers. It is in this way that further, more rewarding, contracts will be gained. This interest places pressure upon him to pay more attention to 'packaging' his expertise in a form that is acceptable to the problem orientated manager than to meeting the requirements of scientific precision that are acceptable to theory orientated academics. It seems that problems of occupying a position between these extremes are considerable and the tendency to be drawn towards one or other of them is fairly great.

Just as behavioural scientists' orientations to work in organizations are various, so are the reasons why organizations make use of them. Challis[6] suggests that there are six possible reasons why behavioural scientists might be employed. The first reason she terms the 'chaos thesis', which implies that organization will turn to behavioural science when it is experiencing a problem of such intensity that it generates chaos. A milder form of this she terms the 'problem thesis'. In such cases the organization is seeking assistance with a problem, which the management feels it cannot handle, but which is not so extreme that it must 'stake all its chances of smooth running on the one horse'. The 'spare capacity' thesis suggests that organizations are more likely to involve behavioural scientists when things are going well and when organisations can afford to risk an experiment from which there may be some pay-off in terms of preventing problems.

The next three possible reasons have their origin outside rather than inside the organization. The first of these suggests that in many cases the employment of behavioural scientists is a matter of fashion. It is a 'bandwagon' which some managers see as a good one to jump aboard, the main pay-off being in terms of image as an up-to-date organization. In some cases there also seems to be a 'competitor effect'; organizations do employ behavioural scientists because their competitors are seen to. This is not necessarily a question of fashion. It is a response to a fear that competitors may gain some advantage through the use of this 'secret weapon'.

Finally, it is suggested that some organizations make use of behavioural scientists for no other reason than that they have succumbed to the 'hard-sell' of the behavioural scientists in question.

It seems likely that these different reasons for employing a behavioural scientist will give rise to differing expectations of what his role in the organization should be. These expectations may or may not coincide with the behavioural scientist's own expectations and so will have varying effects on his employment experience.

In exploring the role of the behavioural scientist one important distinction must be pointed out. So far, in discussing the differing orientations, the implication has been that the behavioural scientist will normally be located outside the organization and will come into it on some kind of contract basis, be it academic or consultancy. Some organizations, however, employ behavioural scientists internally as permanent members of their staff. This practice seems to be less common in Britain than in the United States. As Clark[7] suggests, such organizations 'are possible forerunners of the future rather than typical of the current situation'. This fact in itself may have a significant effect on the degree of effective utilization in Britain. Van de Vall et al.,[8] as a result of a fairly extensive study of important influences on utilization, came to the firm conclusion that:

Internal social researchers are superior to external consultants as agents of planned social intervention and policy making.

But what do managers expect of such internal researchers? A survey by Appleby[9] suggests that there are fairly common expectations as to the kind of person required. But she also suggests that these expectations are frequently not fulfilled. Some employers looked for very senior behavioural scientists with extensive industrial experience and a wide range of specified skills. It seems, however, that for the most part they were unable to find all the skills they required in one person. Other employers sought younger individuals who were easier and cheaper to find. In such cases their main concern was that they should have had some prior industrial experience, the aim being to find behavioural scientists 'already socialized into the values and goals of industry'. There also seems to be a safeguard element in such a requirement in that, if the experiment proved to be a failure, it would be easier to absorb the behavioural scientist into the general management of the organization.

But what of the behavioural scientists themselves? What do they expect in their role? Referring again to Appleby:

The incumbents of posts ... might expect personal autonomy and freedom to interpret the role in line with their special interests because the role was new and was not limited by precedent. This could be reinforced by the fact that many of the job descriptions offered ... the opportunity to provide a general advisory role.[10]

In practice this is not the case. The general understanding of and support for the behavioural sciences within organizations is low, often confined almost exclusively to the original sponsor. This seems to have severely limited the range of activities possible for the individuals concerned. In many cases their main activity is teaching managers about the behavioural sciences on training courses. This sometimes extends to a general management information service abstracting, writing and circulating behavioural science papers and books. There seems, however, to be little or no feedback from such information inputs and some have questioned its general utility. Rarely has the role involved any real research even when the behavioural scientists have argued that they could make a genuine contribution by focusing on substantive issues. Research might raise expectations and produce findings unacceptable to the employer and as such may be regarded as a high risk activity. In one area only has there been fairly widespread lip-service paid to the research methods of behavioural sciences and that is in the use of attitude surveys:

> Attitude surveys are comprehensible to the commissioning body and have an obvious technical debt to the social sciences; they have the additional advantage of providing information without requiring a commitment to action following from it.[11]

Clearly, there appears as yet to be little common ground between the ways in which the behavioural scientists believe themselves to be potentially useful and the ways in which employers believe they should be used. There is an obvious conflict of expectations. The employer, however, is in a position of political strength, and such conflicts tend to be resolved by his expectations and definitions taking precedence.

This failure to find common ground is reinforced by the widely held stereotypes of each side by the other. Smith[12] maintains that managers tend to see the researchers as naive and unrealistic. It also seems that in the minds of many there is a link between 'social' science and socialism, and the belief that its main aim is to confront traditional authority. The researchers on the other hand tend to see the management as hard-headed, ignorant, resistant, dull and uncomprehending. Such stereotypes together with different frames of reference, different perceptions of what is important, and different modes of expression, all create a barrier to genuine communication and understanding between the two. And as yet, as Wadell and Naslund[13] point out, there is a lack of people belonging to both cultures who can serve as 'interpreters'.

This interpreter's role is usually left to the sponsor, often one individual, on whose initiative the behavioural scientist(s) was employed. The behavioural scientist's ability to create a meaningful role for himself seems to rest in part on the location and power of this sponsor in the organization structure. But his own location seems also to be significant. In some cases, especially where several behavioural scientists are employed, they have the status of an autonomous department. More often than not, however, they are located within the personnel department. There are advantages and disadvantages in both situations. A separate department may allow greater freedom of choice of work and methods but it may also mean a lack of entry points and power to negotiate, and sympathy from other departments. Within an existing department, behavioural scientists are likely to gain or lose according to the power and status of that department in the organization, and to receive varying degrees of sympathy and support for their work from the department superiors, who will often not be the original sponsors.

Finally, let us look at the relationship between methodology and utilization. It is clear from the work of Van de Vall *et al.* and of Clark[14] that the academic model of 'pure' research is inappropriate. Concern for methodological precision and scientific validity is less likely to lead to implementation than concern for operational feasibility and an acceptable means of disseminating findings. This has implications both for the way information is gathered and the way in which it is fed back. Summarizing the findings, we can say that the more that researchers make use of unstructured, qualitative techniques, the more likely the findings are to have an impact on policy decisions. The more researchers attempt to relate their work to formal theory the less likely it is to lead to utilization. This does not mean that theory has no place but rather that so called 'grounded'[15] theory, which is of a lower level of abstraction and has its origin in the actual data being gathered rather than in 'the body of existing knowledge', is more likely to lead to implementation. As far as method of presentation is concerned, there is an inverse relationship between size of report and the degree of utilization. Managers, it seems, either do not wish to or do not have time to read and digest voluminous research reports. Further, the more tables there are in the report, and the more complex those tables are in terms of number of variables included, the lower will be the rate of utilization in industrial decisions.

The gap, then, between what is acceptable in academic terms and what is usable in management terms is still a wide one. Attempts can be made to close it from both sides. There is a need for the education and training of a new kind of specialist: the applied behavioural scientist. Preferably he should be employed internally, and have the special skills required for ensuring utilization, these skills being quite different from those currently encouraged for academic research. Very recently a few post-graduate training programmes of this kind have been set up in Britain. The gap can also be closed from the other side by making managers more aware of the concepts, methods and language of the behavioural sciences. Hopefully this book is a contribution in that direction.

REFERENCES

1 VAN DE VALL, M., BOLAS, C. and KANG, T. S., 'Applied social research in industrial organizations: an evaluation of functions, theory and methods', *Journal of Applied Behavioural Science*, **12**, pp. 158–77, 1976.
2 CHERNS, A. B., 'Social research and its diffusion', in *Papers on Social Science Utilization, Monograph I*, CUSSR, Loughborough University, 1972.
3 VAN DE VALL *et al.*, *op. cit.*
4 WADELL, B. and NASLUND, B., 'Doctoral research and practical management', *European Training*, **2**, pp. 117–25, 1973.
5 SMITH, P. 'The missing link between research and its application', paper presented to the *Conference of the British Psychological Society*, April 1975.
6 CHALLIS, L. S., 'Components of a model of the utilization of social science research: the employment of social scientists by organisations', in CUSSR, *op. cit.*, 1972.
7 CLARK, P. A., 'Research on the utilization of socio-organizational analysis: problems and approaches', in CUSSR, *op. cit.*, 1972.
8 VAN DE VALL *et al.*, *op. cit.*
9 APPLEBY, B., 'Applied social scientists in industry: expectations and dimensions of their role', CUSSR, *op. cit.*, 1972.
10 *ibid.*
11 *ibid.*
12 SMITH, P., *op. cit.*
13 WADELL, B. and NASLUND, B., *op. cit.*
14 VAN DE VALL, M. *et al.*, *op. cit.* and CLARK, P. A., *op. cit.*
15 GLASER, B. G. and STRAUSS, A., *The discovery of grounded theory*, Aldine, 1967.

AUTHOR INDEX

SUBJECT INDEX